I0126327

What Does *THAT* Stand For?
Stand For?

Acronyms, Abbreviations, and Initialisms for Organizations

Compiled by Geoffrey Brown

BTLG llc

What Does <u>THAT</u> Stand For?
**Acronyms, Abbreviations, and Initialisms
for Organizations**
Compiled by Geoffrey Brown

Copyright © 2016 Between the Lakes Group, LLC.
All rights reserved.

Published by Between the Lakes Group, LLC, Post
Office Box 13, 372 Between the Lakes Road, Taconic,
CT 06079

While every precaution has been taken in the preparation of this
book, the publisher assumes no responsibilities for errors or
omissions, or from damages resulting from the use of the
information contained herein.

ISBN-13: 978-0692675779
ISBN-10: 0692675779

SPQR is the earliest acronym for an organization of which we're aware.

First noted in use circa 80 BC, it appears that Senatus Populesque Romanus was a bit too large a mouthful conveniently to use in referring to the organization that was the combined state and populace of Rome. And SPQR was certainly a far more convenient identifier to carry around on a pike or pole as one sees so frequently in depictions of the Roman legions.

Convenience and economy of space seem to have been the principal drivers behind adoption of this particular acronym. Interestingly, for the most part these are still the reasons for acronym, initialisms, and organizational abbreviations today.

It was that old timer, SPQR, that made us realize that convenience and economy of space frequently beats cleverness, ease of pronunciation, and even clarity in referring to organizations.

What we are trying to do here:

This is a bit more than a beginning at collecting a comprehensive list of abbreviations, initialisms (or initializations, if you wish) and acronyms for organizations that one might encounter in the United States. While we began this project while doing historical, genealogical and similar research, the list has expanded to the point where we think it can serve as a starting point in most attempts to decode abbreviations that contextually suggest they belong to an organization of some kind. So, we intend this to be a resource that permits the researcher – or the casual reader, for that matter -- when confronted with an abbreviation for an unknown organization, to quickly see a list of organizations that likely have been known by this combination of letters at some point in time in the English-speaking part of the western world.

Think of looking up an acronym in this book as a first step in the process of ascertaining what organization those letters might have represented, which, in turn, can become the next step in learning more about the organization in question and the people associated with it.

We propose to help researchers make the jump from the abbreviated name of the organization to the name of the organization itself. Why might this be useful? Examples may help, so here are some.

For someone investigating genealogy, it might help determine the religion or employer or political leanings of an ancestor and thereby suggest avenues for further research. For historians, it will ideally suggest the kinds of organizations that may have been active in a locale at a particular time. For editors, it may help decode a reporter's notes, or perhaps permit better comprehension and contextualization of quoted material. For writers of fiction, we think that checking their fictional organizations against this list could help avoid many kinds of *faux pas.*

For all, we hope that this will help formulate context – about people, about places, about organizations themselves. Really, it is all about context.

What we are NOT trying to do:

- This is NOT intended to be a comprehensive list of all organizations, past and present, not even in our wildest dreams. After working on this project for several years with varying levels of intensity we can confidently say that compiling such a list would be so far beyond the range of the possible for one individual working alone that it's not even a laudable objective. People, after all, are social animals, and social animals form organizations and have been doing so since prehistoric times. There are, and have been, a whole lot of organizations out there.
- It is NOT intended to supply much information about the organization; really, any more information than might be helpful in ruling out possibilities. For example, if you are researching a notorious libertine

and you discover here that some organizational initials associated with him are those of a ascetic religious order, you may have the wrong organization (or you may not).

There are no doubt other functions this list will fulfill that have not yet occurred to us here at Between the Lakes Group – or BTLGllc, if you prefer. Our feeling is that if it helps you, then we hope you will use it!

BACKGROUND:

We've been asked on several occasions how we got started collecting acronyms and abbreviations for organizations, and whether we intended to become the go-to source on organizations that might have existed or some subset thereof. The answer to the first part of the question is simply that we experienced a need.

The answer to the second part is that we don't purport to be an expert on organizations per se and furthermore that we do not aspire to that status. There are people – lots of them, really – who have made knowing everything possible about subsets of this list of organizations their life's work. (A good example thereof would be the people who have published massive tomes about the many organizations that compose Freemasonry. Another would be the people who actively maintain the extensive registry of rail car markings.)

Becoming such an expert is a worthy task, and, as noted, for some subsets of this list such experts already exist. However, it doesn't float our boat, and, if you were looking for an organizational expert to discuss things with, I am not he.

History:

In the 1960s, in the Army, serving as a personnel clerk, organizational acronyms hit me in the face. All military organizations had acronyms, initializations, or abbreviations of their names that were often far less than intuitive. The author's operational unit, a brigade-level military personnel management unit in the Administration Company of the 25th Infantry Division, was called TLAG-PM2. (For the curious, this stood for Tropic Lightning Adjutant General Personnel Management team #2. The 25th Division has been known as "Tropic Lightning" (hence the TL) since its birth as a World War II jungle infantry outfit.)

The division itself, at the time located at Schofield Barracks, Hawaii, was physically located in USARHAW (United States Army, Hawaii) but organizationally was the Pacific quick reaction force for USARPAC (United States Army Pacific Area Command), which was commanded by CINCPAC (Commander in Chief, Pacific Area Command), although, of course, CINCPAC referred not just to the Commanding General (or Admiral) who ran the show, but his entire headquarters. To read Army orders in quantity as my job required, you had to be able to parse this stuff at pretty much a normal reading speed. So, if you did what I did and were any good at it, it quickly became second nature to internalize acronyms as part of the language.

So much for the Army. Skip ahead, over some additional military experience, this time with computers – another area that has never been shy about freely using acronyms -- and a couple of civilian jobs in the early 1970s, and I became a new hire at what was then First National City Bank (or FNCB) – now Citibank/Citigroup – in New York City. I had been hired with an unusual and ambitious title: Agent of Change. In a small sense this meant finding processes that could be quickly automated, hoping to make the business run more efficiently.

In the process, I encountered a bewildering array of acronyms and abbreviations (even more than in the Army, or even when as a computer programmer, working frequently in COBOL – COmmon Business Oriented Language, speaking of acronyms, albeit non-organizational). To do my job, I needed to know what the processes were and did, and that necessitated decoding the various abbreviations and acronyms I encountered – which resulted in another list of acronyms.

A decade later, during the 1980s, having discovered genealogy as a hobby, I began to encounter acronyms of obscure fraternal organizations in the United States while working on the descendents of one John Hodgkin of Guilford, CT. Often these turned up in obituaries published in the small town newspapers of the day. The result was a growing awareness of the historical prevalence of the use of initials to identify organizations.

Fast-forward to the millenium. Citibank career ended and the Hodgkin family history book long since published, I started a retirement business publishing local history and genealogy in digital form. Making a business such as this function required involvement in genealogy groups in geographic areas where we had publications, so I suddenly became very familiar with local histories of hitherto-unknown (to me) small towns.

An online group around then was puzzling over the identity of a lodge or similar organization known as E.O.M.A. There was much speculation about what this group might possibly have been. Suggestions ranged from a Masonic organization to a labor union to a church group, and finally someone came up with the answer: Empire Order of Mutual Aid. It was a mutual benefit society, an antecedent of a mutual insurance company. I decided that it was once again time to make a list.

Eventually I made the list a free download on our website, www.betweenthelakes.com, with the none too subtle purpose of attracting more paying customers to the website where, if I was lucky, they might choose to purchase an electronic download of some ancient town history.

The free download became quite popular, and the list grew. Whether or not it generated sales is a moot point, but I continued to add abbreviations and acronyms to the list, and over the years it got longer and longer.

The gating issue that took the free download list of organizational acronyms, moved it from the back burner to the front, made it mushroom in size and accuracy, and ultimately made it into a book was something totally unrelated to acronyms in business.

I learned that a teenage girl whom I knew at church had self-published an imaginative tale of dragons, knights, princesses and so forth. Since I knew the author, I bought the book from Amazon and read it. It was not really to my taste – although several of her peers quite liked it -- but what was really impressive was that the teenager had been able to successfully self-publish in print. THAT motivated me!

Suddenly the notion that this list could be much more than it had been, or even that I had ever thought it might become, crystallized and work began in earnest on this becoming a book. *Thanks, Rebekah, for showing me the art of the possible!*

What are we really talking about here?

This list was well over 100 pages long before a basic question came up: just what IS an acronym, or initialization (initialism is an interchangeable coinage for the same thing), or abbreviation? What's the difference between them? You know what one is when you see one, but what actually are they?

I tend to use the terms more or less interchangeably, and suspect that most people do, but here are my contribution to the process of defining them.

First, an **acronym** is really a subset of abbreviations where the first letters of words are combined into a brand new word. These are rather less common than one might think, and for well-known examples of acronyms we go to the sciences and produce a classic acronym: SONAR – which stands for SOund NAvigation Radar. That acronym is such a successful one that few can tell you what the underlying words really are.

An **initialism** (or initialization, if you prefer – we use both terms interchangeably) is likewise an abbreviation typically derived from first letter(s) of words, but in this case the result does not become a new word, and the letters usually continue to be pronounced individually. Here we find most organizations: IBM (International Business Machines), AFL/CIO (American Federation of Labor/Congress of Industrial Organizations), KKK (Ku Klux Klan), and SJ (Society of Jesus) demonstrate how wide ranging this category is.

And that's not the half of it: also in this category are **codes** for organizations (airline codes and railcar codes are two obvious examples) that may stray far from the conventional string of initials, but often are clearly connected with the organization to which they refer.

An **abbreviation** is simply a (widely understood) shortened form of a word or phrase. This is really the mother category of which the other two are simply subsets.

WORTH REMEMBERING:

Acronyms, initialisms and abbreviations can be official or unofficial. They can be created by the founders of an organization, by people seeking to publicize the organization, by the members of an organization, and by those who are not members, including those who do not much care for the organization at all. In the latter category we have many sub-categories, including those coined by people who cannot be members for whatever reason, and those who would not be members, again for whatever reason. In fact, we may have people who outright despise the organization creating abbreviations by which they will refer to the organization and by which the organization may become known.

While usually abbreviations and initializations are – and have been – created almost as part of the folk process in order to save space or time, acronyms often show a spark of professional creativity that the other categories do not.

They can also be downright malicious. They can be terribly serious, and they can be self-deprecating. They can also be quite misleading. When you are able to move from a mysterious abbreviation to an actual organization to continue your research, it's occasionally a good idea to consider what the source of the acronym itself might have been.

About Acronyms and Abbreviations in general (a rant)

As time passed and I got deeper into the subject of acronyms and abbreviations, as the list got longer and longer, I began to follow up questions that came up in the process. At this point, I began to encounter scholarly works on the subject and some not-altogether unanticipated tirades by philologists and linguistic purists who seemed generally offended that acronyms and initializations – and most abbreviations – existed at all.

I was reminded that people involved in the teaching of English seem to be of two schools: those who believe that language is continually growing and evolving and that change is not, *per se*, bad -- and the other people. The other people are the ones who seem to feel that anything written since the 1880s that doesn't read like Henry James is hopelessly degenerate and that all efforts must be spent trying to push the English language back into the cage from which it has been continually escaping since the days of Chaucer. (These folks may also secretly think that Henry James just might actually be a little bit suspect, too.)

Interestingly, you can get a pretty quick read on which camp a scholar is in by asking them their opinion about when the use of acronyms became common. Those who are committed to pushing language back into its cage will immediately assure you that abbreviations for organizations simply didn't exist before World War II. If you remind them of the New Deal agencies that were known by letters, or about abbreviations for secret societies on gravestones, they will mutter something about these being outliers, and to pay no attention to the man behind the curtain. Sometimes throwing SPQR at them will quiet them down a bit -- or at least temporarily distract them.

The fact is that shortened forms of the names of organizations have been in use ever since busy people discovered the need to refer to them in a shorter form that would still be readily understood by the reader or hearer; really in any situation where the name of an organization needed to appear in a space too small to hold it in its entirety. Acronyms and initializations are a step above shorthand, because no special skills are needed to read and comprehend most acronyms and initializations, as long as they appear in a recognizable context.

Some obvious applications have been around since people decided that they wanted to have their military or organizational affiliation on their gravestone. They have been around since printers needed to save some space and a lot of repetitive typesetting. And they have certainly been around since people began to write notes about their lives in diaries, journals, and day books.

9

Who remembers telegrams? They charged by message length (conceptually they were a little like Twitter with its original 140 character maximum message length), and no one was going to pay to spell out that dad was a member of the Free and Accepted Masons when F&AM would do the job just as well and be just as comprehensible. Writing an obituary and want to include the deceased's organizations in the obit? Well, if you are paying for space by the column inch (or paying someone to hand-set the type), an acronym will do the job far better than a mouthful of "Internationals" and "Imperials" required to correctly spell out organizational names. Size matters.

"But show me a published use of this acronym referring to that organization" insist the pedants. To you I say: walk around some old cemeteries, read some old diaries, spend some time reading small town newspapers of the 19th century – especially the obituaries -- and you will see all the illustrations you need.

In fact, I'm confident that this collection only scratches the surface in terms of acronyms and abbreviations for organizations. Acronyms and abbreviations for organizations are the abbreviated voice of the people and have been for at least 2000 years. There's no reason to think that they will not be around for 2000 more.

Parenthetically, the oldest corporate abbreviation I've found belongs to an American business and nicely predates the New Deal. That, of course, is A&P. Its official use by the company itself can be precisely dated as having begun on March 17, 1924 when A&P became the sponsor of the radio show called "The A&P Gypsies" which ran until 1936.

Classifying Organizations

Back when this was a free online download, people occasionally asked how I decided to classify an organization. I had been doing it since the list began, mainly so I could mentally keep straight what kinds of organizations I was dealing with. It seemed intuitively obvious that I should do it. But how?

This is the most judgment-dependent part of the project. Deciding whether a secret society that considered itself a fraternal organization oriented toward immigrants from a particular country as well as a specific religious faith and which also provided members with life insurance or other tangible benefits (this is actually a fairly common scenario) was primarily a fraternal organization or a mutual benefit organization, or a religious one, or some other flavor of organization, has not been easy to do even in cases where the organization in question is well known. The obscure ones? Well, I've tried!

I've tried for a best fit based on the information available. The fact is that many organizations, particularly membership organizations, have many aspects to them. They may offer a tangible benefit to their members. They may be secret and have elaborate uniforms, costumes, and rituals. They may actually be honors that are bestowed at some point in one's life and never revisited except for inclusion on a resume or CV. They may be religious denominations or subsets thereof. They may be railroads but at the same time have industrial interests. The list goes on and on.

There are some organizations that I felt uncomfortable classifying at all, such as the KKK. Furthermore, since the KKK lacks a coherent national organization, there are a significant number of organizations on this list that are identified as KKK. Some, such as neo-Nazi groups, may simply be allied with the KKK due to common interests.

I toyed with the idea that fraternal orders perhaps ought to be sub-classified as being either Masonic or non-Masonic, because so many are either Masonic or built on a Masonic model. To some extent you'll find this implemented, but to do so reliably would require a more in-depth knowledge of the organizations in question – and of freemasonry -- than I was prepared to acquire.

Special interest groups that have nominal purposes as one kind of organization but in fact are dedicated toward other ends have posed problems. An example: how to classify the National Rifle Association, while nominally a sports organization, but whose extensive industry alignment and political involvement overshadow the ostensible sporting function at this point in time.

Occasionally an organization was so obscure that I didn't have enough information to classify it accurately, so I took an educated guess. Honestly, the classifications – and some sub-classifications – remain very much a work in progress; hopefully what I've supplied will be a guide to further investigation.

The Future

You'll recall that the example with which we started was SPQR, clearly an initialism designed to save space. One might think that as the technology of electronic communications vastly increases capacity and speed, we might see corresponding increases in the spelling out of names of organizations to take advantage of this increased capacity. We have not; if anything we see more acronyms, initialisms and abbreviations for organizations than we saw even a few years ago.

In fact, the use of handheld technology seems to be encouraging abbreviation of all kinds. It's obvious: if you key with all ten fingers on a full-sized keyboard, it's easier to spit out large numbers of letters quickly than it is when you type with your thumbs on a tiny screen. And as the tiny screen itself (as smartphone screens increased in size, we find wrist watch displays now creating a new incentive to be brief anyway) constrained organization names, life itself seems to be continually speeding up, encouraging brevity via pressure on that dimension of the time-space continuum.

At the same time, we see the number of small town newspapers approaching the vanishing point as they are supplanted by digital media sources, and, as noted, we see life moving at a faster and faster pace. There is no less pressure for brevity in communication now than there was a century ago, and perhaps there is a bit more.

Furthermore, there is a use of a different form of abbreviation, initialism, and acronym that has become a fixture of daily life in the last 30 years: the URL or web address. (URL, by the way, is an abbreviation for Uniform Resource Locator, which in turn actually represents the use of an abbreviation to stand for a series of zeros and ones – an interesting twist on the "what does THAT stand for?" concept.)

The fact is that virtually all organizations with a web presence today have an abbreviates organizational name now, whether they intended to have one or not when they established their internet presence, in the form of the URL of their website. Where did these particular abbreviations come from? In some organizations, marketing people studied ideal shortenings of the organization name. In others, a technician somewhere, trying to find an unclaimed string of letters that was memorable to him, simply signed up for what was available.

How will this change in the future? Well, I don't know. But the forthcoming "internet of things" certainly gives one pause for thought.

And that is about as far as I feel comfortable in predicting the future!

FREQUENTLY ASKED QUESTIONS (FAQ):

Question: If there is an internet link to more information about the organization, why don't you include it?

Answer: The basic answer here is that if there is something that changes faster than organization names, it is URLs. As well, since they tend to be abbreviations themselves, this would expand this work on still another dimension. Once you move from the abbreviation to the name, an internet search engine may be your next best friend.

Question: Okay, now I know that the letters I was looking up actually did stand for an organization, but I still know nothing about the organization and what it was all about. What do you suggest I do now?

Answer: Google and Bing are obvious starting points, but to get past the rather one-sided view of organizations that their websites provide, I like Wikipedia for the next step. You won't find Wikipedia entries for every organization on this list, but you will certainly find many or most of the less obscure among them – and occasionally some of the truly arcane.

Question: I can think of so many organizations that you do not list! Why haven't you included the "*example*"?

Answer: One of three reasons: (1) although I knew of it, I did not run across it or otherwise not think of it while working on the list, or (2) because I flat out never heard of it or encountered it, or (3) because I never realized it was referred to by its initials. In any case, please take the trouble to send an e-mail at geoff@betweenthelakes.com with a subject of "Abbreviation List Addition" and I'll add it to the list of updates for the next editions. Thank you in advance!!

Question: You list abbreviations for a whole bunch of colleges, but you don't list my alma mater. Why not?

Answer: One of the criteria for inclusion here is the likelihood that the organization is/was at least occasionally known by its initials. Perhaps it's a matter of self-satisfaction but some colleges simply are never identified by their initials. For example, have you ever heard Harvard referred to as "HC" or "HU"? I didn't think so! "Ole Miss" is called "Ole Miss", and is never (to my knowledge) called "UM". Did I miss one or make a faulty assumption? I apologize! While I don't expect to frequently offer new editions of this book, you can certainly let me know. I'll make a note of your comment and consider your suggestion for the next edition.

Question: What time periods are you interested in?

Answer: Any time period at all if it is of potential interest. My original emphasis was oriented toward the needs of local historians or genealogists. This cast the list in a loosely defined "history" category and no doubt resulted in my failure to include certain organizations because I didn't consider them as historical.

The historical orientation did not last. Many/most of the organizations that have found their way onto this list are still very much active, and some still exist in different forms and with different names --but many are not! Some are brand new. I originally strove to capture the old and unusual, adding the current but perhaps ephemeral as I went along, but as this project has grown, more emphasis has moved to the present. In short, we're interested in all time periods.

Question: What geographical area does this list cover?

Answer: Good question! The parts of the world that use the Roman alphabet, for starters. There's a heavy bias in favor of the English speaking world, and within that, to North America. There's no question that organizations founded by immigrant ethnic groups from outside the British Isles belong on this list, with the caveat that the list editor is competent in English, remembers a little French and Italian, recalls a smattering of Latin, has sung German in choral groups, and is otherwise linguistically pretty much illiterate. So, if you are interested in the abbreviation or acronym for a mutual benefit association of Latvian immigrants with a Lettish name, for example, you hopefully will cut us a bit of slack, as I do not know Lettish. But use of the Roman alphabet is pretty much a requirement to make this list.

Question: I think that this list is great and I want to make copies of it and distribute it to my (1) students (2) library patrons (3) customers. May I do this?

Answer: Since this book is copyrighted, you are really posing a question of copyright law. We are not attorneys and can only offer our impressions and our intentions. You are advised to consult with a copyright attorney before making copies of portions of this book for any purposes except your own personal, non-commercial use. Likely economics and experience will tell us when, if, and how vigorously we need to enforce our copyright.

Question: I have seen one (or several) of the initializations listed with punctuation – for example, with a period after each letter. How come you don't use punctuation in your list?

Answer: With the exception of some religious orders (which have historically followed each letter in their abbreviation or acronym with a period – fewer and fewer do so today due to the effect that included spaces or punctuation has upon computers attempting to sequence lists) acronyms, initializations, and abbreviations are nowadays generally expressed without punctuation. Even the final period that traditionally has ended such commonplace abbreviations as "Ave" for "Avenue" is no longer a requirement in most cases.

This has not always been the case, of course, and even today some insert punctuation while others do not. So, when using the list you should consider that punctuation – particularly periods, and occasionally hyphens, ampersands, and apostrophes – may be present in the source document you are working from. In the limited cases where punctuation marks appear in this list it is simply because we cannot imagine the acronym or abbreviation in question appearing without it. An example of this is A&P, the food store chain. The punctuation is part of the initialism.

Question: Some of these look really bizarre! How can you be sure that some of these organizations actually ever existed?

Answer: I am not. When you pause to think about it, the fact that quite a few of the fraternal organizations include secrecy as an important part of their program – thus, information about them is difficult to locate and confirm. However, one thing we can say is that we have seen virtually every one of these acronym, initializations, and abbreviations in print (or online) at some point referring to an organization. If we ran into it, you might run into it as well. That is what we are here for: giving you a lead to pursue to get more information, not to validate the existence of a specific organization. (See the next question for a wordier answer).

Question: Are you absolutely sure that "xxx" really stands for "YYYYY" – or even that such an organization ever really existed?

Answer: No to both, of course – and we are definitely skeptical about a few of the organizations that we do list. The acronyms and abbreviations on this list have come to us from many, many sources, and we have not verified the actual existence of a number of them.

"Then why have such a list at all if you're not sure it's 100% right?" is the next logical question, to which the answer is simply the purpose we stated earlier: "to point researchers toward possibilities for further research and study". Nothing more and nothing less. It's a tool, not a building. You get to build the building, and if our tools are helpful to you in that process, well, we're pleased that we were helpful. But don't expect a hammer to be very useful as a screwdriver.

Another way to look at it: consider the possible downside if we listed an acronym that was never used, or one that referred to an organization that never existed. Point one: if the acronym was in fact never used, you would never come into contact with it in the real world, right? If you never came into contact with it in the real world, you would never have occasion to look it up in this book, right?

Point two: if it was used in the real world, and you came into contact with it, and you confidently looked it up here, and we had not listed it, you would have considerably more research to do just to define the mysterious abbreviation. We think the benefits so greatly outweigh the disadvantage that the point is moot.

Our objective is to help rather than to harm.

Question: What about state or local branches of larger organizations?

Answer: We've generally (not always) not included abbreviations that reflect state or local chapters of larger organizations. A tip: if you're stuck decoding an organization abbreviation and you notice that the first letter or letters match the locality, try eliminating the letters indicative of the geography and take another look.

17

SOURCES: Employed and for further reference – and categorization

No compendium like this ever grows by itself. While periodically an acronym comes to mind seemingly at random -- and while, when one is preparing a compilation like this, an acronym or abbreviation does seem to stand out like the proverbial sore thumb from reading in progress for other reasons -- ultimately I would have been remiss not to make use of the resources of the internet to fill in the missing organizations that properly needed to be included.

The longer the project has gone on, the more of these resources I have found and made use of. At the same time, all the more candidates for this volume have come from sources as varied as signs, URLs, blog posts, and, once, even skywriting!

The internet sources have helped in ways that were likely never intended. For example, a general American history website produced some reports by an insurance commissioner from the turn of the 20th century with a list of mutual benefit fraternities. This helped define a number of organizations that we were unaware had an insurance component as mutual benefit societies and also validated their existence as organizational entities – something not easy to do in a few cases, particularly for organizations that used secrecy as part of the appeal of the insurance policies they vended.

What follows are a few notes on the sources we have used over the years and have found to be dependable and helpful as well as relatively durable (internet resources do come and go).

First off, there are two sites of general acronyms (not limited to organizations) we have found and recommend to you.

www.acronymfinder.com

This is a query service that is quite useful for acronyms that are in current use. We've spot checked our collection against this source and found that most of our listings that represent currently active secular organizations are listed here. It's a free service and if you find yourself in a situation where this book isn't close at hand, and you need to quickly find some possible definitions of an acronym that you feel is pretty current, by all means give it a try.

If the acronym is not so current – if you find it in a slightly dated book or newspaper, for example, or it's not listed on acronymfinder.com –you may also want to check:

www.acronymattic.com

This site specializes in acronyms that have been reported but which could not be verified or had not been verified yet – including a few old or obsolete ones. It, like acronymfinder, is at its most useful for secular acronyms that are in current use or recently have been. If you think that the acronym you are looking for is either slang or off-color, it's a good place to start. On both sites you'll find far more acronyms that do NOT relate to organizations than those that do, but they provide a very valuable service nonetheless and we are happy to mention them here.

These two are not likely to be terribly helpful in tracking down religious organizations, especially the more obscure, nor are they particularly good as some initializations that have not ever gained real traction in the media. Finally they are a bit weak with organizations that are no longer around or are not generally known by an acronym or set of initials today. However, as a place to begin, do consider them.

If you have a particular interest in collecting emblems, swords, badges, etc. of fraternal organizations, especially those of some organizations that are so small or esoteric (or vaporous?) as to not be of interest to much of anyone anymore, but which may at some time have issued fraternal regalia: badges, buttons, hats, ribbons, ceremonial swords, that sort of thing, we enthusiastically recommend the massive list the following people have compiled, especially since the limitations of space posed by medals, ribbons, etc. particularly are – like the Roman centurion's SPQR standard -- apt to require the use of acronyms and initializations.

Regalia of this sort is called "exonumia" – should anyone ever ask you.

www.exonumia.com/art/society.htm

A caveat here: if you think about it, you do not actually have to be an organization to create fraternal regalia; really, anyone can do it. All you need is a vendor who will print or cast or enamel or sew the regalia you want. Thus, it's entirely possible that organizational regalia exists that purports to represent an organization that actually never existed outside one person's imagination or aspirations!

Genealogists seem to encounter more acronyms for organizations than many people, probably because genealogists search for people, and people belong to organizations. Some years ago, an organization called Black Sheep Genealogy developed a good acronym list of the acronyms for organizations that genealogists routinely encounter. (At least we think that Black Sheep was the organization that developed it. We encountered it there first, at any rate, back before a large number of genealogy sites produced their own lists of organizations (some of which are astonishingly similar to the one that Black Sheep put together – or to the old free one on our own website.)

www.ibssg.org/blacksheep/acronym.html

Gravestones and other funerary monuments were (and still are) a place where there was a real need for brevity. Nearly as much as in designing a lapel button or a centurion's standard, space on a tombstone is apt to be very limited, and an additional factor plays as well: the cost of cutting additional letters into stone. Thus, just as names of the deceased were abbreviated or initialized, just as "Born" became "b." and "Died" became "d.", when the name of an organization needed to be added because of an important affiliation, it was (and remains) an occasion when the full organizational name is rarely used.

Thus, another large and fruitful field for abbreviations, acronyms, initialization), and symbols was created and still exists (witness the currently ongoing controversy over religious symbols on military gravestones). The trend toward cremation might have been assumed to be likely to permit more organizational names to be spelled out, but it does not seem to have worked out that way. We think that the use of organizational abbreviations and acronyms on gravestones or burial markers is likely to continue long into the future.

In our quest, we encountered a book that is oriented toward those who are interested in gravestones and all that goes with them. In addition to abbreviations for organizations, you may have noticed that there is an elaborate symbology in terms of gravestone carvings, ranging from the commonplace cross and Star of David, to less obvious ones such as relationships between family members (designated, often, by a single lower-case letter). Even the carved vegetation used to decorate the stone can have complex meanings.

The book we found, Douglas Keister's *Stories in Stone* (2009) is available via Amazon, and if your interests frequently take you to the graveyard, you really ought to have this book to accompany you. (It also has a list of abbreviations for organizations, by the way.)

The user of this book will see "mutual benefit" cited frequently as the type of organization. It's an umbrella term, and it's helpful to understand some history here.

In an age after the fragmentation of large agriculture-based family units in the face of migration to jobs in large cities, before pensions, before employer-sponsored medical insurance, and before life insurance companies that catered to individuals, particularly individuals who were not wealthy, and certainly before there was a governmental safety net, people still wanted to ensure the wellbeing of spouses, children, and other dependents.

Churches tried to care for the poor in their precincts, usually with little success – there were always too many poor and too little money. In England, organizations called friendly societies began to spring up. Often they were sponsored by churches seeking a way to get the poor to contribute to caring for each other and at the same time provide an umbrella under which funds collected from wealthier parishioners could be disbursed in a thoughtful manner to "the deserving poor".

21

At the same time, fraternal organizations, often secret, began to appear frequently. There had been secret societies for many years at that point – most notably the Masons – but these new secret societies had the ritualistic trappings but few of the learning requirements of the Masons. Lacking the elaborate constructs of the Masonic movement, it was convenient to mix the mutual insurance aspects of friendly societies with these new secret rites, regalia, and titles.

Ethnicity, often accompanied by religious affiliation, was another ingredient. Here, organizations attempted to advance the interests of the particular ethnicity or religion involved – and this category included a number of nativist organizations as well as those targeting immigrants. Occupational affiliation represented another.

The key elements in all cases was that the membership had sufficient aspirations to be able to consider the future and perceived some capability for influencing it to some extent, had sufficient free time to participate in an activity outside the home, and had at least a minimum level of disposable income to contribute to an insurance kitty.

These organizations acquired similarities to insurance companies, particularly life insurance companies. In fact, one wonders if people intent on starting an insurance company might not have felt that the role of a fraternal mutual benefit association was one that would sell particularly well in their target market. Some mutual benefits became quite quickly insurance companies in all but name, while others continued for decades as fraternal organizations with only limited insurance capabilities and orientation.

To research these generally requires going to the insurance commissioner of the state in which the organization was headquartered or did business. We have not located a comprehensive online source of these groups, but we found that a fair number of reports of state insurance commissioners are available online, and these often will devote several pages to organizations that provided sufficient insurance functions that reporting to the insurance commissioner was required.

Rather late in the game, we discovered a major ongoing Wikipedia project investigating secret societies of all kinds. Obviously its purpose is to capture general knowledge rather than simply acronyms and abbreviations, but we expect that most of the societies this project will also yield acronyms or initializations. It is something to keep in mind for the future.

Several of the organizations listed herein are described in considerably more detail at the following site:

> www.meta-religion.com/Secret_societies/Groups/secret_organizations.htm

It's certainly worth taking a look, at any rate.

Again we suggest that you routinely take a look at Wikipedia when confronted with an unknown organization. Because that online encyclopedia has contributors all over the world, they just might have what you are looking for, particularly if it's not an organization that was popular in the United States.

> www.wikipedia.org

Religious orders and denominations are a whole subject unto themselves. Heavy users of abbreviations and acronyms, generally, the religious community has given rise to a very large number of abbreviations and acronyms.

We again recommend Wikipedia is the place to start in terms of getting more information about individual orders, denominations, etc., and as a source for current links to material in this area. Despite the seeming permanence of organized religion, changes occur very rapidly in this sector. We have noted that the tendency for organizations/denominations and their acronyms to proliferate seems to be more active among the more fundamentalist protestant denominations at present, so considerably more research may be needed to pin down an organization from the acronym here than in other faith communities.

Organized religious denominations fade almost imperceptibly into sects (of which there are many) and then into cults. We found J. Gordon Melton's 1986 book, *Encyclopedic Handbook of Cults in America* very helpful in understanding the distinctions and differences between the three categories. Denominations? There seems to be little question what they are. Sects? These tend to be breakaways from denominations that tend to be a bit more strict and demanding of their followers than conventional mainline denominations.

Cults, in Melton's taxonomy, tend to have a particular structure, and tend also to espouse foreign and alien theologies in preference to locally prevalent denominations. Lest the "cult" designation be perceived as entirely pejorative, by the way, that author notes that cults are often a source of innovation in mainstream denominations.

Several months ago, we were waiting at a railroad crossing, watching a freight train slowly and painfully inch its way through the crossing. Since we were the first car in line, there was little to command our attention besides the freight cars, and these were passing at such a slow rate that there was time to scrutinize each care carefully.

Perhaps you have noticed the three or four letter codes appearing on each and every railroad car in use in the United States today? It's safe to say that all railroad rolling stock today has them. It's through these codes that railroads can tell what rolling stock is their own, which belongs to some other railroad, or to a company that owns its own cars, or which leasing company owns a particular piece of rolling stock.

By the time the train had finally passed that day, it had occurred to us that these three and four letter codes were actually important abbreviations for organizations! From some of them, one could easily identify the railroad that owned the car. In some cases, the codes matched the initialization by which the railroad in question is popularly known.

In other cases, particularly for railroads where an ampersand appears in the popular name for the railroad, the rail car codes are generally NOT the same as the initials by which the railroad in question is popularly known. Further, since rolling stock leasing companies own much railroad equipment – and have their own car codes, and since many companies in the manufacturing and extractive sectors also have their own car fleets, the picture gets even more complex. That, basically, is why rail car codes – in addition to popular initializations for railroads – appear in this book.

The railroads have been at this rolling stock interchange thing for a long time, and have their system of coding down to something approaching a science. Indeed, it is so well organized today that the AAR (American Association of Railroads) has outsourced the maintenance of this common coding structure to an outside firm. Have a look here:

http://www.railserve.com/aar_railroad_reporting_marks.html

It didn't take long before we had moved logically beyond including a sampling of rail car codes to a newer portion of the transportation industry, airlines. Airline codes – and there are two separate and completely independent coding schemes run by different organizations and used for different purposes – often are clear abbreviations for air carriers.

The two schemes are:

IATA (the International Air Transport Association) provides two character codes:

https://www.iata.org/services/pages/codes.aspx

Conversely, the ICAO (International Civil Aviation Organization, a UN agency) assigns three character codes to aircraft operating agencies and related parties.

We've found that Wikipedia sorts this out better than the individual players, and we refer you to that source for more information:

https://en.wikipedia.org/wiki/List_of_airline_codes

Let it suffice here that two schemes – two character and three letter – exist. We have not attempted to be comprehensive here, and have concentrated on the better known carriers that are apt to be seen in the United States, with a few extras from more

25

obscure airlines thrown in to illustrate such oddities as IATA codes that begin with a numeric character.

Finally, the *World Almanac*, published annually, has a list of Associations and Societies where organizations that are currently known to be in existence are listed. There are other categories in the *World Almanac* as well, including religions and religious organizations, fraternities and sororities, and labor unions, which you may want to see. *The Encyclopedia of Associations* is usually available in the reference section of large and academic libraries and is considered a standard source. You may also find a copy of *The Encyclopedia of Associations* in sections of libraries dedicated to helping people find jobs.

(Note that the sites and other sources mentioned in this section are not under the control of Between the Lakes Group, no matter how enthusiastic we are about them or how highly we recommend them to you.)

Acknowledgements:

This book would never have moved past being a downloadable list of historical acronyms on the Between the Lakes Group website if a then-fourteen year old Rebekah Larson had not self-published her "young adult" novel, *Flaming Rain*, on Amazon. She provided the proof of concept for self-publication and that got the ball rolling.

My wife, Judith Sherman, was left undisturbed for many hours as I searched for acronyms and put them into publishable format. She was also responsible for a critically important decision. The hardest part of compiling this directory was deciding when to stop. There is a near-infinite number of organizations out there, and most are known by at least one abbreviation, acronym, or initialism. When this compilation seemed to be on the verge of becoming a life's work, she said "Just stop." Ultimately, that is what I did.

Others contributed as well in great and small – but always important – ways. Eleanore Jenks as a summer intern inspired me to perceive Between the Lakes Group, by which entity this is published, as an open-ended information business instead of one man's retirement business publishing for the genealogy community.

Ed Kirby, historian, scientist, educator that he is, and his wife Mary, provided encouragement, likely without realizing they were doing so.

Looking backwards, the late Timothy Field Beard was instrumental in encouraging my interest in the past – and this list began as one of historical acronyms. Further back, the late Thomas Johnson, my English master at Lawrenceville, encouraged me in general at a critical time in my life many years ago. Jim Kuhn, my advisor at Columbia Business School, winked and let me run with my MBA master's essay on *The Decline of Union Singing* – a bit of a stretch, to be sure, although he did insist that I bring my guitar to my oral defense. The late Bill Engert, by sticking his neck a mile out and hiring me as an almost 12 year old to be the bugler at Beech Mountain Boy Scout Camp, thereby gave me an early lesson in making my way alone, pursuing a purpose of uncertain merit that was, particularly in the case of first call each morning, detested by many. It was an important life lesson. So were life experiences shared with me by people whom I knew when their lives were not going as well as they could have been -- a barroom drunk and a failed keypunch operator, in fact -- who later turned out to be the late Lee Marvin and the late Janis Joplin.

Len Farano and Ed Burchianti at Citibank gave me solitude for nearly a year to work at thinking about the meanings of words in several dimensions, an exercise that I am sure benefitted me far more than it did Citi. They encouraged me to apply several layers of abstraction to the analysis process, and some of this process is implicitly on display here.

Numerics

100BM: One Hundred Black Men of America (community betterment)

1812: Society of the War of 1812 (lineage)

1812: Military Society of the War of 1812 (lineage)

21CF: Twenty-first Century Foundation (charitable)

2AF: 2nd Amendment Foundation (lobby)

2B: Bahrain Air B.S.C. (IATA airline code)

2M: Moldavian Airlines (IATA airline code)

3M: Minnesota Mining and Manufacturing Company (business)

4C: Child Care Coordinating Council (benevolent)

4C: Conservative Congregational Christian Conference (also CCCC) (religious denomination)

4G: Gazpromavia Aviation Company Ltd. (IATA airline code)

4H: 4-H clubs (see also HHHH) (youth)

4Y: Airbus Transport International (IATA airline code)

40&8: Forty and Eight. WWI veterans' organization taking its name from the capacity of French freight cars of the time – 40 men or 8 horses (honor society of the American Legion) (veterans)

5L: Compania Boliviana de Transporte Aereo (IATA airline code)

5N: Aeroflot-Nord (IATA airline code)

5X: UPS (IATA airline code)

6D: Air Dominicana SA (IATA airline code)

82ADA: 82nd Airborne Division Association (military)

8C: Air Transport International Ltd (IATA airline code)

8J: Jet 4 You (IATA airline code)

8M: Myanmar Airways International (IATA airline code)

9U: Air Moldova (IATA airline code)

9W: Jet Airways (India) Limited (IATA airline code)

A

A: Alton Railroad
A3: Aegean Airlines SA (IATA airline code)
A∴A∴ – Argentium Astrum (occult)
A∴A∴S∴R∴. Ancient and Accepted Scottish Rite (Masonic)
A&AA: A & A Academy (school)
A&E: Alexander & Eastern Railway (railroad)
A&N: Atlantic & Northwestern Railroad
A&P: Great Atlantic and Pacific Tea Company (company)
A&R: Aberdeen & Rockfish Railroad
A&RM: Alexander & Rich Mountain Railroad
A&W: Allegheny & Western Railroad
A&WMA: Air & Waste Management Association (professional)
AA: Alcoholics Anonymous (self-help)
AA: Augustinians of the Assumption (Assumptionists) (religious order)
AA: Addictions Anonymous (self-help)
AA: Alzheimer's Association (benevolent)
AA: American Atheists (religious denomination)
AA: Argentium Astrum (spiritual, mystical)
AA: Ann Arbor Railroad
AA: Americans for the Arts (civic)
AA: American Airlines (airline code)
AAofISandTW: Amalgamated Association of Iron, Steel, and Tin Workers (labor union)
AAof SREofA: Amalgamated Association of Street Railroad Employees of America (labor union)
AAA: Army Aviation Association (veterans)
AAA: American Anthropological Association (learned)
AAA: American Automobile Association (interest group)
AAA: Agricultural Adjustment Administration (New Deal) (governmental)
AAA: Amateur Athletic Association (hobby)
AAA: All-American Association (patriotic, anti-KKK)
AAA: Adventist Accrediting Association (education, religious)
AAA: American Academy of Actuaries (professional)
AAA: American Ambulance Association (trade group)
AAAA: Associated Actors and Artistes of America (labor union)

30

AAAA: American Association of Advertising Agencies (trade group)

AAAAI: American Academy of Allergy, Asthma and Immunology (professional)

AAAE: American Association of Airport Executives (professional)

AAAE: Association of Arts Administration Executives (professional)

AAAI: American Association for Artificial Intelligence (learned)

AAAIMH: American Association for the Abolition of Involuntary Mental Hospitalization (political)

AAAL: American Association for Applied Linguistics (learned)

AAANZ: Anabaptist Association of Australia and New Zealand (religious denomination)

AAAS: American Association for the Advancement of Science (learned)

AAAS: American Academy of Arts and Sciences (learned)

AAAX: AAA Warehouse Corporation (Shell Oil) (railcar marking)

AABB: American Association of Blood Banks (trade group)

AABC: American Amateur Baseball Congress (sports)

AABF: Africa Asia Business Forum (business)

AABP: American Association of Bovine Practitioners (professional)

AAC: Army Air Corps (military)

AAC: Armenian Apostolic Church (religious denomination)

AAC: Alaskan Air Command (military)

AAC: American Anglican Council (religious)

AACA: Antique Automobile Club of America (hobby)

AACAP: American Academy of Child and Adolescent Psychiatry (professional)

AACC: American Association of Cereal Chemists (professional)

AACE: American Association of Clinical Endocrinologists (professional)

AACE: Association for the Advancement of Computing in Education (professional)

AACE: American Association of Cost Engineering (professional)

AACE: American Association of Code Enforcement (professional)

AACH: American Academy of Communication in Healthcare (professional)

AACN: American Association of Colleges of Nursing (education)

AACOM: American Association of Colleges of Osteopathic Medicine (education)

AACP: American Association of College of Pharmacy (education)

AACR: American Association for Cancer Research (scientific)

AACS: American Association of Christian Schools (religion, education)

AACS: Association of American Cemetery Superintendents (professional)

AACS: American Academy of Cosmetic Surgery (professional)

AACSB: The International Association for Management Education (education)

AACSB: Association to Advance Collegiate Schools of Business (education, accrediting)

AACU: American Association of Clinical Urologists (professional)

AAD: American Academy of Dermatology (professional)

AADB: American Association of the Deaf-Blind (support, advocacy)

AADEP: American Academy of Disability Evaluating Physicians (professional)

AAE: Association of American Educators (professional)

AAEA: American Agricultural Economics Association (professional)

AAEC: Association of American Editorial Cartoonists (professional)

AAEE: American Academy of Environmental Engineers (professional)

AAEES: American Academy of Environmental Engineers and Scientists (professional)

AAF: (United States) Army Air Force (military)

AAF: American Adaptive Freemasonry (Masonic)

AAF: American Advertising Federation (trade group)

AAFA: American Apparel and Footwear Association (trade group)

AAFCS: American Association of Family and Consumer Sciences (professional)

AAFCS-CFA: AAFCS Council for Accreditation (accrediting)

AAFFES: Army and Air Force Exchange Services (military)

AAFLN: American Association of Foreign Language Newspapers (trade group)

AAFM: American Academy of Financial Management (professional)

AAFMAA: Army and Air Force Mutual Aid Association (veterans, mutual benefit)

AAFP: American Academy of Family Physicians (professional)

AAFPRS: American Academy of Facial Plastic and Reconstructive Surgery (professional)

AAG: Association of American Geographers (learned)

AAG: American Authors Guild (trade group)

AAGL: American Association of Gynecologic Laproscopists (professional)

AAGP: American Academy for Geriatric Psychiatry (professional)

AAH: Association of Ancient Historians (learned)

AAHA: American Animal Hospital Association (trade group)

AAHC: American Association for History and Computing (learned)

AAHKS: American Association of Hip and Knee Surgeons (professional)

AAHOA: Asian American Hotel Owners Association (trade group)

AAHPM: American Academy of Hospice and Palliative Care Medicine (professional)

AAHS: Association of American Horse Shows (equestrian)

AAHS: American Association for Hand Surgery (professional)

AAIA: Automotive Aftermarket Industry Association (trade group)

AAIM: Alliance for Academic Internal Medicine (professional)

AAIM: American Academy for Insurance Medicine (professional)

AAIM: American Association of Independent Music (trade group)

AAISTW: Amalgamated Association of Iron, Steel and Tin Workers (labor union)

AAL: Aid Association for (or of) Lutherans (mutual benefit)

AAL: American Airlines (airline code)

AALAS: American Association for Laboratory Animal Science (science)

AALC: American Association of Lutheran Churches (religious denomination)

AALE: American Academy for Liberal Education (education, accrediting)

AALJ: Association of Administrative Law Judges (lobbying organization)

AAM: Alabama A&M University (higher education)

AAM: American Association of Museums (trade organization)

AAM: Alliance of Automobile Manufacturers (trade group)

AAMA: American Amusement Machine Association (trade group)

AAMC: Association of American Medical Colleges (umbrella group)

AAMDC: US Army Air and Missile Defense Command (military)

AAMFT: American Association for Marriage and Family Therapy (education)

AAMFT/COAMFTE: AAMFT Commission on Accreditation from Marriage and Family Therapy Education (accrediting)

AAMVA: American Association of Motor Vehicle Administrators (professional)

AAN: American Academy of Neurology (professional)

AANEM: American Association of Neuromuscular & Electrodiaganostic Medicine (professional)

AANS: American Association of Neurological Surgeons (professional)

AANSMG: Aryan Ancestry National Socialist Minority (KKK)

AAO: Ancient Arabic Order (Masonic)

AAO: American Academy of Ophthalmology (professional)

AAO: American Association of Orthodontists (professional)

AAOA: American Academy of Otolaryngic Allergy (professional)

AAofISandTW: Amalgamated Association of Iron, Steel, and Tin Workers (labor union)

AAofSRE: Amalgamated Association of Street Railway Employees (labor union)

AAONMS: Ancient Arabic Order of the Nobles of the Mystic Shrine (the Shriners) (Masonic)

AAONNS: American Academy of Otolaryngology, Head and Neck Surgery (professional)

AAOPAC: American Association of Orthodontists Political Action Committee (political)

AAORRAC: Antiquus Arcanus Ordo Rosae Rubae Aureae Crucis (fraternal, Rosicrucian)

AAOS: American Academy of Orthopedic Surgeons (professional)

AAP: Aloha Aina Party (political party)

AAP: American Academy of Pediatrics (professional)
AAP: Association of American Publishers (trade group)
AAPA: Asian American Political Alliance (political)
AAPA: American Association of Physicians Assistants (professional)
AAPA: American Association of Tort Authorities (trade group)
AAPC: American Association of Political Consultants (trade group)
AAPC: American Association of Pastoral Counselors (professional)
AAPHP: American Association of Public Health Physicians (professional)
AAPIO: American Association of Physicians of Indian Origin (professional)
AAPL: American Association of Professional Landmen (trade group)
AAPL: American Academy of Psychiatry and the Law (professional)
AAPL: Afro-American Patrolmen's League (ethnic)
AAPM: American Academy of Pain Medicine (professional)
AAPOR: American Association for Public Opinion Research (research)
AAPP: American Academy on Physician and Patient (professional)
AAPS: American Association of Plastic Surgeons (professional)
AAPT: American Association of Physics Teachers (professional, education)
AAPT: American Association of Philosophy Teachers (professional, education)
AAR: American Association of Railroads (or Association of American Railroads) (trade group)
AAR: American Association of Rabbis (religious, professional)
AAR: American Academy of Religion (professional)
AARA: Antique Auto Racing Association (motorsports)
AARHMS: American Academy of Research Historians of Medieval Spain (learned)
AARP: American Association of Retired Persons (civic, mutual benefit)
AARTS: Association of Advanced Rabbinical and Talmudic Schools (education)
AAS: American Ambulance Service (World War I)
AAS: American Astronomical Society (learned)
AAS: Association for Asian Studies (academic)

AASA: American Association of School Administrators (education, trade)

AASC: Handmaids of the Blessed Sacrament and of Charity (religious order)

AASC: Handmaids of the Sacred Heart of Jesus (religious order)

AASC: American Association of State Climatologists (professional)

AASCE: Amalgamated Association of Street Car Employees (labor union)

AASD: Afro-American Sons and Daughters (fraternal)

AASI: American Association of Snowboard Instructors (professional, sports)

AASL: American Association of School Librarians (professional)

AASLD: American Association of the Study of Liver Diseases (professional)

AASLH: American Association for State and Local History (learned)

AASM: American Academy of Sleep Medicine (professional)

AASP: Alliance of Automotive Service Providers (business)

AASR: Ancient and Accepted Scottish Rite (Masonic)

AASREA: Amalgamated Association of Street Railway Employees of America (labor union)

AASS: American Anti-Slavery Society (religious)

AAST: American Association of State Troopers (civic)

AATS: American Association for Thoracic Surgery (professional)

AATSP: American Association of Teachers of Spanish and Portuguese (professional, education)

AAU: Amateur Athletic Union (sports)

AAUP: American Association of University Professors (professional, education)

AAUW: American Association of University Women (women, civic)

AAVS: American Anti-Vivisection Society (political)

AAWF: Army Against War and Fascism (political, 1930s)

AAWR: American Association of Women Radiologists (professional, women)

AB: American Brotherhood (fraternal)

AB: Arctic Brotherhood (fraternal, mutual benefit)

AB: Alliance of Baptists (religious denomination)

AB: Akron Barberton Cluster Railroad

AB: African Brotherhood (ethnic)

AB: American Brethren (also FAA - Free and Accepted
Americans, WA – Wide Awakes, etc.) (nativist)
AB&P: Amherst, Belchertown and Palmer Railroad
ABofD: Apprentice Boys of Derry (fraternal, political)
ABA: American Bankers Association (trade group)
ABA: American Benefit Association (mutual benefit)
ABA: American Bar Association (professional)
ABA: Aaron Burr Accord (historical society)
ABA: American Baptist Association (religious denomination)
ABA: American Benevolent Association (mutual benefit)
ABA: Academic Boniface Association (lay order)
ABA: Ayrshire Breeders Association (cattle)
ABA: American Bantam Club (poultry)
ABA: American Brabant Association (equine)
ABA: American Bulldog Association (canine)
ABA: American Board of Anesthesiology (accrediting)
ABA: American Beverage Association (trade group)
ABA: American Booksellers Association (trade group)
ABA: American Bus Association (trade group)
ABAA: American Bearing Manufacturers Association (trade
group)
ABAI: American Board of Allergy and Immunology
(accrediting)
ABANY: American Benefit Association of New York (mutual
benefit)
ABB: Akron & Barberton Belt (railroad)
ABB: American Brotherhood for the Blind (charitable)
ABB: African Blood Brotherhood (ethnic, charitable)
ABC: Assam Baptist Convention (religious denomination)
ABC: American Banking Congress (business)
ABC: Appalachian Bible College (West Virginia) (higher
education)
ABC: American Broadcasting Company (business)
ABC: American Baptist Churches (in the USA) (religious
denomination)
ABC: Alliance of Baptist Churches (religious denomination)
ABC: American Buckeye Club (poultry)
ABC: American Brahma Club (poultry)
ABC: American Buttercup Club (poultry)
ABC: Associated Builders and Contractors (trade group)
ABC: Association of Booksellers for Children (trade group)
ABCA: American, British, Canadian, Australian Armies
Program (military)

ABCFM: American Board of Commissioners for Foreign Missions (religious)

ABCK: Alaska British Columbia Transportation (railroad)

ABCL: American Birth Control League (civic)

ABCM: American Board of Catholic Missions (religious)

ABCRS: American Board of Colon and Rectal Surgery (accrediting)

ABCUSA: American Baptist Churches USA (religious denomination)

ABD: Apprentice Boys of Derry (fraternal, service)

ABD: American Board of Dermatology (accrediting)

ABEM: American Board of Emergency Medicine (accrediting)

ABET: Accreditation Board for Engineering and Technology (education, accrediting)

ABFM: American Board of Family Medicine (accrediting)

ABFMS: American Baptist Foreign Missionary Society (religious)

ABFSE: American Board of Funeral Service Education (education)

ABG: Alpha Beta Gamma (business) (academic honorary)

ABH: Association for the Bibliography of History (learned)

ABHE: Association for Biblical Higher Education (religious)

ABHES: Accrediting Bureau of Health Education Schools (education)

ABHMS: American Baptist Home Mission Society (religious)

ABHS: American Baptist Historical Society (religious)

ABI: Allentown Bible Institute (religious)

ABI: American Beverage Institute (trade group)

ABIM: American Board of Internal Medicine (accrediting)

ABL: Alameda Belt Line (railroad)

ABL: American Benevolent Legion (mutual benefit)

ABLC: American Brown Leghorn Club (poultry)

ABM: Texas and Pacific Railway (railroad)

ABM: Anderson Boy Movement (religious, youth)

ABMC: American Battle Monuments Commission (governmental)

ABMG: American Board of Medical Genetics (accrediting)

ABMS: American Board of Medical Specialties (umbrella organization)

ABMU: American Baptist Missionary Union (religious)

ABN: Alabama Northern Railway (Ashland Railway) (railroad)

ABNM: American Board of Nuclear Medicine (accrediting)

ABNS: American Board of Neurological Surgery (accrediting)

ABO: Association of British Orchestras (musical)
ABO: American Board of Optometry (professional)
ABO: American Board of Ophthalmology (accrediting)
ABoD: Apprentice Boys of Derry (anti-Catholic)
ABOG: American Board of Obstetrics and Gynecology (accrediting)
ABOS: American Board of Orthopaedic Surgery (accrediting)
ABOto): American Board of Otolaryngology (accrediting)
ABOX: RailBox/RailGon (also RBOX and GONX) (rail car leasing company)
ABP: Association of Black Psychologists (professional)
ABP: American Board of Pathology (accrediting)
ABP: American Board of Pediatrics (accrediting)
ABPC: American Buckeye Poultry Club (poultry)
ABPM: American Board of Preventative Medicine (accrediting)
ABPMR: American Board of Physical Medicine and Rehabilitation (accrediting)
ABPN: American Board of Psychiatry and Neurology (accrediting)
ABPR: Aberdeen and Briar Patch Railway (Aberdeen, Carolina and Western Railway) (railroad)
ABPS: American Baptist Publications Society (religious)
ABPS: American Board of Plastic Surgery (accrediting)
ABR: Athens Line (railroad)
ABR: American Bulldog Registry (canine)
ABR: American Board of Radiology (accrediting)
ABS: American Bible Society (religious)
ABS: American Bethel Society (religious)
ABS: American Benefit Society (mutual benefit)
ABS: Alabama Southern Railroad
ABS: American Board of Surgery (accrediting)
ABSNY: American Benefit Society of New York (mutual benefit)
ABT: American Ballet Theatre (dance)
ABTA: American Brain Tumor Association (medical research)
ABTS: American Board of Thoracic Surgery (accrediting)
ABU: American Benevolent Union (mutual benefit)
ABU: American Board of Urology (accrediting)
ABW: A Better World (religious, education)
ABWA: American Business Women's Association (trade group)
ABWE: Association of Baptists for World Evangelism (religious)

ABWE: Association of Black Women Entrepreneurs (business group)

ABWH: Association of Black Women Historians (professional)

AC: Anglican Communion (religious denomination)

AC: Algoma Central and Hudson Bay Railway (railroad)

AC: Apostolic Church (religious denomination)

AC: Aztec Club (lineage)

AC: Anglican Cistercians (religious order)

AC: Air Canada (airline code)

ACA: Air Canada (airline code)

ACA: American Camping Association (professional)

ACA: American Canoe Association (recreation)

ACA: Association Canado-Americaine (fraternal)

ACA: Association of Collegiate Alumnae (civic)

ACA: Academy of Certified Archivists (professional)

ACA: American Combat Association (sport, martial arts)

ACA: American Counseling Association (professional)

ACA: American Composers Alliance (musical)

ACA: Araucana Club of America (poultry)

ACA: American Collectors Association (trade group)

ACA International: was previously American Collectors Association (trade group)

ACAAI: American College of Allergy, Asthma, and Immunology (professional)

ACAOM: Accreditation Commission for Acupuncture and Oriental Medicine (accrediting)

ACB: American Council of the Blind (charitable)

ACBSP: Accreditation Council for Business Schools and Programs (accrediting)

ACC: Anglican Catholic Church (religious denomination)

ACC: Adventist Christian Church (religious denomination)

ACC: Apostolic Christian Church (religious denomination)

ACC: American Conference of Cantors (religious, professional)

ACC: American College of Cardiology (professional)

ACC: American Chemistry Council (trade group)

ACCA: Antiochian Catholic Church in America (religious denomination)

ACCA: Air Conditioning Contractors of America (trade group)

ACCE: American Council for Construction Education (education)

ACCESS: Arab Community Center for Economic and Social Services (ethnic, musical)

40

ACCET: Accrediting Council for Continuing Education and Training (education, accrediting)

ACCJC: Accreditation Commission for Community and Junior Colleges (education, accrediting)

ACCM: Accreditation Commission of Colleges of Medicine (education, accrediting)

ACCP: Army Correspondence Course Program (military)

ACCSC: Accrediting Commission of Career Schools and Colleges (education)

ACCUS: American Catholic Church in the United States (religious denomination)

ACCUS: Automobile Competition Committee for the United States (motorsports)

ACDA: American Choral Directors Association (professional)

ACDA: Association of Catholic Diocesan Archivists (trade, religious)

ACDA: Arms Control and Disarmament Agency (governmental)

ACDHA: American Cream Draft Horse Association (equine)

ACE: American Council on Exercise (professional)

ACEMJ: Accrediting Council on Education in Journalism and Mass Communications (accrediting)

ACEP: American College of Emergency Physicians (professional)

ACERS: American Ceramic Society (research, trade)

ACF: formerly American Car and Foundry (business)

ACF: American Culinary Federation (trade group, education)

ACF: American Composers Forum (musical)

ACF: Administration for Children and Families (governmental)

ACFE: Association of Certified Fraud Examiners (professional)

ACG: American College of Gastroenterology (professional)

ACGA: American Corn Growers Association (trade group)

ACGME: Accreditation Council for Graduate Medical Education (accrediting)

ACHE: American College of Healthcare Executives (professional organization)

ACHF: African Christian Hospital Foundation (religious charitable)

ACHP: Anthropological Committee for Homeless People (good works)

ACHP: Advisory Council on Historic Preservation (governmental)

41

ACHRI: Air Conditioning, Heating and Refrigeration Institute (trade group)
ACHS: Association of College Honor Societies (education)
ACI: Awana Clubs International (civic)
ACI: Association of Catholics in Ireland (lay order)
ACI: Airports Council International (trade group)
ACICS: Accrediting Council for Independent Colleges and Schools (education, accrediting)
ACIS: Algoma Central Railway
ACJ: American Council for Judaism (religious, political)
ACJR: Ashtabula, Carson and Jefferson Railroad
ACJU: American Coastal Lines (railroad)
ACL: Atlantic Coast Line (railroad)
ACL: Australian Christian Lobby (political/religious)
ACL: African Communities League (fraternal, ethnic)
ACL: Administration for Community Living (governmental)
ACL: Association of Christian Libraries (religious)
ACLI: American Council of Life Insurers (trade group)
ACLJ: American Center for Law and Justice (political/religious)
ACLM: American College of Legal Medicine (professional)
ACLS: American Council of Learned Societies (learned)
ACLU: American Civil Liberties Union (civic)
ACLU: Atlantic Container Line (railroad)
ACM: American Church Mission (religious)
ACM: Association for Computing Machinery (learned)
ACMA: American Composites Manufacturers Association (trade group)
ACMGG: American College of Medical Genetics and Genomics (professional)
ACMI: American College of Medical Informatics (professional)
ACMP: Amateur Chamber Music Players (musical)
ACMP: Association of Comics Magazine Publishers (trade group)
ACMQ: American College of Medical Quality (professional)
ACMS: American College of Mohs Surgery (professional)
ACMT: American College of Medical Toxicology (professional)
ACN: American College of Nutrition (professional)
ACNA: Anglican Church in North America (religious denomination)
ACNM: American College of Nuclear Medicine (professional)
ACNM: American College of Nurse-Midwives (professional)
ACNS: American Clinical Neurophysiology Society (professional)

ACOEM: American College of Occupational and Environmental Medicine (professional)
ACOG: American Congress of Obstetricians and Gynecologists (professional)
ACOM: U. S. Atlantic Command (military)
ACOM: Association for Convention Operations Management (trade group)
ACORN: American College of Operating Room Nurses (professional)
ACORN: Abandoned Children and Orphans Resource Network (self-help)
ACP: Adventist Church of Promise (religious denomination)
ACP: A Connecticut Party (political party)
ACP: American Conservative Party (political party)
ACP: American College of Physicians (professional)
ACP: American College of Phlebology (professional)
ACPAQ: Advisory Committee on Post Adjustment Questions (UN activity)
ACPE: Arnold College of Physical Education (Connecticut) (higher education)
ACPE: American College of Physical Education (Illinois) (higher education)
ACPE: Accreditation Council for Pharmacy Education (accrediting)
ACPE: Association for Clinical Pastoral Education (education, accrediting)
ACPF: American College of Physicians Foundation (research)
ACPM: American College of Preventive Medicine (professional)
ACQUIN: Accreditation, Certification and Quality Assurance Institute (education)
ACR: American College of Rheumatology (professional)
ACR: American College of Radiology (professional)
ACRC: Andalusia and Conecuh Railroad
ACREC: Advocacy Committee for Racial Ethnic Concerns (religious)
ACRL: Association of College and Research Libraries (professional)
ACRO: American College of Radiation Oncology (professional)
ACRP: Association of Clinical Research Professionals (professional)
ACS: American Cancer Society (medical research, advocacy)
ACS: American Chemical Society (learned)
ACS: American Colonization Society (religious)

ACS: Allendale Columbia School (New York) (school)
ACS: American College of Surgeons (professional)
ACSCA: Anglican Church of the Southern Cone of American (religious denomination)
ACSM: American Congress on Surveying and Mapping (professional)
ACT: American Council for Technology (quasi-governmental)
ACT: Association for Competitive Technology (lobby)
ACTA: American Christmas Tree Association (trade group)
ACTIAC: American Council for Technology and Industry Advisory Council (trade group)
ACUMA: American Credit Union Mortgage Association (trade group)
ACTWU: Amalgamated Clothing and Textile Workers Union (labor union)
ACUNY: Associated Colleges of Upper New York (higher education)
ACUS: Administrative Conference of the United States (governmental)
ACVS: American College of Veterinary Surgeons (professional)
ACWA: Amalgamated Clothing Workers of America (labor union)
ACWR: Aberdeen, Carolina & Western (railroad)
ACWR: Archivists for Congregations of Women Religious (religious, trade)
ACY: Akron, Canton & Youngstown (railroad)
AD: Alpha Delta Phi (college fraternity)
AD: Atlantic & Danville (railroad)
Ad2: Young Professionals in Advertising (trade group)
ADA: American Dental Association (professional)
ADA: Americans for Democratic Action (political)
ADA: American Diabetes Foundation (medical research, advocacy)
ADA: American Diabetes Association (medical research, advocacy)
ADA: American Diabetic Association (medical research, advocacy)
ADA: Air Defense Artillery (Army branch)
ADA: American Donkey Association (donkeys)
ADBA: American Dog Breeders Association (trade, advocacy)
ADBF: Adrian & Blissfield Railroad
ADC: Air Defense Command (military)
ADDA: Alamo Defenders Descendents Association (lineage)

ADCA: American Dexter Cattle Association (cattle)
ADEAW: Associated Daughters of Early American Witches (lineage)
ADG: Alpha Delta Gamma (college fraternity)
ADIR: Adirondack Scenic Railroad
ADK: Alpha Delta Kappa (honorary)
ADL: Anti Defamation League of B'nai B'rith (political)
ADM: Archer Daniels Midland (company)
ADM: Alpha Delta Mu (social work) (academic honorary)
ADMS: American Donkey and Mule Society (donkeys)
ADN: Ashley, Drew & Northern (railroad)
ADP: Association of Directory Publishers (trade group)
ADPA: American Dartmoor Pony Association (equine)
ADPi: Alpha Delta Pi (college fraternity)
ADRA: American Drag Racing Association (motorsports)
ADS: American Driving Society (equestrian)
ADS: Alpha Delta Sigma (advertising) (academic honorary)
ADT: American District Telegraph (company)
ADVA: Americal Division Veterans Association (Vietnam veterans)
AdvaMed: Advanced Medical Technology Association (trade group)
AE: Arizona Eastern Railroad
AE: Armed Forces Europe (military)
AE: Alpha Epsilon (biological engineering) (honorary fraternity)
AEA: American Economic Association (professional, learned)
AEA: Actors' Equity Association (labor union)
AEA: American Electrology Association (professional)
AEC: Anglican Episcopal Church (religious denomination)
AEC: Atlantic & East Carolina (railroad)
AEC: Atomic Energy Commission (governmental)
AECOM: Albert Einstein College of Medicine (higher education)
AED: Alpha Epsilon Delta (pre-med) (academic honorary)
AED: Association for Episcopal Deacons (religious)
AEE: Aegean Airlines SA (airline code)
AEF: American Expeditionary Forces (WWI) (military)
AEF: Association of Evangelical Friends (religious denomination)
AEIF: Armco Employees Independent Federation (labor union)
AEL: Alpha Epsilon Lambda (honorary fraternity)
AEM: Association of Evangelical Missions (religious)

AEMB: Alpha Eta Mu Beta (biomedical engineering) (honorary fraternity)
AEO: Ancient Egyptian Order (of SCIOTS) (also AEOS) (fraternal)
AEO: Ancient Essenic Order (fraternal)
AEOPS: Ancient Egyptian Order of Princesses of Sharemkhu (Masonic)
AEOS: Ancient Egyptian Order (of SCIOTS) (also AEO) (Masonic)
AEPi: Alpha Epsilon Pi (college fraternity)
AEPOW: American Ex-Prisoners of War (veterans)
AER: Army Emergency Relief (mutual benefit)
AER: Algoma Eastern Railway (railroad)
AERC: Albany and Eastern Railroad
AERE: Association of Environmental and Resource Economists (professional)
AES: Association of Educational Sororities (umbrella organization)
AES: American Ethnological Society (learned)
AES: Audio Engineering Society (professional)
AESS: Association of Environmental Studies and Sciences (education)
AETA: American Equestrian Trade Association (trade group)
AEX: Andersons (rail car lessor)
AF: Asiatic Fleet (military)
AF: American Freemen (nativist, anti-Catholic)
AF: Anamchara Fellowship (religious denomination)
AF: Alabama & Florida Railway (railroad)
AF: Air Force (military)
AF: Air France (airline code)
AF: Anarchist Federation (political)
AF&AM: Ancient Free & Accepted Masons (also AFAM) (Blue Lodge) (Masonic)
AFA: American Foundrymen's Association (labor union)
AFA: Association of Flight Attendants (labor union)
AFA: Air Force Association (Military support)
AFA: Associated Fraternities of America (trade group)
AFA: Admiral Farragut Academy (school)
AFA: American Family Association (political/religious)
AFA: US Air Force Academy (higher education)
AFA: Assembly of the Friends of Azerbaijan (lobby)
AFA: American Fraternal Alliance (fraternal, service)
AFA: American Finance Association (business)

AFAA: Aerobics and Fitness Association of America (professional)

AFAM: Ancient Free & Accepted Masons (also AF&AM) (Blue Lodge) (Masonic)

AFBA: Armed Forces Benefit Association (veterans)

AFBS: American and Foreign Bible Society (religious)

AFBF: American Farm Bureau Federation (agricultural)

AF&AM: (see AFAM) Ancient Free and Accepted Masons (fraternal, Masonic)

AFC: American Fraternal Congress (mutual benefit)

AFC: American Fraternal Circle (mutual benefit)

AFC: Apostolic Faith Church (religious denomination)

AFC: Apostolate for Family Consecration (lay order)

AFCEA: Armed Forces Communications and Electronics Association (military)

AFCS: American Federation of Catholic Societies (religious)

AFCU: American and Foreign Christian Union (religious)

AFE: Armed Forces Entertainment (military support)

AFEA: Agency for French Education Abroad (education)

AFEDJ: American Friends of the Episcopal Diocese of Jerusalem (religious)

AFF: Armed Forces Foundation (military support)

AFFI: American Frozen Food Institute (trade group)

AFGA: American Fainting Goat Association (goats)

AFGE: American Federation of Government Employees (labor union)

AFHF: Air Force Historical Foundation (learned)

AFI: American Film Institute (California) (higher education)

AFIU: American Fraternal Insurance Union (mutual benefit)

AFL: American Federation of Labor (labor union)

AFL: American Football League (sports)

AFL: Anglicans For Life (religious)

AFL: Aeroflot Russian Airlines (airline code)

AFL: American Fraternal League (mutual benefit)

AFL-CIO: American Federation of Labor – Congress of Industrial Organizations (labor union)

AFLC: Association of Free Lutheran Congregations (religious denomination)

AFLC: Air Force Logistics Command (military)

AFLR: Alabama & Florida Railroad

AFM: American Federation of Musicians of the United States and Canada (labor union)

AFMC: Air Force Materiel Command (military)

AFME: American Friends of the Middle East (political)
AFOSI: Air Force Office of Special Investigations (military)
AFP: America First Party (political party)
AFP: American Freedom Party (political party)
AFP: American Falangist Party (political)
AFPA: American Forest & Paper Association (trade group)
AFPMBAI: Armed Forces and Police Mutual Benefit Association, Inc. (mutual benefit)
AFR: Air France (airline code)
AFRC: Air Force Reserve Command (military)
AFRES: Air Force Reserve (military)
AFRH: Armed Forces Retirement Home (governmental)
AFRS: Armed Forces Recreation Society (professional)
AFRTC: Air Force Reserve Training Center (military)
AFS: American Foundrymen's Society (labor union)
AFS: American Foundry Society (trade group)
AFS: American Field Service (educational)
AFS: American Field Service (humanitarian, WWI)
AFS: American Folklore Society (learned)
AFS: American Federation of Scientists (learned)
AFS: American Fern Society (learned)
AFS: American Fisheries Society (professional)
AFSA: American Federation of School Administrators (labor union)
AFSA: Air Force Sergeants Association (military support)
AFSA: American Foreign Service Association (professional)
AFSA: American Financial Services Association (trade group)
AFSC: Air Force Systems Command (military)
AFSCME: American Federation of State, County and Municipal Employees (labor union)
AFSI: Americans For a Safe Israel (religious, political)
AFSOC: Air Force Special Operations Command (military)
AFT: American Federation of Teachers (labor union)
AFT: American Farmland Trust (civic)
AFTRA: American Federation of Television and Radio Artists (see SAG-AFTRA) (labor union)
AFU: American Fraternal Union (mutual benefit)
AFU: Acme Fraternal Union (See also TAFU) (mutual benefit)
AFWA: Association of Fish and Wildlife Agencies (umbrella organization)
AG: Abbeville-Grimes Railway (railroad)
AG: Assemblies of God (religious denomination)
AG: Adjutant General Corps (Army branch)

AG: Authors Guild (professional)
AGA: American Grandprix Association (equestrian)
AGA: Asian Greek Association (umbrella organization)
AGA: American Guernsey Association (cattle)
AGA: American Gastroenterological Association (professional)
AGA: American Gas Association (trade group)
AGB: Arapawa Goat Breeders (goats)
AGBA: American Galloway Breeders Association (cattle)
AGBell: Alexander Graham Bell Association for the Deaf (special interest)
AGC: Adjutant General's Corps (military)
AGCR: Alamo Gulf Coast Railroad
AGCRA: Adjutant General's Corps Regimental Association (military)
AGF: Association of German Freemasons (Masonic)
AGI: Allan Guttmacher Institute (research)
AGI: American Gamelan Institute (musical, archival)
AGJA: American Guild of Judaic Art (religious, cultural)
AGLF: Atlantic & Gulf Coast Railroad
AGMA: American Guild of Musical Artists (labor union)
AGMA: American Gear Manufacturers Association (trade group)
AGO: American Guild of Organists (professional)
AGPX: Ag Processing (rail car marking)
AGR: Alabama and Gulf Coast Railroad
AGS: Alabama Great Southern Railroad
AGS: Alpha Gamma Sigma (California two year schools) (academic honorary)
AGS: American Gem Society (trade group)
AGS: American Goat Society (goats)
AGS: American Geriatrics Society (professional)
AGU: American Geophysical Union (learned)
AGVA: American Guild of Variety Artists (labor union)
AGWVA: American Gulf War Veterans Association (veterans)
AH: American Hunters (also CA for Cacciatore Americani) (political, Italian)
AHA: American Historical Association (academic)
AHA: American Hospital Association (trade group)
AHA: Arabian Horse Association (equestrian)
AHA: American Humane Association (civic, political)
AHA: American Heart Association (professional)
AHA: Amateur Hockey Association (sports)
AHA: American Hereford Association (trade group)

AHAC: Ancient and Honorable Artillery Company (lineage)

AHAC: Amateur Hockey Association of Canada (sports)

AHAM: Association of Home Appliance Manufacturers (trade group)

AHC: Appaloosa Horse Club (equestrian)

AHC: American Horse Council (trade group)

AHC: Alfred Holbrook College (Ohio) (higher education)

AHC: All Hallows College (Utah) (higher education)

AHC: Association of the Holy Childhood (lay order)

AHC: American Health College (Ohio) (higher education)

AHC: Asian Hardfeather Club (poultry)

AHCA: American Health Care Association (trade group)

AHCA: American Highland Cattle Association (cattle)

AHCA: Alexander Hamilton Christian Academy (school)

AHCS: American Hungarian Catholic Society (ethnic, mutual benefit)

AHEPA: American Hellenic Educational Progressive Association (fraternal)

AHF: Army Historical Foundation (learned)

AHFA: American Home Furnishings Alliance (trade group)

AHFC: Adolph Hitler Free Corps (KKK)

AHFOPG: Ancient, Honorable and Fragrant Order of the Pink Goats (social, civic)

AHHS: American Hackney Horse Society (equine)

AHIP: America's Health Insurance Plans (trade group)

AHIRC: Artists Health Insurance Resource Center (musical)

AHJCE: Association of Hillel/Jewish Campus Professional (religious, professional)

AHL: American Hockey League (sports)

AHLA: American Health Lawyers Association (professional)

AHMA: American Hardware Manufacturers Association (trade group)

AHMP: Alliance of Hazardous Materials Professionals (professional)

AHMS: American Home Missionary Society (religious)

AHOBG: Ancient and Honorable Order of the Blue Goose (also HOBG) (fraternal, insurance industry)

AHOJB: Ancient and Honourable Order of the Jersey Blues (lineage)

AHP: American Heritage Party (political party)

AHPA: American Herbal Products Association (trade group)

AHRQ: Agency for Healthcare Research and Quality (professional)

AHS: American Heraldry Society (learned)
AHS: American Harp Society (musical)
AHSA: American Horse Shows Association (equestrian)
AHTA: Anti-Horse Thief Association (protective assn, became fraternal)
AHUA: American Highway Users Alliance (lobby)
AHW: American Home Watchmen (mutual benefit)
AHW: Ahnapee and Western Railway (railroad)
AI: Ahvas (or Avath) Israel (religious, mutual benefit)
AI: Americus Institute (Georgia) (higher education)
AI: Air India (airline code)
AIA: American Institute of Architects (professional)
AIA: Air Intelligence Agency (military)
AIA: Agudath Israel of America (youth, religious)
AIA: America's Infrastructure Alliance (lobby)
AIA: Aerospace Industries Association (trade group)
AIAA: American Institute of Aeronautics and Astronautics (professional)
AIAG: Automotive Industry Action Group (trade group)
AIB: Association for International Broadcasting (trade group)
AIBA: American Independent Business Alliance (trade group)
AIBS: American Institution of Biological Sciences (learned)
AIC: Aviation Instruction Center (military – World War I)
AIC: American International College (Massachusetts) (higher education)
AIC: American Institute for Conservation of Historic and Artistic Works (civic)
AIC: American Institute of Constructors (trade group)
AICF: American Indian College Fund (humanitarian)
AICHE: American Institute of Chemical Engineers (learned)
AICPA: American Institute of Certified Public Accountants (professional)
AICTE: All India Council for Technical Education (education)
AID: Alpha Iota Delta (decision sciences) (academic honorary)
AIF: Atomic Industrial Forum (trade group)
AIFD: American Institute of Floral Designers (professional)
AIGA: American Institute of Graphic Arts (professional)
AIHA: American Industrial Hygiene Association (professional)
AIHA: American Italian Historical Association (learned)
AIHR: American Indian Horse Registry (equine)
AIIM: Association for Information and Image Management (trade group)
AIL: American-Israeli Lighthouse (religious, charitable)

AIM: American Indian Movement (political)

AIM: Association of Independent Methodists (religious denomination)

AIMDS: Association of Independent Maryland and DC Schools (education)

AIMR: Association for Investment Management and Research (business)

AIO: American Indian Order (also TO - Teepee Order) (fraternal)

AIOBA: Ancient and Independent Order of Buffaloes of America (fraternal)

AIOKM: Ancient and Illustrious Order of the Knights of Malta (fraternal, protestant)

AIOSB: Ancient and Illustrious Order of the Star of Bethlehem (mutual benefit)

AIP: America's Independent Party (political party)

AIPAC: American Israel Public Affairs Committee (lobby)

AIPD: Army Institute for Professional Development (military)

AIPE: American Institute of Parks Executives (professional)

AIPLA: American Intellectual Property Law Association (professional)

AIPMM: Association of International Product Marketing & Management (professional)

AIRI: Alabama Industrial Railroad

AISB: Ancient and Illustrious Star of Bethlehem (fraternal)

AISI: American Iron and Steel Institute (trade group)

AISIP: Association of Independent School Admission Professionals (professional)

AISNE: Association of Independent Schools in New England (education)

AIST: Association for Information Science and Technology (professional)

AIT: Armour Institute of Technology (Illinois) (higher education)

AITP: Association of Information Technology Professionals (professional)

AIU: American Insurance Union (mutual benefit)

AIUM: American Institute of Ultrasound in Medicine (professional)

AJ: Alma and Jonquieres Railway (railroad)

AJ: Anti-Jackson Party (political party)

AJA: Association of Japanese Aimations (trade group)

AJAZ: American Jewish Alternatives to Zionism (religious)

AJBP: Association of Jewish Book Publishers (religious, trade association)

AJC: American Jewish Congress (religious)

AJC: American Jewish Committee (religious, political)

AJCCA: American Jewish Correctional Chaplains Association, Inc. (religious, professional)

AJCOP: Association of Jewish Community Organization Personnel (religious)

AJCP: Association of Jewish Center Professionals (religious, professional)

AJCRA: Association of Jewish Community Relations Workers (religious)

AJFCA: Association of Jewish Family and Children's Agencies (umbrella organization)

AJGS: Association of Jewish Genealogical Societies (cultural)

AJHS: American Jewish Historical Society (religious, cultural)

AJLA: American Junior League Association (social, service, World War I era)

AJLI: American Jewish League for Israel (religious, political)

AJM: Air Jamaica (airline code)

AJOKSB: (meaning appears to be secret) (ethnic, fraternal)

AJPA: American Jewish Press Association (media, religious)

AJPRS: American Jewish Public Relations Society (religious, professional)

AJR: Artemus-Jellico Railroad

AK: American Krusaders (KKK)

AKA: Alpha Kappa Alpha (fraternal)

AKA: Alden Kindred of America (lineage)

AKC: American Kennel Club (sports)

AKC: Arkansas Central Railroad

AKCCHF: American Kennel Club Canine Health Foundation (civic)

AKCS: American Kerry Cattle Society (cattle)

AKD: Alpha Kappa Delta (sociology) (honorary fraternity)

AKF: American Kidney Fund (civic)

AKFM: Congress Party for Malagasy Independence (political)

AKIA: "A Klansman I Am" (KKK)

AKIA: Aircraft Kit Industry Association (lobby)

AKL: Alpha Kappa Lambda (college fraternity)

AKM: Alpha Kappa Mu (honorary fraternity)

AKMD: Arkansas Midland (railroad)

AKO: Aryan Kindred Organization (KKK)

AKP: American Knights of Protection (mutual benefit)

AKUV: Arbeiter Kranken Unterstuetzungs-Verein) (Workmen's Sick Benevolent Society) (mutual benefit)

AL: American League (sports)

AL: American Legion (veterans)

AL: African Legion (ethnic, paramilitary)

AL&G: Arkansas, Louisiana & Gulf Railroad

AL-ANON: Self-help for families of alcoholics (see also ALANON) (self-help)

ALA: American Legion Auxiliary (veterans)

ALA: American Library Association (trade group)

ALA-CoA: American Library Association Committee on Accreditation (accrediting)

ALA: Amalgamated Lithographers of America (labor union)

ALA: Association of Landscape Architects (trade group)

ALA: American Lung Association (civic)

ALA: Assembly on Literature for Adolescents (education)

ALAB: Alabama Railroad

ALAC: Knights Templar Ladies Auxiliary (fraternal)

ALANON: Self-help for families of alcoholics (see also AL-ANON) (self-help)

ALASU: Alabama State University (higher education)

ALATEEN: Self-help for younger family members of alcoholics (self-help)

ALAUS: American Latvian Association in the United States (mutual benefit)

ALCA: Apostolic Lutheran Church of America (religious denomination)

ALCM: Association of Lutheran Church Musicians (religious, musical)

ALCO: American Locomotive Company (business)

ALCOA: Aluminum Company of America (business)

ALCTS: Association for Library Collections & Technical Services (professional)

ALD: National Alpha Lambda Delta (honorary fraternity)

ALDE: Alliance of Liberals and Democrats for Europe (political)

ALDF: Animal Legal Defense Fund (good works)

ALDF: American Lyme Disease Foundation (self help)

ALEC: American Legislative Exchange Council (lobby)

ALH: American Legion of Honor (mutual benefit) (also ALOH)

ALISE: Association for Library and Information Science Education (professional)

ALK: Sri Lankan Airlines Limited (airline code)
ALM: American Lutheran Mission (religious)
ALM: Arkansas, Louisiana & Mississippi Railroad
ALMC: Army Logistics Management College (military, education)
ALOH: American Legion of Honor (also ALH) (mutual benefit)
ALP: American Labor Party (political party)
ALPA: Air Line Pilots Association (labor union)
ALPSP: Association for Learned and Professional Society Publishers (trade group)
ALQS: Aliquippa and Southern Railroad
ALR: Association of the Living Rosary (lay order)
ALRMM: American Lodge of Research Master Masons (Masonic)
ALS: Alton & Southern Railroad
ALS: American Lombardi Society (mutual benefit, entertainment venue)
ALTA: American Library Trustee Association (professional)
ALTA: American Land Title Association (trade group)
ALU: American Labor Union (labor union)
ALW: Association of Lithuanian Workers (ethnic, charitable)
ALY: Allegheny Railroad
ALZ: Alzheimers Association (special interest)
AM: Anglican Mainstream (political/religious)
AM: Arkansas & Missouri (railroad)
AM: American Mechanics (mutual benefit)
AM: Aeromexico (airline code)
Am: American Party (political party)
AMA: American Medical Association (professional)
AMA: American Missionary Association (religious)
AMA: American Motorcycle Association (sports)
AMA: Anglican Mission in the Americas (religious)
AMA: American Marketing Association (trade group)
AMA: Americana Music Association (trade group)
AMA: Aerospace Medical Association (professional)
AMA: Automobile Manufacturers Association (trade group)
AMAC: Association of Mature American Citizens (lobby)
AMAX: American Metal Climax, Inc. (company)
AMB: Anti-Mission Baptist Church, a/k/a Old School Baptist Church (religious denomination)
AMBA: Association of MBAs (professional)
AMBUCS: American Business Clubs (fraternal, service)

AMC: Amalgamated Meat Cutters (labor union)
AMC: American Music Conference (musical)
AMC: American Motors Corporation (business)
AMC: Appalachian Mountain Club (recreation)
AMC: Albany Medical College (New York) (higher education)
AMC: Albertus Magnus College (Connecticut) (higher education)
AMC: American Metals Company (company)
AMC: Amador Central Railroad
AMC: Arkansas, Louisiana and Mississippi Railroad
AMC: U. S. Army Materiel Command (military)
AMC: Air Mobility Command (military)
AMC: Atlantic Medical College (Maryland) (higher education)
AMC: American Medical College (Ohio) (higher education)
AMcA: American McCall Association (religious, missionary)
AMC&BWofNA: Amalgamated Meat Cutters and Butcher Workers of North America (same as AMCBW?) (labor union)
AMCBW: Amalgamated Meat Cutters and Butchers' Workmen (labor union)
AMCHS: American Catholic Historical Society (religious)
AMD: Allied Masonic Degree (of the USA) (Masonic)
AMDA: Society for Post-Acute and Long-Term Care Medicine (professional)
AMDCA: American Milking Devon Cattle Association (cattle)
AME: African Methodist Episcopal Church (religious denomination)
AMEC: Alliance of Mennonite Evangelical Congregations (religious denomination)
AMETALCO: American Metal Company (business)
AMEX: American Express Company (company)
AMEZ: African Methodist Episcopal (Zion) Church (religious denomination)
AMFA: Aircraft Mechanics Fraternal Association (labor union)
AMG: Alpha Mu Gamma (foreign languages) (academic honorary)
AMGA: American Medical Group Association (trade group)
AMHA: American Morgan Horse Association (sports)
AMI: American Meat Institute (trade group)
AMI: American Mushroom Institute (trade group)
AMIA: Association of Moving Image Archivists (professional)
AMIA: American Medical Informatics Association (professional)

AMICC: Arthritis and Musculoskeletal Interagency Coordinating Committee (governmental)

AMIDEAST: American & Mideast Educational and Training Services (?)

AMIS: American Musical Instrument Society (musical)

AMJR: American Mammoth Jackstock Registry (donkeys)

AML: American Motor League (lobby)

AMMF: Ave Maria Mutual Funds (mutual benefit)

AMNLAE: Luisa Amanda Espinoza Association of Nicaraguan Women (women)

AMOBB: Ancient Mystic Order of Bagmen of Bagdad (mutual benefit)

AMOCO: American Oil Company (company)

AMORC: Ancient and Mystical Order Rosae Crucis (Rosicrucian, cult)

AMOS: Ancient Mystic Order of Samaritans (fraternal, IOOF)

AMP: Anti-Masonic Party (political party)

AMP: Anti-Monopoly Party (political party)

AMP: Applied Mathematics Panel (governmental)

AMPB: Archconfraternity for the Most Precious Blood (lay order)

AMPTP: Alliance of Motion Picture and Television Producers (trade group)

AMR: Arcata and Mad River Railroad

AMS: Army Medical School (military, WWI)

AMS: American Mathematical Society (professional)

AMS: American Meteorological Society (professional)

AMS: American Musicological Society (professional)

AMS: Agricultural Marketing Service (governmental)

AMSA: American Moving & Storage Association (trade group)

AMSUS: Association of Military Surgeons of the United States (professional)

AMSS: American Milking Shorthorn Society (cattle)

AMT: Alpha Mu Tau (high school fraternity)

AMT: Association for Manufacturing Technology (trade group)

AMTA: Antenna Measurement Techniques Association (professional)

AMTA: American Music Therapy Association (professional, musical)

AMTK: Amtrak (railroad)

AMTRAK: National Railroad Passenger Corporation (railroad)

AMVETS: American Veterans (lobby)

AMWA: American Medical Women's Association (professional, civic)
AMWA: American Medical Writers Association (professional)
AMX: Aeromexico (airline code)
AN: Apalachicola Northern (railroad)
AN: Alliance Nationale (mutual benefit)
AN: Aryan Nation (KKK)
ANA: American Nursing Association (or American Nurses Association)(professional)
ANA: American Nyckelharpa Association (musical)
ANA: Association of National Advertisers (trade group)
ANA: American Numismatic Association (trade group, hobby)
ANA: Army and Navy Academy (school)
ANA: Administration for Native Americans (governmental)
ANA: Australian Natives' Association (fraternal, service)
ANAC: Augustinian Nuns in the Anglican Communion (religious order)
ANAK: Secret Society at Georgia Institute of Technology
ANARC: Association of North American Radio Clubs
ANB: Alaskan Native Brotherhood (fraternal, ethnic)
ANC: Army Nurse Corps (Army branch)
ANC: African National Congress (guerilla organization)
ANC: Atlantic & North Carolina Railroad
ANC: Air Navigation Commission (UN organization)
ANCF: American Negro College Fund (humanitarian)
AND: Alliance for National Defense (veteran)
AND: Academy of Nutrition and Dietetics (education)
ANG: American Newspaper Guild (political front)
ANG: Air National Guard (military)
ANK: Aryan Nation Knights (KKK)
ANOG: Ancient and Noble Order of the Gormogons (Catholic, anti-Masonic)
ANP: American Nazi Party (political)
ANP: Anti Nebraska Party (political party)
ANPE: African National People's Empire (ethnic)
ANRC: American National Red Cross
ANS: American Numismatic Society (hobby)
ANS: Alpha Nu Sigma (nuclear engineering) (honorary fraternity)
ANS: American Nuclear Society (professional)
ANS: Alaskan Native Sisterhood (fraternal, mutual benefit)
ANSI: American National Standards Institute (trade group)
ANUUSA: Army and Navy Union of the USA (lobby)

ANY: Athabasca Northern Railway (railroad)

ANZAC: Australia/New Zealand Army Corps (WW I) (military)

AO: Appalachian and Ohio Railroad

AoA: Administration on Aging (governmental)

AOA: Aviation Ordinance men Association (fraternal, military)

AOA: Academy of the Assumption (school)

AOA: Ancient Order of Aguthusians (?)

AOA: Alpha Omega Alpha (medicine) (honorary)

AOA: American Osteopathic Association (professional)

AOA-COCA: Commission on Osteopathic College Accreditation (accrediting)

AOA: American Outdoors Association (trade group)

AOA: American Orthopaedic Association (professional)

AOA: American Optometric Association (professional)

AOA-ACOE: Accreditation Council on Optometric Education (accrediting)

AOC: American Order of Clansmen (mutual benefit – not KKK)

AOC: African Orthodox Church (religious denomination)

AOC: Anglican Orthodox Church (religious denomination)

AOD: American (or Ancient) Order of Druids (fraternal, mutual benefit)

AOEC: Association of Occupational and Environmental Clinics (research)

AOF: American Order of Foresters (fraternal, mutual benefit)

AOF: Ancient Order of Foresters (also AOofF) (fraternal, mutual benefit)

AOF: Ancient Order of Freesmiths (originated in Germany) (fraternal, mutual benefit)

AOF: Actors Order of Friendship (fraternal)

AOF: American Orchestra Forum (musical)

AOFAS: American Orthopaedic Foot and Ankle Society (professional)

AOFB: Ancient Order of Froth Blowers (English, charitable)

AOFB: Angelic Order of Fairy Belles (auxiliary of Ancient Order of Froth Blowers) (English, charitable)

AOG: Ancient Order of Gleaners (mutual benefit)

AOGF: Ancient Order of Good Fellows (perhaps same as ROGF – Royal Society of Good Fellows) (mutual benefit)

AOH: Ancient Order of Hibernians (lay religious, mutual benefit)

AOK: Arkansas-Oklahoma Railroad

AOKJ: Ancient Order of Knights of Jerusalem (mutual benefit)
AOKMC: Ancient Order of Knights of the Mystic Chain (fraternal) (also KMC)
AOLA: Ancient Order of Loyal Americans (anti-Catholic)
AOM: Ancient Order of Mysteries (Masonic)
AOM: Ancient Order of Muts (fraternal)
AOMA: Academy of Oriental Medicine at Austin (Texas) (higher education)
AOMP: Artisans' Order of Mutual Protection (also known simply as Order of Mutual Protection) (mutual benefit)
AOO: American Order of Owls (fraternal)
AOO: Ancient Order of Osiris (fraternal)
AOofF: Ancient Order of Foresters (also AOF) (fraternal, mutual benefit)
AOOG: Ancient Order of Gleaners (farmers, mutual protective)
AOP: Anglican Order of Preachers (religious order)
AOP: Ancient Order of Pyramids (mutual benefit)
AOPA: Aircraft Owners and Pilots Association (hobby)
AOPi: Alpha Omicron Pi (sorority)
AOR: Aliquippa & Ohio River Railroad
AORCS: Ancient Order of the Red Cross Society (Masonic)
AOS: Ancient Order of Sanhedrins (fraternal, mutual benefit)
AOS: American Order of the Square (mutual benefit)
AOS: Ancient Order of Shepherds (mutual benefit)
AOTA: American Occupational Therapy Association (professional)
AOTA-ACOTE: American Occupational Therapy Association Accreditation Council for Occupational Therapy Education (accrediting)
AOU: American Ornithologists' Union (professional)
AOUC: American Order of United Catholics (mutual benefit)
AOUW: Ancient Order of United Workmen (mutual benefit)
AOZ: Ancient Order of Zuzumites (service club)
AP: Associated Press (journalism)
AP: Alliance of Poles (in America) (ethnic)
AP: The American Party (nativist, political party)
AP: American Party (a/k/a Know Nothings) (nativist, political party)
AP: America's Party (political party)
AP: Associated Parishes (religious)
AP: Air One (airline code)
AP: Armed Forces Pacific (military)

APA: Administrative Personnel Association (religious)
APA: American Protective Association (nativist, anti-Catholic)
APA: American Psychological Association (professional)
APA-CoA: American Psychological Association Committee on Accreditation (accrediting)
APA: American Planning Association (professional)
APA: American Polocrosse Association (equestrian)
APA: Anglican Province of American (religious)
APA: American Protestant Association (anti-immigrant, anti-Catholic)
APA: Apache Railway (railroad)
APA: American Pharmaceutical Association (trade group)
APA: American Pharmacists Association (trade group)
APA: Alliance of Poles in America (mutual benefit)
APA: American Psychoanalytic Association (education)
APA: American Philosophical Association (professional)
APA: American Polygraph Association (professional)
APA: American Poultry Association (poultry)
APA: All Peoples Association (fraternal, service)
APA: American Psychiatric Association (professional)
APA: American Publishers Association (trade group)
APA: American Pyrotechnics Association (trade group)
APAB: American Polygraph Accreditation Board (education)
APAHS: Association for the Publication of African Historical Sources (learned)
APAJ: American Protestant Association Junior (anti-immigrant, anti-Catholic)
APAP: Association of Performing Arts Presenters (professional)
APB: Sisters Adorers of the Precious Blood (religious order)
APC: Associate Presbyterian Church (religious denomination)
APC: Alabama Presbyterian College (higher education)
APC: Apostolic Pastoral Congress (religious denomination)
APC: American Pie Council (trade group)
APC: American Plastics Council (trade group)
APCA: Association of Pentecostal Churches of America (religious denomination)
APCF: Association for the Preservation of Chanticleer Fowl (poultry)
APCK: Anglican Province of Christ the King (religious)
APCR: Academy of Physicians in Clinical Research (professional)
APDD: Association of Pizza Delivery Drivers (labor union)
APDF: Association of Professional Design Firms (trade group)

APEA: American Physical Education Association (professional)
APGA: American Public Gas Association (trade group)
APHA: American Public Health Association (professional)
APHA: American Paint Horse Association (equestrian)
APhA: American Pharmaceutical Association (trade group)
APhi: Alpha Phi (sorority)
APHIS: Animal and Plant Health Inspection Service (governmental)
API: Animal Protection Institute (humanitarian)
API: Americans for a Progressive Israel (religious, political)
API: American Petroleum Institute (trade group)
APICS: American Production and Inventory Control Society (professional)
APiMu: Alpha Pi Mu (industrial engineering) (academic honorary)
APL: American Protective League (quasi-governmental, WWI)
APMA: American Podiatric Medicine Association (professional)
APMA-CPME: American Podiatric Medicine Association Council on Podiatric Medical Education (accrediting)
APN: Americans for Peace Now (religious, political)
APO: American Post Office (military – World War I)
APO: Alpha Psi Omega (theatre) (academic honorary)
APO: Alpha Phi Omega (fraternal, service)
APP: American Populist Party (political party)
APPA: American Public Power Association (trade group)
APPMA: American Pet Products Manufacturers Association (trade group)
APR: Association of Postconsumer Plastic Recyclers (trade group)
APRI: A. Philip Randolph Institute (political)
APRR: Albany Port Railroad
APS: American Philatelic Society (hobby)
APS: American Philosophical Society (learned)
APS: American Psychological Society (learned)
APS: American Physical Society (learned)
APS: Alpha Phi Sigma (criminal justice) (academic honorary)
APS: Association of Pedagogical Sororities (umbrella organization)
APS: Academic Physician Section (professional)
APSA: American Political Science Association (learned)
APSE: Associated Press Sports Editors (professional)
APSU: Austin Peay State University (higher education)
APTA: American Public Transit Association (trade group)

APTA: American Physical Therapy Association (professional)
APTA-CAPTE: American Physical Therapy Association
Commission on Accreditation in Physical Therapy Education
(accrediting)
APVA: Association for the Preservation of Virginia Antiquities
(civic)
APWA: American Public Works Association (professional)
APWU: American Postal Workers Union (labor union)
APWU: Ale and Porter Workers Union (labor union)
APY: All-Polish Youth (political/religious)
AQ: Aloha Air (airline code)
AQAS: Agency for Quality Assurance through Accreditation of
Study Programs (Germany, professional)
AQHA: American Quarter Horse Association (equestrian)
AR: Aberdeen & Rockfish (railroad)
AR: American Redoubt (political/religious)
AR: Armor (Army branch)
AR: Aerolineas (airline code)
ARA: Army Reserve Association (military)
ARA: American Radio Association (labor union)
ARA: Arcade & Attica Railroad Corp (railroad)
ARA: American Relief Administration (governmental)
ARA: American Railway Association (trade group)
ARA: Awards and Recognition Association (trade group)
ARADCOM: Army Air Defense Command (military)
ARBC: Association of Regular Baptist Churches (Canada –
religious)
ARBC: Association of Reformed Baptist Churches (religious
denomination)
ARBCA: Association of Reformed Baptist Churches of America
(religious denomination)
ARC: American Red Cross (humanitarian)
ARC: Alexander Railroad
ARC: Ancient Rosae Crucis (fraternal, Rosicrucian)
ARC: Arctic Research Commission (governmental)
ARC-PA: Accreditation Review Commission on Education for
the Physician Assistant (accrediting)
ARCA: Automobile Racing Club of America (motorsports)
ARD: Sovereign Colonial Society Americans of Royal Descent
(lineage)
ARDA: American Resort Development Association (trade
group)
ARDC: American Racing Drivers Club (motorsports)

ARDF: Anglican Relief and Development Fund (religious)
ARF: American Revolutionary Federation (also known as Armenian Revolutionary Federation) (political)
ARF: Armenian Revolutionary Federation (political)
ARF: Animal Research Foundation (research)
ARI: American Rangers, Inc. (business)
ARI: Army Research Institute (military)
ARIA: Arthritis Research Institute of America (medical research)
ARIA: Australian Recording Industry Association (trade group)
ARL: Association of Research Libraries (trade group)
ARLIS: Art Libraries Society of North America (umbrella organization)
ARM: Atlantic Region Ministries (religious – Canada)
ARMA: Association of Records Managers and Administrators (professional)
ARMA: Association of Information Management Professionals (professional)
ARMDI: American Red Magen David for Israel (religious, political)
ARNG: Army National Guard (military)
ARP: American Republican Party (political party)
ARP: American Reform Party (political)
ARPA: Advanced Research Projects Agency (governmental)
ARPA: American Red Poll Association (cattle)
ARPC: Associate Reformed Presbyterian Church (religious denomination)
ARPG: American Rangers Protective Group (business)
ARR: Alaska Railroad (railroad)
ARRL: American Radio Relay League (hobby)
ARRS: American Roentgen Ray Society (professional)
ARS: American Recreation Society (professional)
ARS: Arkansas Southern Railroad
ARS: American Recorder Society (musical)
ARS: Agricultural Research Service (governmental)
ARSAR: American Red Star Animal Relief (humane)
ARSP: Action Reconciliation Service for Peace (religious)
ARTBA: American Road and Transportation Builders Association (trade group)
ARU: American Railway Union (labor union)
ARUSA: Arena Racing USA (motorsports)
ARVN: Army of the Republic of (South) Viet Nam (military)
ARW: Arkansas Western Railway (railroad)

ARW: American Rescue Workers (religious)
ARZA: Association of Reform Zionists of America (religious)
ARZC: Arizona & California Railroad
AS: Alton & Southern (railroad)
AS: Alaska Airlines (airline code)
AS: Abilene and Southern Railway (railroad)
ASA: Anthroposophical Society in America (religious denomination)
ASA: Army Security Agency (also USASA) (governmental)
ASA: American Swedenborgian Association (religious denomination)
ASA: American Statistical Association (learned)
ASA: American Sociological Association (professional)
ASA: American Sportscasters Association (professional)
ASA: American Society of Agronomy (professional)
ASA: Army Air Service (military – World War I)
ASA: Alpha Sigma Alpha (sorority)
ASA: Acoustical Society of America (professional)
ASA: American Screenwriters Association (professional)
ASA: American Society of Appraisers (professional)
ASA: Alaska Airlines (airline code)
ASA: American Sanctuary Association (accrediting)
ASA: American Sumatra Association (poultry)
ASA: American Sussex Association (poultry)
ASA: American Society of Anesthesiologists (professional)
ASA: American Subcontractors Association (trade group)
ASA: American Speed Association (motorsports)
ASAB: Atlanta & St. Andrew's Bay (railroad)
ASABE: American Society of Agricultural and Biological Engineers (professional)
ASAE: American Society of Association Executives (professional)
ASAE: American Society of Agricultural Engineers (professional)
ASAIL: Association for the Study of American Indian Literatures (learned)
ASALH: Association for the Study of African-American Life and History (scholarly)
ASAM: American Society of Addiction Medicine (professional)
ASAP: American Students to Activate Pride (religious, youth)
ASAPS: American Society for Aesthetic Plastic Surgery (professional)
ASAS: American Society of Abdominal Surgeons (professional)

ASBMB: American Society for Biochemistry and Molecular Biology (learned)
ASBPE: American Society of Business Publication Editors (professional)
ASBS: American Society of Breast Surgeons (professional)
ASC: Adorers of the Blood of Christ (religious order)
ASC: Adams State College (Colorado) (higher education)
ASC: American Society of Cytopathology (professional)
ASCAP: American Society of Composers, Arrangers, and Publishers (business)
ASCC: American Stock Car Challenge (motorsports)
ASCE: American Society of Civil Engineers (professional)
ASCH: American Society of Clinical Hypnosis (professional)
ASCJ: Apostles of the Sacred Heart of Jesus (religious order)
ASCLA: Association of Specialized and Cooperative Library Agencies (umbrella organization)
ASCLS: American Society for Clinical Laboratory Science (professional)
ASCO: American Society of Clinical Oncology (professional)
ASCP: American Society of Clinical Pathology (professional)
ASCRA: American Stock Car Racing Association (motorsports)
ASCRS: American Society of Cataract and Refractive Surgery (professional)
ASCRS: American Society of Colon and Rectal Surgeons (professional)
ASCS: Agricultural Stabilization and Conservation Service (governmental)
ASCU: American Slovenian Catholic Union (mutual benefit)
ASD: Alliance of Socialist Democracy (anarchist)
ASDAH: Association of Seventh-Day Adventist Historians (religious, learned)
ASDS: American Society for Dermatologic Surgery (professional)
ASDSO: Association of State Dam Safety Officials (professional)
ASE: American Stars of Equity (mutual benefit)
ASE: American Society of Echocardiography (professional)
ASEA: American Society for Eastern Arts (musical, artistic)
ASEA: Atlantic Self-Endowment Association (mutual benefit)
ASEAA: Atlantic Self-Endowment Association of America (mutual benefit)
ASEAN: Association of South East Asian Nations (governmental)

ASEEES: Association for Slavic, East European, and Eurasian Studies (academic)

ASEH: American Society for Environmental History (research)

ASEP: American Society of Exercise Physiologists (professional, accrediting)

ASES: American Solar Energy Society (research, advocacy)

ASF: Army Service Forces (military)

ASFS: American Seamen's Friend Society (religious)

ASG: Alexander Strategy Group (lobby)

ASGE: American Society of Gastrointestinal Endoscopy (professional)

ASGS: American Society of General Surgeons (professional)

ASH: American Society of Hematology (professional)

ASHA: American School Health Association (education)

ASHA: American Shire Horse Association (equine)

ASHA: American Suffolk Horse Association (equine)

ASHA: American Speech-Language-Hearing Association (professional, accrediting)

ASHE: American Society of Hispanic Economists (professional)

ASHI: American Society of Home Inspectors (professional)

ASHIM: American Society of Health Informatics Managers (professional)

ASHRACE: American Society of Heating, Refrigeration and Air Conditioning Engineers (professional)

ASIPP: American Society of Interventional Pain Physicians (professional)

ASIS: American Society for Industrial Security (business)

ASIS: Army Signals Intelligence Service (governmental)

ASIS: American Society for Information Sciences (professional)

ASJ: Apostles of the Sacred Heart of Jesus (religious order)

ASJ: Association for Jewish Studies (religious, education)

ASJM: Augustinian Sisters, Servants of Jesus and Mary (religious order)

ASJM: American Society for Jewish Music (religious, cultural)

ASL: Anti-Saloon League (political, civic)

ASL: Alpha Sigma Lambda (honorary fraternity)

ASLA: American Society of Landscape Architects (professional)

ASLA-LAAB: American Society of Landscape Architects Landscape Architectural Accreditation Board (accrediting)

ASLHS: American Sign Language Honor Society (academic honorary)

ASLO: American Society of Limnology and Oceanography (learned)
ASM: Alpha Sigma Mu (metallurgy) (honorary fraternity)
ASM: American Society of Mammalogists (professional)
ASMA: Aerospace Medical Association (professional)
ASMBS: American Society of Metabolic and Bariatric Surgery (professional)
ASME: American Society of Mechanical Engineers (professional)
ASMA: American Society of Magazine Editors (professional)
ASML: Atlanta, Stone Mountain & Lithonia Railroad
ASMS: American Society of Maxillofacial Surgeons (professional)
ASN: Army School of Nursing (military, WWI)
ASN: Alpha Sigma Nu (honorary fraternity, religious)
ASN: American Society of Nephrology (professional)
ASN: American Society of Neuroimaging (professional)
ASN: American Society of Neuroradiology (professional)
ASNC: Albion State Normal College (Idaho) (higher education)
ASO: Atlanta Symphony Orchestra (musical)
ASO: American Star Order (fraternal, ethnic, mutual benefit)
ASOB: Association of Shrine Oriental Bands of North America (Masonic, musical)
ASOPRS: American Society of Opthalmic, Plastic and Reconstructive Surgery (professional)
ASP: Association of the Sons of Poland (lineage)
ASP: Advocates of Saint Peter (lay order)
ASP: American Society of Parasitologists (professional)
ASPA: American Society for Public Administration (professional)
ASPB: American Society of Plant Biologists (professional)
ASPC: Air Service Production Center (military – World War I)
ASPCA: American Society for Prevention of Cruelty to Animals (charity)
ASPE: American Society of Plumbing Engineers (professional)
ASPL: American Society for Pharmacy Law (professional)
ASPPA: American Society of Pension Professionals & Actuaries (professional)
ASPPH: Association of Schools & Programs of Public Health (umbrella association)
ASPS: American Society of Plastic Surgeons (professional)
ASQ: American Society for Quality (professional)
ASR: Ancient Scottish Rite (Masonic)

ASR: Allegheny Southern Railroad

ASRM: American Society for Reproductive Medicine (professional)

ASRO: American Society for Radiation Oncology (professional)

ASRS: American Society of Retina Specialists (professional)

ASRY: Ashland Railroad

ASS: Arion Singing Society (ethnic)

ASSC: Aviation Section Signal Corps (military, World War I)

ASSH: American Society for Surgery of the Hand (professional)

ASSIST: American Secondary Schools for International Students and Teachers (Connecticut) (school)

ASSP: Angelic Sisters of St. Paul (religious order)

ASSP: Society of All Saints Sisters of the Poor (religious community)

ASSU: American Sunday School Union (religious)

ASTA: American String Teachers Association (professional, music)

ASTA: American Society of Travel Agents (trade group)

ASTC: American Society of Theatre Consultants (professional)

ASTD: American Society for Training & Development (professional)

ASTHO: Association of State and Territorial Health Officials (professional)

ASTL: American Society for Transportation and Logistics (professional)

ASTM: American Society for Testing and Materials (standards)

ASU: Angelo State University (Texas) (higher education)

ASU: Appalachian State University (North Carolina) (higher education)

ASU: Arizona State University (Arizona) (higher education)

ASU: Arkansas State University (Arkansas) (higher education)

ASU: Athens State University (Alabama) (higher education)

ASU: Alabama State University (Alabama) (higher education)

ASUV: Auxiliary to the Sons of Union Veterans of the Civil War (also ASUVCW) (veterans, hereditary)

ASUVCW: Auxiliary to the Sons of Union Veterans of the Civil War (also ASUV) (veterans, hereditary)

ASWPL: Association of Southern Women for the Prevention of Lynching (civic)

ASY: America Supports You (military support)

AT: Auto Train (railroad service)

AT: Royal Air Maroc (airline code)

AT&T: American Telephone and Telegraph Company (also ATT) (business)
ATA: Anti Thief Association (or Anti Horse Thief Association – AHTA) (mutual benefit, but became fraternal)
ATA: Asia Theological Association (religious)
ATA: American Translators Association (professional)
ATA: Association of Teaching Artists (musical, educational)
ATA: American Teachers Association (professional)
ATA: American Trucking Associations (trade group)
ATA: Archery Trade Association (trade group)
ATAA: Akhal-Teke Association of America (equine)
ATBA: American Ticket Brokers Association (trade group)
ATC: Appalachian Trail Conservancy (recreational)
ATC: Air Training Command (military)
ATC: Air Transport Command (military)
ATC: Australian Turf Club (equestrian)
ATC: Agriculture Transportation Coalition (trade group)
ATCA: American Theatre Critics Association (professional)
ATDD: American Train Dispatchers Department (labor union)
ATF: Alcohol, Tobacco, Firearms, and Explosives Bureau (governmental)
ATIS: Allied Translator and Interrogator Section (military)
ATLA: American Theological Library Association (professional)
ATLC: Atomic Trades and Labor Council (labor union)
ATMAE: Association of Technology, Management, and Applied Engineering (education)
ATN: Alabama & Tennessee River Railroad
ATO: Alpha Tau Omega (college fraternity)
ATOS: American Theatre Organ Society (musical)
ATPAM: Association of Theatrical Press Agents & Managers (professional)
ATPP: American Third Position Party (political party)
ATR: Alliance Terminal Railroad
ATR: Ancient Toltec Rite (Masonic)
ATRW: Anthracite Railroad
ATS: American Tract Society (religious)
ATS: Alliance of Transylvanian Saxons (mutual benefit)
ATS: Asbury Theological Seminary (higher learning, religious)
ATS: Association of Theological Schools in the United States and Canada (education)
ATS: American Thoracic Society (professional)
ATSC: Army Training Support Center (military)
ATSF: Atchison, Topeka and Santa Fe Railway (railroad)

ATT: American Telephone and Telegraph Company (also AT&T) (business)
ATTF: Alaskan Tanker Task Force (military)
ATU: Amalgamated Transit Union (labor union)
ATU: Arkansas Tech University (Arkansas) (higher education)
ATU: American Temperance University (Tennessee) (higher education)
ATW: Atlantic & Western (railroad)
AU: Adelphi University (New York) (higher education)
AU: Alfred University (New York) (higher education)
AU: American University (District of Columbia) (higher education)
AU: Auburn University (Alabama) (higher education)
AU: Americans United for Separation of Church and State (political)
AUA: Alpha Upsilon Alpha (language arts) (honorary fraternity)
AUA: American Urological Association (professional)
AUAM: American Union Against Militarism (political)
AUAR: Austin Area Terminal Railroad
AUB: Apostolic United Brethren (religious cult)
AUC: American Unitarian Conference (religious denomination)
AUC: Association of Ukrainian Choirs (ethnic, umbrella organization)
AUD: Association for Union Democracy (labor union)
AUG: Augusta Railroad
AUI: Ukraine International Airlines (airline code)
AUL: Aeroflot-Nord (airline code)
AUM: Ancient Order of Mysteries (fraternal, Masonic)
AUNW: Austin and Northwestern Railroad
AUOKDA: Ancient United Order, Knights and Daughters of Africa (ethnic, Masonic, mutual benefit)
AUR: Association of University Radiologists (professional)
AUS: Army of the United States (military)
AUS: Augusta Southern Railroad
AUSA: Association of the United States Army (charitable)
AUSN: Association of the United States Navy (charitable)
AUSS: American Union of Swedish Singers (musical)
AUSWV: American Union of Spanish-American War Veterans (veterans)
AUT: Auto-Train Corporation (railroad)
AUV: Association of Union Veterans (veterans)
AV: Aviation (Army branch)
AV: Avianca (airline code)

AVA: Association of Veterinary Anesthetists (professional)
AVC: Association of Vineyard Churches (religious denomination)
AVC: American Veterans Committee (veterans)
AVER: American Veterans for Equal Rights (military support)
AVL: Aroostook Valley Railroad
AVMA: American Veterinary Medical Association (professional, accrediting)
AVN: American Values Network (political/religious)
AVR: Allegheny Valley Railroad
AVS: American Viola Society (musical)
AVSA: African Violet Society of America, Inc. (hobby)
AW: American Woodmen (mutual benefit)
AW: American Workmen (mutual benefit)
AWAB: Association of Welcoming and Affirming Baptists (religious denomination)
AWC: Aircraft Warning Corps (governmental)
AWCI: American Watchmakers-Clockmakers Institute (trade group)
AWCPS: Ancient White Park Cattle Society of North America (cattle)
AWEA: American Wind Energy Association (trade group)
AWES: American World Exonumia Society (trade group, hobby)
AWF: Armenian Youth Federation (ethnic)
AWI: Air Wisconsin Airlines Corporation (airline code)
AWIR: Ankole Watusi International Registry (cattle)
AWM: American War Mothers (military support)
AWMA: Air & Waste Management Association (trade group)
AWMC: Allegheny Wesleyan Methodist Connection (religious)
AWO: American Waterways Operators (trade group)
AWP: Atlanta and West Point (railroad)
AWP: American Workers Party (political party)
AWPPW: Association of Western Pulp and Paper Workers (labor union)
AWRA: American Water Resources Association (professional)
AWS: American Welding Society (trade group)
AWSA: American Woman Suffrage Association (civic)
AWSPS: Association of Watershed & Stormwater Professionals (professional)
AWW: Algers Winslow & Western (railroad)
AWWA: American Water Works Association (trade group)
AWWP: Army Wounded Warrior Program (military support)

AX: Alpha Chi (high school fraternity)
AX: Alpha Chi (honor society)
AXR: Alpha Chi Rho (college fraternity)
Axi: Alpha Xi Delta (sorority)
AY: Finnair (airline code)
AZ: Alitalia (airline code)
AZA: Aleph Zadik Aleph (high school fraternity)
AZC: Albany Zouave Cadets (youth)
AZM: American Zionist Movement (religious)
AZS: Arizona Southern Railroad
AZYF: American Zionist Youth Foundation (religious, youth)

B

B&A: Boston and Albany (also seen as BA) (railroad)
B&H: Bell and Howell (business)
B&H: B&H Rail Corporation (see BH) (may stand for Bath & Hammondsport) (railroad)
B&LE: Bessemer and Lake Erie (railroad)
B&M: Boston & Maine (also BM) (railroad)
B&N: Buckhannon & Northern Railroad
B&O: Baltimore and Ohio (also BO) (railroad)
BA: Bonus Army (veterans)
BA: Brotherhood of America (fraternal, mutual benefit)
BA: Boston and Albany Railroad (see also B&A) (railroad)
BA: Builders of the Adytum (fraternal)
BA: B'rith Abraham (Jewish, charitable)
BA: British Airways (airline code)
BA: Brewers Association (trade group)
BA: Blue Alliance (military support)
BAC: International Union of Bricklayers and Allied Craftworkers (labor union)
BAC: Brotherhood of the Ascended Christ (religious community)
BACS: Bellevue Avenue Colored School (school)
BAF: Bohemian American Foresters (mutual benefit)
BAF: Babushka Adoption Foundation (fraternal service)
BAM: Born Again Movement (religious denomination)
BANA: B'nei Ariva of North America (religious, youth)
BANKPAC: American Bankers Association Political Action Committee (business)
BAP: Butte, Anaconda and Pacific Railway (railroad)
BAR: Bangor and Aroostook (railroad)
BARA: Black American Racers Association (motorsports)
BARCO: Barnum & Richardson Company (business)
BARE: Benefit Association of Railway Employees (mutual benefit)
BARM: Bureau of Archives and Records Management (governmental)
BART: Bay Area Rapid Transit (railroad)
BAS: Bohemian American Foresters (mutual benefit)

BATF: Bureau of Alcohol, Tobacco, Firearms, and Explosives (governmental)
BAU: Bohemian American Union (mutual benefit)
BAW: Brotherhood of American Workmen (mutual benefit)
BAW: British Airways (airline code)
BAY: Brotherhood of American Yeomen (mutual benefit)
BAYL: Bay Line Railroad
BB: Big Brothers (civic, youth)
BB: Boys' Brigade (youth, religious, inter-denominational)
BB: Buckingham Branch Railroad
BBA: Boston Bar Association (professional)
BBB: Council of Better Business Bureaus (trade group)
BBB: Beta Beta Beta (biology) (honorary fraternity)
BBBSA: Big Brothers/Big Sisters of America (civic)
BBC: Brotherhood of Baptist Churches (religious denomination)
BBC: British Broadcasting Corporation (quasi-governmental)
BBFI: Baptist Bible Fellowship International (religious denomination)
BBGA: Bread Bakers Guild of American (trade group)
BBH: Brown Brothers, Harriman (business)
BBI: B'nai B'rith International (religious)
BBN: Buckingham Browne & Nichols School (Massachusetts) (school)
BBN: Bolt, Beranek & Newman (company)
BBRF: Brain and Behavior Research Foundation (medical research)
BBYO: B'nai B'rith Youth Organization (religious, youth)
BC: Boston College (Massachusetts) (higher education)
BC: Believers Church (religious denomination)
BC: Barnard College (higher education)
BC: Bryson College (Tennessee) (higher education)
BC: Burritt College (Tennessee) (higher education)
BC: Bishop College (Texas) (higher education)
BC: Burleson College (Texas) (higher education)
BCA: Boys Club of America (civic)
BCA: Bureau of Consular Affairs (governmental)
BCC: Brethren in Christ Church (religious denomination)
BCCA: Beer Can Collectors of America (hobby)
BCD: Berkshire County Day School (Massachusetts) (school)
BCD: Buckley Country Day School (New York) (school)
BCFP: Bureau of Consumer Financial Protection (governmental)

BCGI: Blessed Charles Grafton Institute (religious)
BCH: Bureau of Child Hygiene (healthcare, WWI)
BCH: British Columbia Hydro (business)
BCI: Battery Council International (trade group)
BCIM: Bureau of Catholic Indian Missions (religious)
BCJ: Brotherhood of Carpenters and Joiners (trade group)
BCK: Buffalo Creek Railroad
BCL: Brethren of the Common Life (religious order)
BCLR: Bay Colony Railroad
BCM: Bible Christian Mission (religious denomination)
BCMS: Berkshire and Columbia Missionary Society (religious)
BCOQ: Baptist Convention of Ontario and Quebec (religious –
Canadian)
BCPBS: Bible and Common Prayer Book Society (religious)
BCR: British Columbia Railroad
BCR: Bay Coast Railroad
BCRF: Breast Cancer Research Foundation (medical research)
BCTGM: Bakery, Confectionery, Tobacco Workers and Grain
Millers International Union (labor union)
BCU: Brotherhood of Christian Unity (religious)
BD: Branch Davidians (cult)
BDAC: Bureau of Drug Abuse Control (governmental)
BDHCA: Belgian Draft Horse Corps of America (equine)
BDJ: Brotherhood of David and Jonathan (see also OSM -
Order of the Secret Monitor) (Masonic)
BDPA: Black Data Processing Associates (professional)
BDS: Boycott, Divestment and Sanctions (political)
BDU: Beer Drivers Union (labor union)
BE: Baltimore & Eastern Railroad
BE: British Eventing (equestrian)
BEA: Bureau of Economic Analysis (governmental)
BEE: Brotherhood of Electrical Employees (also known as
Benevolent Electricians Everywhere) (trade, fraternal)
BEEM: Beech Mountain Railroad
BEF: Brewery Engineers and Firemen (labor union)
BEF: British Expeditionary Forces (military, World War I)
BEFC: Black Eagle Flying Corps (ethnic)
BEMF: Boston Early Music Festival (musical)
BEP: Blue Enigma Party (State of Delaware) (political party)
BEP: Bureau of Engraving and Printing (governmental)
BETA: British Equestrian Trade Association (trade group)
BEV: British Equestrian Vaulting (equestrian)
BEW: Board of Economic Warfare (governmental)

BFC: Bellefonte Central Railroad
BFC: Bible Fellowship Church (religious denomination)
BFCL: International Order of Rainbow Girls (Masonic)
BFFLA: Big Four Fraternal Life Association (mutual benefit)
BFM: Board of Foreign Missions (religious)
BFS: Brethren of the Free Spirit (religious denomination)
BFS: Bureau of Fiscal Service (governmental)
BGC: Baptist General Conference (religious denomination)
BGCA: Boys and Girls Clubs of America (youth)
BGCC: Baptist General Conference of Canada (religious denomination, Canadian)
BGCT: Baptist General Convention of Texas (religious denomination)
BGS: Little Brothers of the Good Shepherd (religious order)
BGS: Beta Gamma Sigma (business) (academic honorary)
BGSU: Bowling Green State University (Ohio) (higher education)
BH: Brotherhood of Hope (religious order)
BH: Base hospital (military – World War I)
BH: B&H Rail Corporation (see B&H) (railroad)
BH: Bath & Hammondsport Railroad
BH&E: Boston, Hartford and Erie Railroad
BHA: British Horseball Association (equestrian)
BHC: British Home Children (charitable)
BHC: Bible Holiness Church (religious denomination)
BHC: Business History Conference (academic)
BHC: Baca Horse Conservancy (equine)
BHCR: Black Hills Central Railroad
BHDTA: British Horse Driving Trials Association (equestrian)
BHIC: British Horse Industry Confederation (trade group)
BHLA: Ben Hur Life Association (mutual benefit)
BHMC: Bellevue Hospital Medical College (New York) (higher education)
BHMS: Brooklyn Heights Montessori School (New York) (school)
BHR: Brookhaven Rail LLC (railroad)
BHS: British Horse Society (equestrian)
BHS: Barbershop Harmony Society (formerly SPEBSQSA) (hobby)
BHS: Business Honor Society (high school, honorary)
BHSU: Black Hills State University (South Dakota) (higher education)
BIA: Bureau of Indian Affairs (governmental)

BIC: Brethren in Christ (religious denomination)
BIL: Brothers in Love (mutual benefit)
BILS: Bureau of International Labor Affairs (governmental)
BIO: Biotechnology Industry Association (trade group)
BIO: Biotechnology Innovation Organization (trade group)
BIS: Bureau of Industry and Security (governmental)
BISG: Book Industry Study Group (trade group)
BJMS: Bishop James Madison Society (college honorary)
BJS: Bureau of Justice Statistics (governmental)
BK: Blue Key Honor Society (honorary, leadership)
BKA: Benevolent Knights Association (also CBKA –
Commandery, Benevolent Knights Association) (fraternal or
mutual benefit)
BKA: Benevolent Knights of America (mutual benefit)
BKH: Bands and Knights of Hope (youth, temperance)
BK of M: Benevolent (sometimes seen as Black) Knights of
Molders (labor union)
BKP: Bangkok Airways Co., Ltd. (airline code)
BKRR: Batten Kill Railroad Co., Inc. (railroad)
BKRT: Boy Knights of the Round Table (not an organization;
actually a line of sewing patterns)
BKX: Beta Kappa Chi (natural sciences and mathematics)
(honorary fraternity)
BL: Black Legion (vigilante; KKK-related)
BL: Broadway League (trade group)
BLA: Baptists Life Association (mutual benefit)
BLA: Black Liberation Army (political)
BLA: Baltimore & Annapolis Railroad
BLA: Baptist Life Association (mutual benefit)
BLE: Brotherhood of Locomotive Engineers (labor union)
BLE: Bessemer & Lake Erie Railroad
BLF: Brotherhood of Locomotive Firemen (labor union)
BLF&E: Brotherhood of Locomotive Firemen and Engineers
(labor union)
BLM: Bureau of Land Management (governmental)
BLKM: Black Mesa & Lake Powell Railway (railroad)
BLMR: Blue Mountain Railroad
BLS: Bureau of Labor Statistics (governmental)
BLU: Blue Ridge Southern Railroad
BM: Boston and Maine (also B&M) (railroad)
BMAA: Baptist Missionary Association of America (religious
denomination)
BMC: Bennett Medical College (Illinois) (higher education)

BMC: Bingham Military School (North Carolina) (higher education)
BMC: Barnes Medical College (Missouri) (higher education)
BMC: Bible Missionary Church (religious denomination)
BMC: Baltimore Medical College (Maryland) (higher education)
BMC: Berkshire Medical College (Massachusetts) (higher education)
BMC: Bryn Mawr College (Pennsylvania) (higher education)
BMCC: Bible Methodist Connection of Churches (religious denomination)
BMCC: Borough of Manhattan Community College (higher education)
BMCM: Bellevue Medical College of Massachusetts (higher education)
BMEC: British Methodist Episcopal Church (religious denomination)
BMEWS: Ballistic Missile Early Warning System (military)
BMI: Broadcast Music Incorporated (business)
BMI: Bordentown Military Academy (school)
BMI: Bureau of Military Information (governmental)
BMiC: Bible Missionary Church (religious denomination)
BMIN: Bureau of Marine Inspection and Navigation (governmental)
BMISBU: Boiler Makers and Iron Ship Builders Union (labor union)
BML: Belfast & Moosehead Lake Railroad
BMRG: Blue Mountain Lake & Reading Railroad
BMS: Baptist Missionary Society (religious)
BMS: Bowdoin Medical School (Maine) (higher education)
BMT: Brooklyn-Manhattan Transit (subway)
BMW: Brotherhood of Maintenance of Way (labor union)
BMWE: Brotherhood of Maintenance of Way Employees (labor union)
BN: Burlington Northern (railroad)
BNA: Bavarian National Association (of North America) (mutual benefit)
BNAI: Brotherhood of North American Indians (fraternal, ethnic)
BNDD: Bureau of Narcotics and Dangerous Drugs (governmental)
BNL: Brotherhood of the New Life (religious, communal)
BNMB: Beavers National Mutual Benefit (mutual benefit)
BNSF: Burlington Northern Santa Fe (railroad)

BNSI: Bureau of Navigation and Steamoat Inspection (governmental)
BO: Baltimore and Ohio Railroad (also B&O)
BOB: Benevolent Order of Buffaloes (perhaps related to Royal Antediluvian Order of Buffaloes in UK) (fraternal)
BOB: Benevolent Order of Bereans (anti-Catholic but foreign born)
BOC: British Orthodox Church (religious denomination)
BOEM: Bureau of Ocean Energy Management (governmental)
BOF: Brotherhood of Friends (social)
BofA: Bank of America (business)
BofLFandE: Brotherhood of Locomotive Firemen and Engineers (labor union)
BOMC: Baronial Order of Magna Charta (lineage)
BofRTM: Brotherhood of Railroad Track Men (labor union)
BofT: Board of Trade (business)
BOH: Benevolent Order of Hawks (fraternal, ethnic)
BOM: Benevolent Order of Monkeys (fraternal)
BOP: Border Pacific Railroad
BOMC: Baronial Order of the Magna Carta (lineage)
BONY: Bank of New York (business)
BOP: Border Pacific Railroad
BOSC: Benevolent Order of Scottish Clans (see OSC: Order of Scottish Clans) (lineage)
BP: Buffalo & Pittsburgh (railroad)
BP: British Petroleum (business)
BP: Bureau of Prisons (governmental)
BP: Bureau of Prohibition (governmental)
BPA: Brotherhood of Philip and Andrew (religious?)
BPA: Bonneville Power Administration (governmental)
BPBU: Bill Posters and Billers' Union (labor union)
BPC: Bible Presbyterian Church (religious denomination)
BPD: Brotherhood of Painters and Decorators (labor union)
BPD: Bureau of the Public Debt (governmental)
BPD&PofA: Brotherhood of Painters, Decorators & Paperhangers of America (labor union)
BPFNA: Baptist Peace Fellowship of North America (religious)
BPI: Billings Polytechnic Institute (Montana) (higher education)
BPM: Beta Phi Mu (library/information science) (academic honorary)
BPOD: Benevolent and Patriotic Order of Does (BPOE auxiliary) (fraternal)

BPOE: Benevolent and Protective Order of Elks (fraternal, mutual benefit)

BPOEC: Benevolent and Protective Order of Elks of Canada (fraternal)

BPOEW: Benevolent and Protective Order of Elks of the World (fraternal)

BPP: Black Panther Party (political party)

BPRC: Berger Passaic Railway Corporation (railroad)

BPRR: Buffalo & Pittsburgh Railroad, Inc. (railroad)

BPSA: Bio Process Systems Alliance (trade group)

BPTR: Bergen Passaic Terminal Railroad

BPU: Bricklayers and Plasterers' Union (labor union)

BPW: Business and Professional Women

BPW: Business and Professional Women (civic)

BQ: Beanite Quakerism (religious denomination)

BR: British Reining (equestrian)

BRAC: Brotherhood of Railway & Airline Clerks (labor union)

BRAC: Base Realignment and Closure Commission (military)

BRAN: Brandon Corporation (likely railroad car marking) (business)

BRC: Brotherhood of Railway Clerks (see BRRC: Brotherhood of Rail Road Clerks) (labor union)

BRC: Belt Railway of Chicago (railroad)

BRC: Blue Ridge College (Maryland) (higher education)

BRFF: Beavers Reserve Fund Fraternity (mutual benefit)

BRG: Brownsville & Rio Grande International Railroad

BRRB: Brotherhood of Rail Road Brakemen (labor union)

BRRC: Brotherhood of Rail Road Clerks (became BRC) (labor union)

BRRT: Brotherhood of Rail Road Trainmen (became BRT) (labor union)

BRRT: Brotherhood of Rail Road Telegraphers (also BRT) (labor union)

BRS: Brotherhood of Railroad Signalmen (labor union)

BRSR: Blue Ridge Scenic Railroad

BRT: Brotherhood of Railroad Trainmen (also BRRT: Brotherhood of Rail Road Trainmen) (labor union)

BRT: Brotherhood of Railroad Telegraphers (also BRRT) (labor union)

BRTM: Brotherhood of Railroad Track Men (labor union)

BRW: Black River & Western (railroad)

BS: Big Sisters (youth)

BS: Birmingham Southern (railroad)

BS: Brigidine Sisters (religious order)
BS: B'rith Sholom (Jewish, fraternal)
BS&C: Big Sandy & Cumberland Railroad
BS&P: Berkeley Springs & Potomac Railroad
BSA: Boy Scouts of America (youth)
BSA: Brotherhood of St. Andrew (religious –
Episcopalian/Anglican)
BSA: Boston Society of Architects (professional)
BSA: Botanical Society of America (academic)
BSA: British Showjumping Association (equestrian)
BSA: Bearing Specialists Association (trade group)
BSA: Business Software Alliance (trade group)
BSB: Benedictine Sisters of Bethany (religious order)
BSBA: Bohemian Slavonian Benevolent Association (mutual
benefit)
BSC: Brothers and Sisters of Charity (religious order)
BSC: Boston State College (Massachusetts) (higher education)
BSC: Building Security Council (trade group)
BSCP: Brotherhood of Sleeping Car Porters (labor union)
BSEE: Bureau of Safety and Environmental Enforcement
(governmental)
BSEF: Bromine Science and Environmental Forum (trade
group)
BSFBU: Bohemian-Slavonic Fraternal Benefit Union (mutual
benefit)
BSG: Brotherhood of Saint Gregory (religious community)
BSHA: British Show Horse Association (equestrian)
BSMC: Blue Star Mothers Club (military support)
BSPS: British Show Pony Society (equestrian)
BSI: Bureau of Secret Intelligence (governmental)
BSIW: Bridge and Structural Iron Workers (labor union)
BSO: Boston Symphony Orchestra (musical)
BSOR: Buffalo Southern Railroad, Inc. (railroad)
BSP: Beta Sigma Psi (religious)
BSRT: Business Sector Round Table (business)
BStA: Brotherhood of St. Andrew (religious)
BSU: Bridgewater State University (Massachusetts) (higher
education)
BSU: Bohemian Slavonian (or Slavonic) Union (mutual benefit)
BTC: Building Trades Council (labor union)
BTC: Birmingham Terminal Railroad
BTCO: Boston Terminal Railroad
BTJ: Boys Town Jerusalem (charity)

BTLGllc: Between the Lakes Group LLC (business)
BTP: Boston Tea Party (political party)
BTS: Bureau of Transportation Statistics (governmental)
BU: Bakers Union (labor union)
BU: Bartenders Union (labor union)
BU: Brotherhood of the Union (mutual benefit, secret, labor)
BU: Boston University (Massachusetts) (higher education)
BU: Benevolent Union (mutual benefit)
BU: Scandinavian Airlines Norge AS (airline code)
BU: Baylor University (Texas) (higher education)
BUC: Boston Union Club (men's club)
BUGB: Baptist Union of Great Britain (religious denomination)
BUHF: Brotherhood of the Union (fraternal?)
BUL: Boston Union League (men's club)
BUNZ: Baptist Union of New Zealand (religious denomination)
BUS: Baptist Union of Scotland (religious denomination)
BUW: Baptist Union of Wales (religious denomination)
BUWC: Baptist Union of Western Canada (religious denomination, Canadian)
BV: Badischer Volksverein (mutual benefit)
BVA: Blinded Veterans Association (veterans)
BVM: Sisters of Charity of the Blessed Virgin Mary (religious order)
BVS: Bevier & Southern Railroad
BW: Caribbean Airlines Limited (airline code)
BWA: Caribbean Airlines Limited (airline code)
BWA: Baptist World Alliance (religious denomination)
BWG: Brotherhood of the West Gate (Rosicrucian-related) (fraternal)
BWPBS: Bishop White Prayer Book Society (religious)
BWRS: British War Relief Society (military support)
BXN: Bauxite Northern (railroad)
BYC: Brigham Young College (Utah) (higher education)
BYPU: Baptist Young People's Union of America (religious)
BYM: Britain Yearly Meeting (religious denomination)
BYU: Brigham Young University (Utah) (higher education)
BZ: B'nai Zion (religious, fraternal, mutual benefit)

C

C: Conservative Party (political party)

C&A: Camden & Amboy Railroad

C&A: Charlottesville and Albemarle Railway (railroad)

C&C: Coal and Coke Railroad

C&NW: Chicago and Northwestern Railroad (also CNW)

C&O: Chesapeake & Ohio (also CO) (railroad)

C&PA: Cumberland and Pennsylvania Railroad (see also CPA)

C&S: Colorado & Southern Railway (railroad)

CA: Coast Artillery (military – World War I)

CA: Chesapeake & Albemarle Railroad

CA: Christian Alliance (religious)

CA: Cacciatore Americani (also AH: American Hunters) (political, Italian)

CA: Catholic Action (lay order, political)

CA: Cantors' Assembly (religious, professional)

CA: Chorus America (musical)

CA: Compete America (trade group)

CAA: Catholic Aid Association (religious; mutual benefit)

CAA: Council on Aviation Accreditation (accrediting)

CAAHEP: Commission on Accreditation of Allied Health Education Programs (accrediting)

CABC: Convention of Atlantic Baptist Churches (religious denomination)

CAC: Coast Artillery Corps (Military – World War I)

CAC: Catholic Apostolic Church (religious denomination)

CAC: Christ Apostolic Church (religious denomination)

CAC: Children of the American Colonists (lineage)

CAC: California Avocado Commission (trade group)

CACAP: Catholic Academy for Communication Arts Professionals (religious)

CACREP: Council for Accreditation of Counseling and Related Educational Programs (accrediting)

CACTS: Coast Artillery Corps Training School (military – World War I)

CACV: Cooperstown & Charlotte Valley Railroad

CAD: Cadiz Railroad

CADE-ADA: American Dietetic Association Commission on Accreditiation for Dietetics Education (education, accrediting)

CAEG: Coffeen and Western Railroad

CAEP: Council for the Accreditation of Educator Preparation (accrediting)

CAES: Central American Education Society (religious)

CAGI: Compressed Air and Gas Institute (trade group)

CAGY: Columbus & Greenville (railroad)

CAH: Community of All Hallows (religious community)

CAHA: Canadian Amateur Hockey Association (sports)

CAHL: Canadian Amateur Hockey League (sports)

CAHME: Commission of Accreditation of Healthcare Management Education (accrediting)

CAI: Community Associations Institute (trade group)

CAIS: Connecticut Association of Independent Schools (education)

CAL: China Airlines (airline code)

CALA: Carolina Southern Railroad

CalPoly: California Polytechnic State University (higher education)

Caltech: California Institute of Technology (higher education)

CAMERA: Committee for Accuracy in Middle East Reporting in America (religious, political)

CANRA: Committee for Army and Navy Religious Affairs (military, Jewish)

CANSO: Civil Air Navigation Services Organization (trade group)

CAOF: Catholic Association of Foresters (mutual benefit)

CAOTC: Coast Artillery Officers Training Camp (military, World War I)

CAP: Civil Air Patrol (youth)

CAP: Community Action Program (political)

CAP: College of American Pathologists (professional)

CAPE: Council for American Private Education (education)

CAPS: Christian Association for Psychological Studies (professional)

CAPWIP: Center for Asia Pacific Women in Politics (political)

CAQ: Center for Audit Quality (trade group)

CAR: Children of the American Revolution (also NSCAR) (lineage)

CARA: Center for Applied Research in the Apostolate (religious)

CARC: Commission on Accreditation for Respiratory Care (education)

CARE: Christian Action Research and Education (political/religious)
CAROA: Conference of the Anglican Religious (religious)
CARR: Carrollton Railroad
CARSO: Council of American Survey Research Organizations (trade group)
CAS: Concordia Aid Society (mutual benefit)
CAS: Casualty Actuarial Society (professional)
CAS: Congregation of American Sisters (religious order)
CASCOM: U. S. Army Combined Arms Support Command (military)
CASO: Canada Southern Railroad
CASRO: Council of American Survey Research Organizations (trade group)
CATHLA: Catholic Library Association (religious)
CAWK: Christian American Knights of the Ku Klux Klan (KKK)
CAYW: Catholic Association for Young Women (religious)
CB: Church of the Brethren (religious denomination)
CB: Congregational Brotherhood (religious, youth)
CB&Q: Chicago, Burlington & Quincy Railroad
CBA: Christian Brothers Academy (school)
CBA: Central Baptist Association (religious denomination)
CBA: Conservative Baptist Association (religious denomination)
CBA: California Broadcasters Association (trade group)
CBA: Community Broadcasters Association (trade group)
CBA: Consumer Bankers Association (trade group)
CBAA: Conservative Baptist Association of America (religious denomination)
CBBA: Christian Burden Bearers Association (mutual benefit)
CBC: Chillicothe Business College (Missouri) (higher education)
CBC: Christian Brothers College (Missouri) (higher education)
CBC: Carbon County Railway (railroad)
CBC: Continental Baptist Churches (religious denomination)
CBC: Canadian Broadcasting Corporation (quasi-governmental)
CBC: Church of the Bible Covenant (religious denomination)
CBC: Chesapeake Bay Company (lineage)
CBCC: Covenanted Baptist Church of Canada (religious, Canadian)
CBCG: Christian Baptist Church of God (religious denomination)
CBDNA: College Band Directors National Association (musical)

CBF: Cooperative Baptist Fellowship (religious denomination)
CBH: Church of the Blessed Hope (religious denomination)
CBHS: Cleveland Bay Horse Society of North America (equine)
CBI: China-Burma-India Theater (military)
CBI: Council for a Beautiful Israel (religious, civic)
CBIA: California Building Industry Association (trade group)
CBJO: Coordinating Board of Jewish Organizations (religious)
CBKA: Commandery, Benevolent Knights Association (also
BKA – Benevolent Knights Association) (fraternal, mutual
benefit)
CBL: Catholic Benevolent Legion (mutual benefit)
CBL: Conemaugh & Black Lick Railroad
CBLM: Community of the Blessed Lady Mary (religious
community)
CBM: Church of the Brethren Mission (religious denomination)
CBM: Canadian Baptist Ministries (religious denomination)
CBM: Citizens Bank of Maryland (company)
CBNS: Cape Breton & Central Nova Scotia Railway (railroad)
CBO: Congressional Budget Office (governmental)
CBQ: Chicago, Burlington and Quincy (railroad)
CBRW: Columbia Basin Railroad
CBS: Columbia Broadcasting System (business)
CBSA: Catholic Boarding Schools Association (education,
religious)
CBSH: Colored Brotherhood & Sisterhood of Honor (mutual
benefit, ethnic)
CBTU: Coalition of Black Trade Unionists (labor union)
CBUSA: Clydesdale Breeders of the USA (equine)
CBWL: Cogan, Berlind, Weill & Levitt (company)
CC: The Christian Connexion (religious denomination)
CC: Columbian Circle (mutual benefit)
CC: Cannon Club (Princeton University eating club)
CC: Chemical Corps (military)
CC: Companions of the Cross (religious order)
CC: Children of the Confederacy (lineage)
CC: Community of Christ (religious denomination)
CC: Columbia College (Florida) (higher education)
CC: Columbia College (New York) (higher education)
CC: Columbia College (Oregon) (higher education)
CC: Columbus College (South Dakota) (higher education)
CC: Claverack College (New York) (higher education)
CC: Carleton College (Missouri) (higher education)
CC: Chicago Central & Pacific (also CCP) (railroad)

CC: Catholics for Choice (political/religious)
CC: Christian Concern (political/religious)
CC: Calvary Chapel (religious denomination)
CC: Christian Church (Disciples of Christ) (religious denomination)
CC: Churches of Christ (religious denomination)
CC: Concordia College (higher education)
CC: Colorado College (higher education)
CC: Confederation Club (fraternal, service)
CC&O: Carolina, Clinchfield and Ohio Railway (railroad)
CC&S: Charleston, Clendedin & Sutton Railroad
CC&V: Cripple Creek and Victor Railroad
CCA: Conference of Consulting Actuaries (professional)
CCAF: Catholic Charities Aid Association (religious)
CCB: Colored Consolidated Brotherhood (mutual benefit, charitable, ethnic)
CCBC: Central Canada Baptist Conference (religious denomination, Canadian)
CCBT: Central Carolina Bank & Trust (company)
CCC: Civilian Conservation Corps (New Deal) (governmental)
CCC: Celtic Catholic Church (religious denomination)
CCC: Chicago Coin Club (hobby)
CCC: Celestial Church of Christ (religious denomination)
CCC: Charisma Christian Church (religious denomination)
CCC: Christian City Churches (religious denomination)
CCC: China Christian Council (religious denomination)
CCC: Charles City College (higher education)
CCC: Council of Conservative Citizens (KKK)
CCC: Catholic Chippewa Congress (religious)
CCCA: Christian Consultive Church of America (cult)
CCCC: Congregational Christian Churches in Canada (religious denomination)
CCCC: Conservative Congregational Christian Conference (also 4C) (religious denomination)
CCCL: Connecticut Central Railroad
CCCU: Churches of Christ in Christian Union (religious denomination)
CCDS: Committees of Correspondence for Democracy and Socialism (political)
CCDS: Chicago College of Dental Surgery (Illinois) (higher education)
CCE: Council on Chiropractic Education (education, accrediting)

CCEJ: Center of Concern's Education for Justice (religious)
CCEM: Church of Christ with the Elijah Message (religious denomination)
CCES: Canadian Centre for Ethics in Sport (sports)
CCES: Catholic Church Extension Society of the USA (religious)
CCF: Congress for Cultural Freedom (political front)
CCF: Conservative Christian Fellowship (political/religious)
CCF: Chinese Communist Forces (Korean War) (military)
CCF: Catholic Communication Foundation (religious)
CC(H): Church of Christ (Holiness) (in the U.S.A.) (religious denomination)
CCI: Church of Christ, Instrumental (religious denomination)
CCIM: Corpus Christi Terminal Railroad
CCJM: Congregation of the Sacred Hears of Jesus and Mary (Picpus Fathers) (religious order)
CCJO: Consultative Council of Jewish Organizations (religious)
CCJS: Cleveland College of Jewish Studies (religious, higher education)
CCK: Community of Christ the King (Benedictine) (religious community)
CCK: Campbell's Creek Railroad
CCKY: Chattanooga & Chicamauga Railway (railroad)
CCLDS: Church of Christ of the Latter Day Saints (religious denomination)
CCMA: Canadian Country Music Association (trade group)
CCMA: Closure & Container Manufacturers Association (trade group)
CCMC: Chicago College of Medicine & Surgery (higher education)
CCMCCI: Commission for Catholic Missions among the Colored People and the Indians (religious)
CCNA: Christian Church of North America (religious denomination)
CCNE: Commission on Collegiate Nursing Education (education, accrediting)
CCNY: City College of New York (higher education)
CCP: Chicago Central & Pacific (also CC) (railroad)
CCP: Concerned Citizens Party (political party)
CCPR: Chelatchie Prairie Railroad
CCR: Communion of Christ the Redeemer (religious denomination)
CCR: Corinth & Counce (railroad)

CCR: Catholic Charismatic Renewal (lay order)

CCRA: Camp Chase Industrial Railroad

CCRKBA: Citizens' Committee for the Right to Keep and Bear Arms (lobby)

CCRL: Catholic Civil Rights League (political/religious)

CCRR: Claremont Concord Railroad

CCRY: Charles City Railway (railroad)

CCSA: Congress of Chiropractic State Associations (trade group)

CCSB: Canadian Convention of Southern Baptists (religious denomination, Canadian)

CCSI: Congregatio Canonicorum Sancti Augustini (religious order)

CCSSF: Common Computing Security Standards Forum (professional)

CCSU: Central Connecticut State University (Connecticut) (higher education)

CCT: Central California Traction (railroad)

CCTAS: Crusaders-Catholic Total Abstinence Society (religious, civic)

CCTC: California Commission on Teacher Credentialing (education)

CCTI: Chartered Clinical Trialist Institute (professional)

CCU: Croatian Catholic Union of the United States of America (and Canada) (ethnic, mutual benefit)

CCU: Czech Catholic Union (ethnic, charitable)

CCU: Catholic Central Union (mutual benefit)

CCUO: Chicago-Chemung Railroad

CCUS: Christian Congregation in the United States (religious denomination)

CCUSA: Catholic Charities USA (religious)

CCVA: Catholic Central Verein of America (religious)

CD: Colonial Dames (lineage)

CD: Christian Democrats (political party)

CD: Catholic Democrats (religious, political)

CDA: Colonial Dames of America (also NSCDA) (lineage)

CDA: Catholic Daughters of the Americas (sometimes CDofA or CDoA) (religious)

CDAC: Canadian American Railroad

CDC: Center for Disease Control and Prevention (governmental)

CDCA: Canadian Dexter Cattle Association (cattle)

CDD: Congregation of the Disciples of the Lord (religious order)

CDI: Centrist Democrat International (political/religious)

CDL: Christian Defense League (cult)

CDMA: Canadian Donkey and Mule Association (donkeys)

CDoA: Catholic Daughters of America (also CDofA and CDA) (religious)

CDofA: Catholic Daughters of American (also CDoA and CDA) (religious)

CDP: Sisters of Divine Providence – Congregation of Divine Providence (religious order)

CDXVII: Colonial Dames of the XVII Century (lineage)

CE: Christian Endeavor (religious)

CEA: Consumer Electronics Association (trade group)

CE(C): Church of England (Continuing) (religious denomination)

CEC: Christian Episcopal Church (religious denomination)

CEC: Charismatic Episcopal Church (religious denomination)

CEC: Council for Exceptional Children (civic)

CEDR: Cedar River Railroad

CEDS: Citizens Emergency Defense System (paramilitary, cult)

CEEC: Communion of Evangelical Episcopal Churches (religious denomination)

CEF: Canadian Expeditionary Forces (military, World War I)

CEFX: CIT Group/Capital Finance, Inc. (rail car markings) (rail car leasing company)

CEI: Chicago & Eastern Illinois (railroad)

CEI: Chicago Evangelistic Institute (religious)

CEIW: Central Indiana and Western Railroad

CELC: Confessional Evangelical Lutheran Conference (religious denomination)

CEMR: Central Manitoba Railway (railroad)

CENTCOM: U. S. Central Command (military)

CEPH: Council on Education for Public Health (education)

CEQ: Council on Environmental Quality (governmental)

CERA: Central Railroad of Indianapolis (railroad)

CERT: Computer Emergency Readiness Team (governmental)

CES: Christian Endeavor Society (religious)

CES: Catholic Extension Society (religious)

CET: Canadian Equestrian Team (equestrian, sports)

CF: Council of Fifty (political/religious)

CF: Cape Fear Railroad

CF: Conservative Friends (religious denomination)

CF: Church Fraternal (mutual benefit)
CFA: Columbian Fraternal Association (mutual benefit)
CFA: Canadian Fraternal Association (mutual benefit)
CFA: Cat Fanciers Association (interest)
CFA: Congregatio Fratrus Cellitarum seu Alexianorum (Alexian Brothers) (religious order)
CFA: Companions of the Forest of America (auxiliary of Foresters of America) (mutual benefit)
CFA: Cancer Fund of American (medical research, advocacy)
CFANV: Commodore Foote Association of Naval Veterans (affiliated with GAR) (veterans)
CFB: Church of the First Born (cult)
CFC: Chosen Friends of Canada (mutual benefit)
CFC: Columbian Fraternal Circle (mutual benefit)
CFC: Couples For Christ (religious)
CFC: Court of Federal Claims (governmental)
CFFT: Catholic Family Fraternal of Texas (religious)
CFG: Camp Fire Girls (youth)
CFG: Church of the Foursquare Gospel (religious denomination)
CFH: The Conference on Faith and History (academic)
CFI: Coalition for Israel (religious)
CFI: Chanticleer Fanciers International (poultry)
CFL: Catholic Fraternal League (mutual benefit)
CFL: Catholic Fraternal Life (mutual benefit)
CFL: Connecticut For Lieberman (political party)
CFL: Catholic Financial Life (mutual benefit)
CFLA: Catholic Fraternal Life Association (mutual benefit)
CFLCC: Combined Forces Land Component Command (military)
CFLI: Catholic Fraternal Life Insurance Society (mutual benefit)
CFLI: Catholic Family Life Insurance (mutual benefit)
CFLIS: Canadian Foresters Life Insurance Society (mutual benefit)
CFNR: California Northern Railroad
CFO: Ottawa Central Railroad
CFP: Christian Freedom Party (political party)
CFPA: Catholic Family Protective Association (mutual benefit)
CFPB: Consumer Financial Protection Bureau (governmental)
CFQC: Quebec Central Railway (railroad)
CFR: Corona Fellowship of Rosicrucians (fraternal, Rosicrucian)
CFS: Cambridge Friends School (Massachusetts) (school)

CFSG: Confederate Flag Support Group (KKK)
CFTC: Commodity Futures Trading Commission (governmental)
CFU: Continental Fraternal Union, Order of (fraternal)
CFU: Caribbean Football Union (sport)
CFUA: Croatian Fraternal Union of America (mutual benefit)
CFUSA: Camp Fire USA (youth)
CFX: Brothers of St. Francis Xavier (Xaverians) (religious order)
CG: Campfire Girls (see CFUSA) (youth)
CG: Cleveland Grays (lineage)
CG: California Grays (social, paramilitary)
CG: Hereditary Order of Descendents of Colonial Governors (lineage)
CG: Central of Georgia Railway (railroad)
CG: Church of God (religious denomination)
CG: Community of the Gospel (religious order)
CG: Conductors Guild (musical)
CGA: Community of the Glorious Ascension (religious community)
CGA: Canadian Galloway Association (cattle)
CGA: Canadian Guernsey Association (cattle)
CG(A): Church of God (Anderson) (religious denomination)
CGAA: Coast Guard Aviation Association (fraternal, service)
CGAF: Church of God of the Abrahamic Faith (religious denomination)
CGBCI: Conservative Grace Brethren Churches International (religious denomination)
CGCI: Christ Gospel Churches International (religious denomination)
CGCM: Church of God in Christ, Mennonite (religious denomination)
CGEU: Coalition of Graduate Employee Unions (labor union)
CGF: Church of God by Faith (religious denomination)
CGGC: Church of God General Conference (religious denomination)
CG(H): Church of God (Holiness) (religious denomination)
CGI: Church of God International (religious denomination)
CGIHP: Churches of God Independent Holiness People (religious denomination)
CGMA: Coast Guard Mutual Assistance (military support)
CGOC: Company Grade Officers' Council (military support)
CG(R): Church of God (Restoration) (religious denomination)

CGS: Community of the Good Shepherd (religious community)
CGS: Canadian Goat Society (goats)
CGS: Sisters of the Good Shepherd (religious order)
CGSC: U. S. Army Command and General Staff College (military)
CGSD: Church of God, Seventh Day (religious denomination)
CGT: Canada and Gulf Terminal Railroad
CGW: Chicago Great Western Railway (railroad)
CGWA: Church of God, a Worldwide Association (religious denomination)
CH: Court of Honor (mutual benefit)
CHA: Calvary Holiness Association (religious denomination)
CHA: Chamberlain Hunt Academy (school)
CHA: Canadian Historical Association (learned)
CHA: Canadian Hockey Association (sports)
CHA: Christian Holiness Association (religious denomination)
CHA: Catholic Health Association (religious)
CHA: Clearing House Association (lobby)
CHAC: Clydesdale Horse Association of Canada (equine)
CHAMPUS Civilian Health and Medical Program of the Uniformed Services (see also TRICARE:) (governmental)
CHAT: Chattahoochee and Gulf Railroad
CHAUS: Catholic Health Association of the United States (trade group)
CHC: Community of the Holy Cross (Benedictine) (Rempstone) (religious community)
CHC: Congregational Holiness Church (religious denomination)
CHC: City Harvest Church (religious denomination)
CHC: Calvary Holiness Church (religious denomination)
CHCS: Canadian Highland Cattle Society (cattle)
CHEST: American College of Chest Physicians (professional)
CHHPS: Canadian Horse Heritage and Preservation Society (equine)
CHI: Catholic Health Initiatives (religious)
CHILD: Children's Healthcare Is a Legal Duty (lobby)
CHIME: College of Healthcare Information Management Executives (professional)
ChiO: Chi Omega (sorority)
CHL: Canadian Hockey League (sports)
CHL: Central Hockey League (sports)
CHM: Congregation of the Humility of Mary (religious order)
CHMA: Cheviot Hills Military Academy (school)

CHMC: Chicago Homeopathic Medical College (Illinois) (higher education)

CHMC: Charity Hospital Medical College (Louisiana) (higher education)

CHN: Community of the Holy Name (Australia) (religious community)

CHN: Community of the Holy Name (Lesotho) (religious community)

CHN: Community of the Holy Name (Zulu Province) (religious community)

CHN: Community of the Holy Name (UK) (religious community)

CHP: Christian Holiness Partnership (religious denomination)

CHR: Chestnut Ridge Railroad

CHRR: Chesapeake Railroad

CHS: Community of the Holy Spirit (religious community)

CHS: Charlotte Southern Railroad

CHS: United States Catholic Historical Society (religious)

CHS: Canadian Hackney Society (equine)

CHSA: Caspian Horse Society of the Americas (equine)

CHT: Community of the Holy Transfiguration (religious community)

CHTS: Chester Valley Railroad

CHTT: Chicago Heights Terminal Transfer Railroad

CHV: Chattahoochee Valley Railroad

CHW: Chesapeake and Western (railroad)

CI: Cambria and Indiana Railroad

CI: China Airlines (airline code)

CI: Cochins International (poultry)

CI: Cordage Institute (trade group)

CIA: Catholic Institute Association (religious)

CIA: Connecticut Indian Association (ethnic)

CIA: Culinary Institute of American (higher education)

CIA: Central Intelligence Organization (governmental)

CIC: Christian Israelite Church (religious denomination)

CIC: Women's Committee of the Commission on Interracial Cooperation (civic)

CIC: Cedar Rapids and Iowa City Railway (railroad)

CIC: Catholic Interracial Council (religious)

CIC: Counterintelligence Corps (governmental)

CICM: Congregation of the Immaculate Heart of Mary (religious order)

CID: Center for Intercultural Dialogue (academic)

CIDA: Council for Interior Design Accreditation (accrediting)
CIJ: Congregation of the Infant Jesus (religious order)
CIL: Christian Israelite Church (religious denomination)
CIM: China Inland Mission (religious)
CIM: Congregation of Jesus and Mary (Eudists) (religious order)
CIM: Chicago and Illinois Midland (railroad)
CINCLANT: Commander in Chief Atlantic Forces (military)
CINCLANTFLT: Commander in Chief, Atlantic Fleet (military)
CINCPAC: Commander in Chief Pacific Forces (military)
CIND: Central Railroad of Indiana (railroad)
CIO: Congress of Industrial Organizations (labor union)
CIO: Committee for Industrial Organization (political)
CIP: Christians in Politics (political/religious)
CIP: Corps of Intelligence Police (governmental)
CIPFM: Chartered Institute of Professional Financial Managers (professional)
CIPS: Canadian Information Processing Society (professional)
CIRA: Continuity Irish Republican Army (guerilla organization)
CIRR: Chattahoochee Industrial Railroad
CIS: Council of International Schools (education)
CIT: Core Issues Trust (political/religious)
CIT: Case Institute of Technology (Ohio) (higher education)
CITA: Committee for the Implementation of Textile Agreements (governmental)
CITRA: Commission on International and Trans-Regional Accreditation (education)
CIU: Cigarmakers International Union (labor union)
CIU: Coopers International Union (labor union)
CIW: Illinois Central Gulf (railroad)
CJ: Congregation of Jesus (religious order)
CJC: Poor Sisters of Jesus Crucified and the Sorrowful Mother (religious order)
CJC: Commission on Jewish Chaplaincy (religious, military)
CJC: Canadian Jewish Congress (religious)
CJCS: Conference of Jewish Communal Service (see JCSA – Jewish Communal Service Association) (Jewish, civic)
CJCS: Center for Jewish Community Studies (religious)
CJE: Council for Jewish Education (religious)
CJF: Council of Jewish Federations, Inc. (religious, civic)
CJGS: Community of Companions of Jesus the Good Shepherd (religious community)
CJH: Chimes Junior Honorary (two year colleges) (academic honorary)

CJOCS: Council of Jewish Organizations in Civil Service (religious, political)

CJR: Connecticut Junior Republic (school)

CJSA: China Judaic Studies Association (learned)

CJT: Cargojet Airways Ltd. (airline code)

CK: Catholic Knights (mutual benefit)

CK&HEEWH: Christian Knights & Heroines of the Eastern and Western Hemispheres (fraternal, ethnic)

CK&LI: Catholic Knights & Ladies of Illinois (commercial, gambling establishment)

CKA: Catholic Knights of America (mutual benefit)

CKIN: Chesapeake and Indiana Railroad

CKIS: Catholic Knights Insurance Society (mutual benefit)

CKKKK: Carolina Knights of the Ku Klux Klan (KKK)

CKLA: Catholic Knights and Ladies of America (mutual benefit)

CKLI: Catholic Knights and Ladies of Illinois (mutual benefit)

CKO: Catholic Knights of Ohio (religious, mutual benefit?)

CKofA: Catholic Knights of America (mutual benefit)

CKofW: Catholic Knights of Wisconsin (mutual benefit)

CKP: Colorado, Kansas & Pacific Railroad

CKP: Colored Knights of Pythias (ethnic, fraternal, mutual benefit)

CKRY: Central Kansas Railway (railroad)

CKSG: Catholic Knights of St. George (mutual benefit)

CKSI: Carthage, Knightstown and Shirley Railroad

CKW: Catholic Knights of Wisconsin (religious, mutual benefit)

CL: Columbian League (mutual benefit)

CL: Colored League (sports)

CL: Croatian League (mutual benefit)

CLA: Commonwealth Lawyers Association (professional)

CLA: Communist League of America (political party)

CLAH: Conference of Latin American History (learned)

CLAN: Community of the Lady of All Nations (religious)

CLAO: Contact Lens Association of Ophthalmologists (professional)

CLBA: Church of the Lutheran Brethren of America (religious denomination)

CLC: Church of the Lutheran Confession (religious denomination)

CLC: Catholic Ladies of Columbia (mutual benefit)

CLC: Christian Legal Centre (political/religious)

CLC: Columbia and Cowlitz Railroad

CLCO: Claremont and Concord Railroad
CLG: Church of the Lamb of God (cult)
CLGR: Central Louisiana and Gulf Railroad
CLK: Cadillac and Lake City Railroad
CLMA: Carson Long Military Academy (school)
CLNA: Carolina Coastal Railroad
CLP: Clarendon & Pittsford Railroad Co. (railroad)
CLP: Christian Liberty Party (political party)
CLS: Christian Literature Society (religious)
CLSA: Canon Law Society of America (religious)
CLUW: Coalition of Labor Union Women (labor union)
CL: Columbian League (baseball league)
CL: Columbus League (mutual benefit)
CLA: CropLife America (trade group)
CLC: Christian Life Community (religious)
CLE: Consistent Life Ethic (political/religious)
CLI: CropLife International (trade group)
CLID: Church League for Industrial Democracy (religious, political)
CLIR: Council on Library and Information Resources (professional)
CLM: Christian Life Movement (religious)
CLMI: Carson Long Military Academy (school)
CLS: Cum Laude Society (high school, honorary)
CLSL: Columbia & Silver Creek Railroad
CM: Congregation of the Mission (Lazarists or Vincentians) (religious order)
CM: Vincentian Priests and Brothers (religious order)
CM: The Congregational Methodist Church (religious denomination)
CM: Conference of Mayors (political)
CM: College of Montana (higher education)
CM: Colorado Midland (railroad)
CM: Central Montana Rail (railroad)
CM: Chemical Corps (Army branch)
CMA: Coal Merchants' Association (business)
CMA: Coming Men of America (youth, fraternal, perhaps Masonic)
CMA: Camden Military Academy (school)
CMA: Culver Military Academy (school)
CMA: Christian and Missionary Alliance (religious)
CMA: Chamber Music America (musical)
CMA: Christian Motorcyclists of America (religious)

CMAA: Church Music Association of America (musical)
CMAA: Crane Manufacturers Association of America (trade group)
CMBA: Catholic Men's Benevolent Association (religious, mutual benefit)
CMBA: Catholic Mutual Benefit Association (religious, mutual benefit)
CMBA: Columbus Mutual Benefit Association (mutual benefit)
CMBU: Catholic Mutual Benevolent Union (mutual benefit)
CMC: Congregation of the Mother Coredemptrix (religious order)
CMC: Calvinistic Methodist Church (religious denomination)
CMC: Congregational Methodist Church (religious denomination)
CMC: Chortizer Mennonite Conference (religious denomination)
CMC: Conservative Mennonite Conference (religious denomination)
CMC: Claremont McKenna College (higher education)
CMEC: Christian Methodist Episcopal Church (religious denomination)
CMEP: Christians for Middle East Peace (religious)
CMER: Curtis, Milburn and Eastern Railroad
CMF: Claretian Missionaries (religious order)
CMG: Central Michigan Railway (railroad)
CMG: Catholic Mutual Group (religious, mutual benefit)
CMGA: Canadian Mounted Games Association (sports)
CMHC: Cornerstone Morgan Horse Club (equine)
CMHS: Congressional Medal of Honor Society (military)
CMI: Christian Missions International (religious)
CMI: Carmelites of Mary Immaculate (religious order)
CMI: Can Manufacturers Institute (trade group)
CMIU: Cigar Makers International Union (labor union)
CMLA: Concordia Mutual Life Association (mutual benefit)
CMLAS: Columbian Mutual Life Assurance Society (mutual benefit)
CMM: Community of St. Mary of Nazareth and Cavalry (religious community)
CMMB: Catholic Medical Missions Board (humanitarian, religious)
CMML: Christian Missions in Many Lands (religious)
CMO: Chicago, St. Paul, Minneapolis & Omaha Railroad
CMQ: Central Maine and Quebec Railroad

CMPB: Community Motion Picture Bureau (military support)
CMR: Central Massachusetts Railroad
CMR: Central Midland Railway (railroad)
CMRR: Catskill Mountain Railroad, Inc. (railroad)
CMRS: Catholic Mutual Relief Society (religious, mutual benefit)
CMS: Church Missionary Society (religious)
CMS: Connecticut Missionary Society (religious)
CMS: Cambridge Montessori School (Massachusetts) (school)
CMS: College Music Society (musical)
CMS: Centers for Medicare and Medicaid Services (governmental)
CMSA: Case Management Society of America (professional)
CMTA: Caroline Marsh Tacky Association (equine)
CMU: Christian Mothers' Union (religious)
CMU: Carnegie Mellon University (higher education)
CN: Community of Nazareth (religious community)
CN: Canadian National (railroad)
CN: Church of the Nazarene (religious denomination)
CNA: California Nurses Association (labor union)
CNB: Crocker National Bank (company)
CNC: Central Normal College (higher education)
CND: Council of National Defense (governmental, WWI)
CND: Congregation of Notre Dame (religious order)
CNE: Central New England Railroad
CNI: Confederate Nations of Israel (political/religious)
CNI: Coalition for Networked Information (professional)
CNJ: Central Railroad of New Jersey (railroad)
CNN: Cable News Network (business)
CNO: SAS Scandinavian Airlines Norge AS (airline code)
CNOR: Cincinnati Northern (railroad)
CNOW: Columbia & Northern (railroad)
CNP: Council for National Policy (political/religious)
CNPZ: Nestor Paz Zamora Commission (guerilla group)
CNR: Chicago Numismatic Roundtable (hobby)
CNRR: Carolina Northern Rail Road (railroad)
CNorR: Canadian Northern Railway (railroad)
CNS: Chicago Numismatic Society (hobby)
CNS: Catholic News Service (religious)
CNS: Congress of Neurological Surgeons (professional)
CNTP: Cincinnati, New Orleans and Texas Pacific Railway (railroad)
CNW: Chicago and North Western Transportation Company (also C&NW) (railroad)

CO: Columbian Order (Tammany Society) (fraternal)
CO: Oratory of St. Philip Neri (Oratorians, Oratory) (religious order)
CO: Chesapeake and Ohio Railway (also C&O) (railroad)
CO: Continental Airlines (airline code)
COA: Continental Airlines (airline code)
COA: Colonial Order of the Acorn (lineage)
CoA-NA: American Association of Nurse Anesthetists Council on Accreditation of Nurse Anesthesia Educational Programs (accrediting)
COC: Colonial Order of the Crown (lineage)
COC: Celtic Orthodox Church (religious denomination)
COCA: Commission on Osteopathic College Accreditation (education)
COCF: Canadian Order of Chosen Friends (mutual benefit)
CODA: College Orchestra Directors Association (professional)
COE: Church of England (religious denomination)
COE: Colorado & Eastern Railroad
COE: Council on Occupational Education (education)
COER: Crab Orchard and Egyptian Railroad
COF: Catholic Order of Foresters (also COOF) (mutual benefit)
COF: Canadian Order of Foresters (mutual benefit)
CofC: Community of Celebration (religious)
CofC: Children of the Confederacy (lineage)
CofE: Corps of Engineers (military)
CofS: Church of Scotland (religious denomination)
COH: Court of Honor (perhaps Boy Scouts)
COH: Circle of Honor (appears to be generic)
COHA: Central Ontario Hockey Association (sports)
COHL: Central Ontario Hockey League (sports)
COHH: Concatenated Order of Hoo-Hoo (fraternal, forest products industry, service)
COI: Church of Ireland (religious denomination)
COLPA: National Jewish Commission on Law and Public Affairs (religious, political)
COMPACFLT: Commander, Pacific Fleet (military)
CompTIA: Computing Technology Industry Association (trade group)
CONAD: Continental Air Defense Command (military)
Conrail: Consolidated Rail Corporation (railroad)
Conoco: Continental Oil Company (business)

COOF: Catholic Order of Foresters (also COF) (mutual benefit)
CoOL: Conservation OnLine (professional)
COP: City of Prineville Railroad
COPS: Community Oriented Policing Services (governmental)
CORE: Congress of Racial Equality (political)
CORE: Council on Rehabilitation Education (education, accrediting)
CORP: Central Oregon and Pacific Railroad
CORR: Championship Off-Road Racing (motorsports)
COSH: Committees for Occupational Safety and Health (labor union)
COST: Council On State Taxation (trade group)
COTC: Central Officers Training Camp (military – World War I)
COTS: Central Officers Training School (WWI-era military)
COTW: Camels of the World (anti-prohibition)
CP: Congregation of the Passion (Passionists) (religious order)
CP: Passionist Missionaries (religious order)
CP: Passionist Community (religious order)
CP: Canadian Pacific (railroad)
CP: Constitution Party (political party)
CP: Citizens Party (political party)
CP: Chevaliers of Pythias (mutual benefit, charitable)
CP: College of Preachers (religious)
CPA: Chauffeurs Protective Association (labor union)
CPA: Cumberland and Pennsylvania Railroad (see also C&PA)
CPA: Cathay Pacific Airways, Ltd. (airline code)
CPC: Capuchin Poor Clares (religious order)
CPC: Cumberland Presbyterian Church (religious denomination)
CPC: Central Pennsylvania College (higher education)
CPC: Covenant Presbyterian Church (religious denomination)
CPC: Church Periodical Club (religious)
CPCA: Chinese Patriotic Catholic Association (religious)
CPCA: Cumberland Presbyterian Church in America (religious denomination)
CPDL: Christian-Patriots Defense League (cult)
CPDR: Carolina Piedmont Railway (railroad)
CPF: Coalition for Patent Fairness (lobby)
CPG: Catholic Police Guild (religious)
CPGS: Cotton Patch Goose Society (poultry)
CPHL: Canadian Professional Hockey League (sports)

CPI: Committee on Public Information (governmental, WWI)
CPI: Church Publishing, Inc. (religious, company)
CPI: Committee on Public Information (governmental)
CPJ: Citizens for Public Justice (religious, education)
CPL: Christian Protective League (anti-semitic)
CPL: Citizens' Protective League (WWI)
CPL: Council of Prison Locals (labor union)
CPLJ: Camp Lejeune Railroad
CPLT: Camino, Placerville and Lake Tahoe Railroad
CPM: Chosen People Ministries (religious denomination)
CPNY: Conservative Party of New York State (political party)
CPPS: Society of the Precious Blood (religious order)
CPPS: Sisters of the Precious Blood (religious order)
CPR: Canadian Pacific Railroad
CPRR: Central Pacific (railroad)
CPS: Missionary Sisters of the Precious Blood (religious order)
CPS: Canadian Pony Society (equine)
CPSC: Consumer Product Safety Commission (governmental)
CPT: Christian Peacemaker Teams (political/religious)
CPUS: Citizens Party of the United States (political party)
CPUSA: Communist Party of the United States of America
(political party)
CPV: Communist Party of Vietnam (political)
CPY: Communist Party of Yugoslavia (political)
CR: Cradle Roll (religious, youth)
CR: Community of the Resurrection (Resurrectionists) (religious
order)
CR: Congregation of Clerics Regular (Theatines) (religious
order)
CR: Sisters of the Resurrection (religious order)
CR: Community of the Resurrection (religious community)
CR: Community of the Resurrection of our Lord (religious
community)
CR: Conrail (Consolidated Rail Corporation) (railroad)
CR+C: Confraternity Rosae + Crucis (fraternal, Rosicrucian)
CR: Canonesses Regular (religious order)
CR&N: Carolina and Northwestern Railway (also CRN)
(railroad)
CRA: Champion Racing Association (motorsports)
CRBA: Catholic Relief and Beneficiary Association (religious,
mutual benefit)
CRC: Order of the Temple and the Grail and of the Catholic
Order of the Rose-Croix (fraternal, Rosicrucian)

CRDX: Chicago Freight Car Leasing (rail car markings) (rail car leasing company)

CRE: Center for Regulatory Effectiveness (lobby)

CREC: Communion of Reformed Evangelical Churches (religious denomination)

CREW: Commercial Real Estate Women (professional)

CRF/TCT: Transcatheter Cardiovascular Therapeutics (professional)

CRFE: Caucus of Rank and File Educators (labor reform group)

CRH: Choate Rosemary Hall (Connecticut) (school)

CRI: Church on the Rock, International (religious denomination)

CRJ: Center for Russian Jewry (religious)

CRL: Chicago Rail Link (railroad)

CRM: Clerics Regular Minor (religious order)

CRMA: City and Regional Magazine Association (trade group)

CRME: Commission on Religious and Moral Education (Baptist) (religious)

CRN: Carolina and Northwestern Railway (also CR&N) (railroad)

CRN: Council for Responsible Nutrition (trade group)

CRNJ: Canons Regular of the New Jerusalem (religious order)

CROSA: Canonesses of St. Augustine (religious order)

CRP: Canons Regular of Premontre (Norbertines or Premonstartensians) (religious order)

CRP: Central Railroad of Pennsylvania (railroad)

CRPCA: Canadian Red Poll Cattle Association (cattle)

CRR: Clinchfield Railroad

CRR: Connecticut River Railroad

CRR: Crawford Republican Party (political party)

CRS: Catholic Relief Services (religious, civic)

CRS: Christian Relief Services (religious, civic)

CRS: Congressional Research Service (governmental)

CRSG: Covenant of Religious Socialists of Germany (political/religious)

CRSH: Conrail (railroad)

CRSM: Council of Royal and Select Masters (Masonic)

CRSP: Clerics Regular of St. Paul (Barnabites) (religious order)

CRSP: Angelics of St. Paul (religious order)

CRT: Children of the Republic of Texas (lineage)

CRYX: Cryo-Trans (rail car marking) (rail car leasing company)

CofS: Church of Scotland (religious denomination)

CS: Church of Satan (cult)
CS: Congregation of the Missionaries of St. Charles Borromeo (Scalabrians) (religious order)
CS: Colorado & Southern (railroad)
CS: Columbian Squares (youth, KofC)
CS: Church of Scotland (religious denomination)
CS: Claretian Sisters (religious order)
CSA: Confederate States of America (governmental)
CSA: Confederate States Army (military)
CSA: Confederate States Army (KKK)
CSA: Community of Saint Andrew (religious community)
CSA: Czechoslovak Society of America (fraternal, mutual benefit)
CSA: Christian Science Association (religious denomination)
CSA: The Covenant, the Sword, the Arm of the Lord (paramilitary, cult)
CSA: Casting Society of America (trade group)
CSA: Sisters of St. Agnes (religious order)
CSAI: Carmelite Sisters of the Aged and Infirm (religious order)
CSARJ: Commission on Social Action of Reform Judaism (religious, political)
CSAS: Czechoslovak Society of Arts and Sciences (professional)
CSB: Congregation of St. Basil (Basilians) (religious order)
CSB: Order of Our Savior (Bridgettines) (religious order)
CSB: Catholic Slovak Brotherhood (mutual benefit)
CSB: Church of Satanic Brotherhood (cult)
CSBO: Catholic Slovak Benefit Organization (mutual benefit)
CSC: Congregation of the Holy Cross (Holy Cross Fathers/Brothers) (religious order)
CSC: Community of Servants of the Cross (religious community)
CSC: Community of Sisters of the Church (UK, Canada, Australia, Solomon Islands) (religious community)
CSC: Catholic Sioux Congress (religious)
CSC: Sisters of the Holy Cross (religious order)
CSCA: Central States Communication Association (education)
CSCD: Cascade and Columbia River Railroad
CSD: Community of St. Denys (religious community)
CSDAC: Creation Seventh Day Adventist Church (religious denomination)
CSDIW: Continental Society Daughters of Indian Wars (lineage)
CSE: Council of Science Editors (professional)

CSEA: California School Employees Association (labor union)
CSF: Community of St. Francis (religious community)
CSF: California Scholarship Federation (high school, honorary)
CSF: Commercial Spaceflight Federation (trade group)
CSG: Council of State Governments (quasi-governmental)
CSH: Convent of the Sacred Heart (school)
CSHC: Christ's Sanctified Holy Church (religious denomination)
CSI: Christian Sports International (religious)
CSIDA: College Sports Information Directors of America (professional)
CSIS: Center for Strategic and International Studies (political)
CSJ: Congregation of St. Joseph (religious order)
CSJB: Sisters of St. John the Baptist (Baptistine Sisters) (religious order)
CSJB: Community of St. John, Baptist (religious community)
CSJD: Community of St. John the Divine (religious community)
CSJE: Community of St. John the Evangelist (Ireland) (religious community)
CSJO: Congress of Secular Jewish Organizations (religious)
CSL: Community of St. Laurence (religious community)
CSL: Companions of St. Luke (Benedictine) (religious order/community)
CSL: Chicago Short Line (railroad)
CSM: Community of St. Mary (religious community)
CSM: Community of the Sisters of Melanesia (religious community)
CSM: Colonial Society of Massachusetts (lineage)
CSM&AA: Community of St. Michael and All Angels (religious community)
CSMC: Catholic Students Mission Crusade (religious)
CSMC: Christian Students Mission Club (religious)
CSMV: Community of St. Mary the Virgin (religious community)
CSN: Sisters of Nazareth (religious order)
CSN: Community of the Sacred Name (religious community)
CSN: Confederate States Navy (military)
CSO: Connecticut Southern Railroad
CSP: Congregation of St. Paul (Paulists) (religious order)
CSP: Colonial Society of Pennsylvania (lineage)
CSP: Community of St. Peter (religious community)
CSP: Community of the Sacred Passion (religious community)

CSPH: Community of St. Peter (UK) Horbury (religious community)

CSPS: Czecho-Slovak Protective Society (mutual benefit)

CSPT: Conference for the Study of Political Thought (political)

CSRS: Civil Service Retirement System (governmental)

CSS: Congregation of the Sacred Stigmata (Stigmatines) (religious order)

CSS: Christa Sevika Sangha (Handmaids of Christ) (religious community)

CSS: Chicago South Shore and South Bend Railroad

CSSA: Council of School Supervisors & Administrators (professional)

CSSF: Congregation of the Sisters of St. Felix of Cantalice (Felician sisters) (religious order)

CSSIW: Continental Society, Sons of Indian Wars (lineage)

CSSL: Caledonian Society of St. Louis (mutual benefit)

CSSp: Congregation of the Holy Ghost (Spiritans) (religious order)

CSSR: (see CSsR – Redemptorists) (religious order)

CSsR: Congregation of the Most Holy Redeemer (Redemptorists) (religious order)

CSSSB: Chicago, South Shore, South Bend (railroad)

CST: Carmelites of St. Therese of the Infant Jesus (religious order)

CSTE: Council of State and Territorial Epidemiologists (professional)

CSU: California State University (usually followed by name of city) (California) (higher education)

CSU: Colorado State University (Colorado) (higher education)

CSU: Catholic Slovak Union (mutual benefit)

CSU: Cleveland Slovak Union (mutual benefit)

CSV: Clerics of St. Viator (Viatorians) (religious order)

CSWE: Council on Social Work Education (education, accrediting)

CSWG: Community of the Servants of the Will of God (religious community)

CSX: CSX Corporation (simply an initialism as a name; Chesapeake & Southern may have contributed the CS part) (railroad)

CSXT: CSX Corporation (see CSX) (railroad)

CSYX: Central Soya (rail car markings of agribusiness)

CT: Community of the Transfiguration (religious community)

CT: Columbia Terminal Railroad

CTAS: Catholic Total Abstinence Society (religious, civic, self-help)

CTAU: Catholic Total Abstinence Union (of America) (self-help)

CTBTO: Comprehensive Nuclear Test Ban Treaty Organization (international organization)

CTC: Chesapeake Transit Company

CTCA: Commission on Training Camp Activities (military, WWI)

CTDFPA: Connecticut Chapter of National Society of Founders and Patriots of America (lineage)

CTE: Cen-Tex Rail Lines (railroad)

CTHU: Coal Teamsters and Handlers Union (labor union)

CTIA: Cellular Telephone Industries Association (trade group)

CTIE: Kansas City Southern Railroad

CTML: Cairo Terminal Railroad

CTN: Canton Railroad

CTR: Clinton Terminal Railroad

CTRN: Central of Tennessee Railroad

CTSA: Catholic Theological Society of America (religious)

CU: Catholic Union (religious)

CU: Cotner University (Nebraska) (higher education)

CU: Catholics United (political/religious)

CUAC: Colleges and Universities of the Anglican Communion (religious, education)

CUBA: Christian Unity Baptist Association (religious denomination)

CUBC: Church of the United Brethren in Christ (religious denomination)

CUBS: unknown (mutual benefit)

CUE: Coalition of University Employees (labor union)

CUGB: Catholic Union of Great Britain (religious)

CUIC: Churches Uniting in Christ (religious)

CUNA: Credit Union National Association (trade group)

CUNY: City University of New York (New York) (higher education)

CUOH: Columbus and Ohio River Railroad

CUOI: Catholic Union of Illinois (mutual benefit)

CUP: Constitutional Union Party (political party)

CURB: Curtis Bay Railroad

CUS: Confederation of Trade Union Unity (political)

CUVA: Cuyahoga Valley (railroad)

CV: Central Vermont (railroad)

CV: Catholic Vote (political/religious)
CV: Christian Voice (political/religious)
CVA: Christian Vegetarian Association (religious, lifestyle)
CVA: Catholic Veterans Association (religious)
CVC: Chicago Veterinary College (Illinois) (higher education)
CVI: Congregation of the Incarnate Word and Blessed Sacrament (religious order)
CVL: Congregation of the Sisters of the Visitation of Our Lady (religious community)
CVO: Communist Voice Organization (political)
CVR: Cimarron Valley Railroad
CVRR: Central Vermont Railroad
CVS: Caecelia Vocal Society (musical)
CVS: Consumer Value Stores (business)
CVS: Cedar Valley Seminary (higher education)
CW: Catholic Workmen (mutual benefit, religious, civic)
CW: Colorado & Wyoming Railroad
CW: Camels of the World (fraternal)
CW: Columbia Woodmen (mutual benefit)
CWA: Communication Workers of America (labor union)
CWA: Cold Water Army (children, temperance)
CWA: Country Women's Association (Australia) (women)
CWA: Civil Works Administration (New Deal) (governmental)
CWA: Canadian Wheelmen's Association (sports)
CWAWIU: Carriage, Wagon and Auto Workers International Union (labor union)
CWBL: Catholic Women's Benevolent Legion (mutual benefit)
CWC: Central Wesleyan College (Missouri) (higher education)
CWHF: Corolla Wild Horse Fund (equine)
CWI: Chicago & Western Indiana (railroad)
CWI: Committee for a Workers' International (political party)
CWK: Confederate White Knights (KKK)
CWL: Catholic Women's League (religious)
CWM: Catholic Worker Movement (religious, political)
CWM: Center for World Music (musical)
CWP: Communist Workers Party (political party)
CWP: Chicago, West Pullman and Southern Railroad
CWR: California Western Railroad
CWRC: Central Wisconsin Railroad
CWRL: Central Western Railroad
CWRO: Cleveland Works Railroad
CWRY: Commonwealth Railway (railroad)
CWS: Chemical Warfare Service (military, World War I)

CWS: Church World Service (religious)
CWSA: Connecticut Women's Suffrage Association (political)
CWSL: Catholic Women's Service League (religious)
CWV: Catholic War Veterans (religious, veterans)
CX: Cathay Pacific Airways Ltd. (airline code)
CYC: China Youth Corps (youth, political)
CYJ: Canadian Young Judaea (religious, youth)
CYMA: Catholic Young Men's Association (religious)
CYMCA: Central YMCA College (Illinois) (higher education)
CYMF: Central Yearly Meeting of Friends (religious denomination)
CYO: Catholic Youth Organization (religious, youth)
CZ: Coalhuila and Zacatecas Railway (railroad)
CZF: Canadian Zionist Federation (religious)
CZM: Chita che Zvipo Zye Moto (Community of the Gifts of the Holy Fire) (religious community)
CZR: Chita Che Zita Rinoyera (Holy Name Community) (religious community)

D

D: Democratic Party (political party)

D0: DHL Air Limited (airline code)

D&H: Delaware & Hudson (also DH) (railroad)

D&H: Delaware & Hudson Canal (canal company)

D&M: Detroit & Mackinac (railroad)

D&MofEBS: Daughters and Mothers of England Benevolent Society (mutual benefit)

D&R: Dardanelle & Russellville (railroad)

D&RGW: Denver and Rio Grande Western (railroad)

D&S: Durango & Silverton Railroad

D&W: Danville and Western Railway (railroad)

DA: Department of the Army (military)

DA: Daughters of America (also DOA and DofA) (fraternal, nativist, mutual benefit)

DA: Dominican Academy (school)

DA: Dominion Atlantic (railroad)

DA: Degree of Anona (youth, fraternal)

DAARA: Daytona Antique Automobile Racing Association (motorsports)

DAC: Daughters of the American Colonists (lineage)

DAF: Department of the Air Force (military)

Dairylea: Dairymen's League Cooperative Association (agriculture)

DAKR: Dakota Rail (railroad)

DAKS: Dakota Short Line (railroad)

DAL: Delta Air Lines Inc. (airline code)

DALT: Dallas Terminal Railway (railroad)

DAN: Daughters of the Nile (Masonic)

DAN: Delta Alpha Nu (dance) (academic honorary)

DAPi: Delta Alpha Pi (students with disabilities) (academic honorary)

DAR: Daughters of the American Revolution (also NSDAR) (lineage)

DARPA: Defense Advance Research Project Agency (governmental)

DAU: Defense Acquisition University (governmental)

DAV: Disabled American Veterans (veterans)

DAVWW: Disabled American Veterans of the World War (veterans)
DB: Dunkard Brethren (religious denomination)
DBA: Danish Brotherhood in America (fraternal, mutual benefit)
DBC: Daniel Baker College (Texas) (higher education)
DBCAA: Dutch Belt Cattle Association of American (cattle)
DBE: Daughters of the British Empire in the USA (lineage)
DC: Daisy Chain of the Congregational Church (youth, religious)
DC: Daughters of Charity of St. Vincent DePaul (religious order)
DC: Disciples of Christ (religious denomination)
DC: Daughters of the Cincinnati (lineage)
DC: Congregazione dei Preti della Dottrina Cristiana (religious order)
DC: Dana College (Nebraska) (higher education)
DC: Delray Connecting Railroad
DC: Daughters of the Cincinnati (lineage)
DC: Daughters of the Confederacy (lineage)
DC: Daughters of Columbia (also DOC) (auxiliary of the American Patriot League (APL)) (World War I, quasi-governmental)
DC: Dental Corps (Army branch)
DCA: Defense Commissary Agency (governmental)
DCA: Dominique Club of America (poultry)
DCAA: Defense Contract Audit Agency (governmental)
DCAL: Dexter Cattle American Legacy (cattle)
DCBOA: Draft Horse Breeders & Owners Association (equine)
DCC: Dames of Colonial Cavaliers (lineage)
DCC: Detroit City College (Michigan) (higher education)
DCCI: Descendants of Cape Cod and the Islands (lineage)
DCLR: Delaware Coast Line Railroad
DCM: Department of Civilian Marksmanship (military)
DCMA: Defense Contract Management Agency (governmental)
DCNA: Dorking Club of North America (poultry)
DCON: Detroit Connecting Railroad
DCRR: Dubois County Railroad
DCTC: District of Columbia Teachers College (higher education)
DCW: Daughters of Colonial Wars (lineage)
DDC: Daughters of Divine Charity (religious order)
DDRA: Dirt Drag Racing Association (motorsports)

DE: Daughters of Erin (may be same as LAOH) (fraternal, hereditary)

DEA: Drug Enforcement Administration (governmental)

DEAC: Distance Education Accreditation Commission (education, accrediting)

DEEX: Detroit Edison (railroad)

DEI: Delta Epsilon Iota (honorary fraternity)

DEKE: Delta Kappa Epsilon (see DKE) (college fraternity)

DEMA: Diving Equipment and Marketing Association (trade group)

DEP: Delta Epsilon Phi (German) (high school, honorary)

DES: Daughters of the Eastern Star (fraternal)

DES: Delta Epsilon Sigma (honorary fraternity, religious)

DET: Delta Epsilon Tau (distance learning) (honorary fraternity)

DFAS: Defense Finance and Accounting Service (governmental)

DFAW: Descendents of the Founders of Ancient Windsor (lineage)

DFMC: Diocesan Fiscal Management Conference (religious)

DFMS: Domestic and Foreign Mission Society of the Episcopal Church (religious)

DFNJ: Descendents of the Founders of New Jersey (lineage)

DFPA: Daughters of Founders and Patriots of America (lineage)

DG: Delta Gamma (sorority)

DGA: Directors Guild of America (labor union)

DGA: Dramatists Guild of America (labor union)

DGH&M: Detroit, Grand Haven and Milwaukee Railway (railroad)

DGL: Diocese of the Great Lakes (religious)

DGNO: Dallas, Garland, and Northeastern Railroad

DGVR: Durbin and Greenbrier Valley Railroad

DH: Daughters of Hawaii (lineage)

DH: Delaware & Hudson Railroad (also D&H)

DH: Degree of Honor (also DOH) (mutual benefit)

DH: Degree of Hiawatha (youth, fraternal)

DH: Daughters of Hope (charitable, mutual benefit)

DHC: Diocese of the Holy Cross (religious)

DHC: Detroit Homeopathic College (Michigan) (higher education)

DHC: Defense Homes Corporation (governmental)

DHHCEU: Drug, Hospital, and Health Care Employees Union (labor union)

DHK: DHL Air Limited (airline code)

DHL: part of the postal and logistics company Deutsche Post DHL Group (business)

DHM: Daughters of the Heart of Mary (religious order)

DHMC: Detroit Homeopathic Medical College (Michigan) (higher education)

DHPA: Degree of Honor Protective Association (mutual benefit)

DHPS: Degree of Honor Protective Society (mutual benefit)

DHS: Daughters of the Holy Spirit (religious order)

DHS: Department of Homeland Security (governmental)

DI: Daughters of Isis (fraternal)

DIA: Drug Information Association (professional)

DIA: Defense Intelligence Agency (governmental)

DIBPOEW: Daughters of the Independent, Benevolent and Protective Order of Elks of the World (fraternal)

DISA: Defense Information Systems Agency (governmental)

DISC: Diocesan Information Systems Conference (religious)

DIT: Detroit Institute of Technology (higher education)

DJC: Duluth Junior College (higher education)

DKB: Descendents of Knights of the Bath (lineage)

DKE: Delta Kappa Epsilon (also DEKE) (college fraternity)

DL: Daughters of Liberty (also DoL) (political, pre-Revolutionary War)

DL: Delaware Lackawanna RR (railroad)

DL: Delta Airlines (airline code)

DLBC: Deeper Life Bible Church (religious denomination)

DLCR: Delaware Coast Line Railroad

DLF: Digital Library Federation (learned)

DLH: Deutsche Lufthansa AG (airline code)

DLJ: Donaldson, Lufkin & Jenrette (company)

DLM: Divine Light Mission (cult)

DLSA: Defense Legal Services Agency (governmental)

DLNW: Denver, Laramie and North Western Railroad

DLW: Delaware, Lackawanna and Western Railroad

DLWR: Depew, Lancaster & Western Railroad

DM: Dames of Malta (also DofM) (fraternal, religious)

DM: Order of DeMolay (fraternal, youth)

DM: Lake State Railroad

DM: Daughters of Mokanna (Masonic)

DM: Daughters of Mary (Lutheran) (religious order)

DM: Discalced Mercedarians (religious order)
DMAA: Disease Management Association of America (trade group)
DMAA: Duke Medical Alumni Association (education)
DMAA: Direct Mail Marketing Association (trade group)
DM&E: Dakota Minnesota & Eastern (also DME) (railroad)
DMC: Dearborn Medical College (higher education)
DMC: Dunham Medical College (higher education)
DMC: Dutton Medical College (higher education)
DMD: Delta Mu Delta (business) (academic honorary)
DMDC: Defense Manpower Data Center (military)
DME: Dakota Minnesota & Eastern (also DM&E) (railroad)
DMI: DeMolay International (youth)
DMIR: Duluth, Mesabi & Iron Range (railroad)
DMJ: Daughters of Mother Jones (labor union)
DMM: Dansville and Mount Morris Railroad
DMU: Des Moines Union Railway (railroad)
DMU: Des Moines University (higher education)
DMVW: Dakota, Missouri Valley and Western Railroad
DMWV: Descendents of Mexican War Veterans (lineage)
DNA: District Nursing Association (civic, public health)
DNC: Division of Naval Communications (military)
DNE: Duluth and Northeastern Railroad
DOA: Daughters of America (see DofA, DA) (fraternal, nativist, mutual benefit)
DOC: Daughters of Columbia (also DC) (auxiliary of the American Patriot League (APL)) (World War I, quasi-governmental)
DO: Delta Omega (public health) (honorary)
DOC: Department of Commerce; Commerce Department (governmental)
DOD: Department of Defense (governmental)
DODR: Daughters of Duke Richard (presumably lineage)
DOE: Department of Energy (governmental)
DofA: Daughters of America (see DOA, DA) (fraternal, nativist, mutual benefit)
DofA: Daughters of America (see DOA, DA)
DofC: Daughters of Confederacy (lineage)
DofE: Daughters of Erin (part of Ancient Order of Hibernians) (Irish-American)
DofI: Daughters of Isabella (female, Knights of Columbus)
DofI: Daughters of Israel (female, Jewish)
DofL: Daughters of Liberty (nativist, anti-Catholic)

DofM: Dames of Malta (also DM) (fraternal, religious)
DofP: Daughters of Pocahontas (also Degree of Pocahontas)
(DOP, DP) (fraternal, Red Men)
DofR: Daughters of Rebekah (see DR) (fraternal)
DOH: Degree of Honor (also DH) (mutual benefit)
DOH: Deutscher Orden der Harguari (ethnic, mutual benefit)
DOHPA: Degree of Honor Protective Association (mutual
benefit)
DOI: Daughters of Isabella (fraternal)
DOI: Daughters of Isis (Masonic)
DOI: Department of the Interior (governmental)
DOJ: Department of Justice (governmental)
DOK: Daughters of the King (religious –
Episcopalian/Anglican, women)
DOKK: Dramatic Order Knights of Khorassan, Knights of
Pythias (fraternal)
DOL: Daughters of Liberty (also DL) (political, pre-
Revolutionary War)
DOL: Department of Labor (governmental)
DOLLUS: Dames of the Loyal Legion of the United States
(lineage)
DOM: Dames of Malta (lineage)
DOM: Daughters of Mokanna (Masonic)
DON: Daughters of the Nile (fraternal, Masonic)
DON: Daughters of Norway (lineage)
DOP: Daughters of Penelope (fraternal)
DOP: Degree of Pocahontas (also Daughters of Pocahontas)
(see also DofP, DP) (fraternal)
DOR: Daughters of Rebekah (see DR) (fraternal)
DOS: Daughters of Scotia (lineage)
DOS: Daughters of Scotland (lineage)
DOS: Daughters of St. Richards (lineage)
DOS: Department of State (governmental)
DOT: Department of Transportation (governmental)
DOV: Daughters of Veterans (lineage)
DP: Daughters of Pocahontas (also Degree of Pocahontas) (see
also DOP, DofP) (fraternal)
DP: Degree of Pocahontas (also Daughters of Pocahontas (see
also DOP, DofP) (fraternal)
DPA: Descendents of the Pioneers of America (lineage)
DPA: Delta Phi Alpha (German) (academic honorary)
DPA: Defense Production Administration (governmental)
DPA: Dales Pony Association of North America (equine)

DPC: Domestic Policy Council (governmental)
DPCU: Delaware Poultry Club United (poultry)
DPE: Delta Phi Epsilon (foreign service) (professional fraternity)
DPhi: Delta Phi (fraternity)
DPMA: Data Processing Management Association (trade group)
DPRA: Dartmoor Pony Registry of America (equine)
DPU: DePaul University (higher education)
SPSA: Dales Pony Society of America (equine)
DQE: DeQueen & Eastern (railroad)
DR: Daughters of Rebekah (also seen as DOR) (fraternal)
DR: Daughters of the Revolution (lineage)
DR: Dardanelle and Russellville Railroad
DR: Democratic Republican Party (Jeffersonian) (political party)
DRA: Dude Ranchers Association (trade group)
DRBC: Delaware River Basin Commission (governmental)
DRC: Dutch Reformed Church (religious denomination)
DRG: Denver and Rio Grande Railroad
DRI: Davenport, Rock Island and North Western Railroad
DRT: Daughters of the Republic of Texas (lineage)
DS: Durham & Southern (railroad)
DS: Danish Sisterhood (fraternal, mutual benefit)
DS: Daughters of Sacajawea (fraternal, ethnic)
DS: Delphian Society (education of women) (academic)
DS: Daughters of Scotland (fraternal, ethnic)
DS: Dorcas Society (religious)
DS: Daughters of Sacajawea (ladies' auxiliary of Teepee Order) (fraternal)
DSA: Duluth, South Shore & Atlantic Railroad
DSA: Democratic Socialists of America (political)
DSAA: Driving Schools Association of the Americas (trade group)
DSC: Daughters of St. Crispin (fraternal)
DSCA: Defense Security Cooperation Agency (governmental)
DSCUS: Distilled Spirits Council of the United States (trade group)
DSDA: Davidian Seventh Day Adventists (religious denomination)
DSDI: Descendents of the Signers of the Declaration of Independence (lineage)
DSF: Daughters of St. Francis (religious community)
DSH: Daughters of the Sacred Heart (religious order)
DSMP: Daughters of St. Mary of Providence (religious order)

DSO: Dallas Symphony Orchestra (musical)
DSP: Delta Sigma Phi (college fraternity)
DSRC: Dakota Southern Railway (railroad)
DSRR: Delta Southern Railroad
DSS: Defense Security Service (governmental)
DSSA: Duluth, South Shore & Atlantic Railway (railroad)
DSU: Dakota State University (South Dakota) (higher education)
DPW: Department of Public Works (governmental)
DPW: Daughters of the Pioneers of Washington (lineage)
DSSA: Dutch Settlers Society of Albany (lineage)
DSU: Delaware State University (Delaware) (higher education)
DT: Dirty Thirteen (college honorary)
DT: Dakota Territory (political subdivision)
DT: Decatur Junction Railroad
DT&P: Danville Traction and Power Company (railroad)
DTA: Delta Tau Alpha (agriculture) (academic honorary)
DTD: Delta Tau Delta (college fraternity)
DTI: Detroit, Toledo and Ironton (railroad)
DTIC: Defense Technical Information Center (governmental)
DTRA: Defense Threat Reduction Agency (governmental)
DTRR: Danbury Terminal Railroad
DTS: Detroit and Toledo Shore Line Railroad
DU: Delta Upsilon (college fraternity)
DU: Denison University (Ohio) (higher education)
DU: Drexel University (higher education)
DUCWV: Daughters of Union Civil War Veterans (lineage)
DUM: Druidic University of Maine (higher education)
DUP: International Society, Daughters of Utah Pioneers (lineage)
DURR: Delaware & Ulster Rail Ride (railroad)
DUT: Denver Union Terminal Railway (railroad)
DUTC: Dallas Union Terminal (railroad)
DUV: Daughters of Union Veterans (of the Civil War) (see also DUVCW) (lineage)
DUVCW: Daughters of Union Veterans (of the Civil War) (see also DUV) (lineage)
DV: Daughters of Vartan (ethnic)
DV: Delaware Valley Railroad
DV: Daughters of Veterans (lineage)
DVFS: Delaware Valley Friends' School (school)
DVS: Secret senior honor society at Emory University (academic honorary)

DX: Delta Chi (fraternity)
DXR: Delta Chi Rho (fraternity)
DVS: Delta Valley and Southern Railroad
DW: Detroit and Western (railroad)
DWC: Duluth, Winnipeg and Pacific Railway (railroad)
DWP: Duluth, Winnipeg and Pacific Railway (railroad)
DZ: Delta Zeta (sorority)

E

EA: Emergency Aid, Philadelphia, PA (healthcare, WWI)
EA: Eclectic Assembly (also The Eclectic Assembly, see TEA) (mutual benefit)
EAA: Experimental Aircraft Association (trade group)
EAC: Election Assistance Commission (governmental)
EACH: East Camden and Highland Railroad
EAEA: East Asian Economic Association (business)
EAL: Eastern Amateur League (sports)
EAMC: Estonian American Singing Club (musical)
EANG: Enlisted Association of the National Guard (military)
EANGUS: Enlisted Association of the National Guard of the United States (military)
EARY: Eastern Alabama Railway
EASA: Electrical Apparatus Service Association (trade group)
EASAS: European Association for South Asian Studies (learned)
EAU: Equitable Aid Union (mutual benefit)
EAUA: Equitable Aid Union of America (mutual benefit)
EB: Exclusive Brethren (religious denomination)
EB: Enterprise Baptists (religious denomination)
EBA: Emerald Benefit (or Beneficial) Association (mutual benefit)
EBC: Eastman Business College (New York) (higher education)
EBC: Elliott's Business College (Iowa) (higher education)
EBC: European Baptist Convention (religious denomination)
EBF: European Baptist Federation (religious denomination)
EBGR: Eastern Berks Gateway Railroad
EBMA: Employers' and Business Men's Association (trade group)
EBSA: Employee Benefits Security Administration (governmental)
EBSR: East Brookfield and Spencer Railroad
EC: Elevator Constructors (labor union)
EC: Emblem Club (of the US) (hobby)
EC: Episcopal Church (see TEC) (religious denomination)
EC: Eastern College (Virginia) (higher education)
EC: Ephrata Cloister (religious denomination)
ECA: Economic Cooperation Administration (governmental)

ECBA: European Council for Business Education (education)

ECBF: Episcopal Church Building Fund (religious)

ECBR: East Cooper and Berkeley Railroad

ECC: Evangelical Covenant Church (religious denomination)

ECC: Evangelical Catholic Church (religious denomination)

ECC: Evangelical Christian Church (religious denomination)

ECC: Edinburgh Cape Club (fraternal, service)

ECC-L: Evangelical Community Church – Lutheran (religious denomination)

ECFMG: Education Commission for Foreign Medical Graduates (education, accrediting)

ECHA: Eastern Canada Hockey Association (sports)

ECHL: East Coast Hockey League (sports)

ECHS: Evander Childs High School (school)

ECK: East Coast Knights (KKK)

ECL: Eastern Canada League (sports)

ECPM: European Christian Political Movement (political/religious)

ECNA: Evangelical Church of North America (religious denomination)

ECOSOC: United National Economic and Social Council (UN organization)

ECOP: Evangelical Covenant Order of Presbyterians (religious denomination)

ECPYM: European Christian Political Youth Network (political/religious)

ECS: Episcopal Community Services (religious)

ECSU: Eastern Connecticut State University (Connecticut) (higher education)

ECTB: East Chattanooga Belt Railway (railroad)

ECUSA: Episcopal Church in the United States of America (religious denomination)

ECV: E Clampsus (or Clampus) Vitus (also ECVE) (mutual benefit)

ECVE: E Clampsus Vitus (or Clampus) (also ECV) (mutual benefit)

ECW: Episcopal Church Women (religious)

ECW: Extreme Competitive Wrestling (sports)

ED: Department of Education (governmental)

EDA: Economic Development Administration (governmental)

EDA: Electrostatic Discharge Association (trade group)

EDF: Environmental Defense Fund (civic, political)

EDPi: Epsilon Delta Pi (computational science) (honorary fraternity)

EDW: El Dorado and Western Railroad

EEA: European Economic Association (business)

EEC: East Erie Commercial (railroad)

EEI: Epworth Evangelistic Institute (religious)

EEI: Equestrian Events Incorporated (equestrian)

EEI: Edison Electric Institute (trade group)

EELC: Estonian Evangelical Lutheran Church (religious denomination)

EEOC: Equal Employment Opportunity Commission (governmental)

EFA: Equal Franchise Association (political)

EFA: Evangelical Friends Alliance (religious denomination)

EFBC: Evangelical Free Baptist Church (religious denomination)

EFCA: Evangelical Free Churches in America (religious denomination)

EFF: Ex Fide Fortis, motto of Royal Neighbors of America (women, mutual benefit)

EFI: Evangelical Friends International (religious denomination)

EFI: Equestrian Federation of Ireland (equestrian, umbrella group)

EFICRP: Education Fund for Israeli Civil Rights and Peace (religious, political)

EFL: Equal Franchise League (political)

EFM: Education For Ministry (religious)

EFMP: Exceptional Family Member Program (military support)

EFRR: Effingham Railroad

EFS: East Florida Seminary (higher education)

EFU: Equitable Fraternal Union (mutual benefit)

EFR: Episcopalians for Global Reconciliation (religious)

EGTA: European Guitar Teachers Association (musical)

EGTK: Tupac Katari Guerilla Army (guerilla group)

EHA: Economic History Association (learned)

EHC: Episcopal Housing Corporation (religious, civic)

EHL: Eastern Hockey League (sports)

EHM: Episcopal Healing Ministry (religious)

EHS: Episcopal High School (school)

EI: Aer Lingus (airline code)

EIA: Electronics Industries Alliance (trade group)

EIN: Aer Lingus (airline code)

EIRC: Eastern Illinois Railroad

EIRR: Eastern Idaho Railroad

EIS: English Institute of Sports (sports)

EIU: Education, Industry, Union – (motto of Select Knights, Ancient Order of United Workmen) (mutual benefit)

EJE: Elgin, Joliet & Eastern (railroad)

EJR: East Jersey Railroad and Terminal (railroad)

EK: Eastern Kentucky Railroad

EK: Emirates Airlines (airline code)

EKN: Eta Kappa Nu (electrical engineering) (honorary fraternity)

EKR: Empire Knights of Relief (fraternal, mutual benefit)

EL: Epworth League, Methodist Episcopal Church (religious)

EL: Emily's List (Australian) (women, labor, politics)

EL: Erie Lackawanna Railroad

ELA: Equitable League of America (mutual benefit)

ELAO: English Language Acquisition Office (governmental)

ELC: Evangelical Lutheran Church (religious denomination)

ELCA: Evangelical Lutheran Church in America (religious denomination)

ELCC: Evangelical Lutheran Church in Canada (religious denomination)

ELCL: Evangelical Lutheran Church in Latvia (religious denomination)

ELDNA: Evangelical Lutheran Diocese of North America (religious denomination)

ELF: Eritrean Liberation Front (guerilla organization)

ELFCN: Evangelical Lutheran Free Church of Norway (religious denomination)

ELGLMC&MS: Elves, Leprechauns, Gnomes and Little Men's Chowder & Marching Society (fraternal, service)

ELHA: Elida Lodge Home Association (mutual benefit)

ELKR: Elk River Railroad

ELL: Estonian Air (airline code)

ELN: National Liberation Army (guerilla group)

ELS: Emerson Literary Society (fraternity)

ELS: Evangelical Lutheran Synod (religious denomination)

ELS: Escabana and Lake Superior Railroad

ELSCNA: Evangelical Lutheran Synodical Conference of North America (religious, umbrella organization)

ELY: El Al Israel Airlines, Ltd. (airline code)

EM: Edgemoor and Manetta Railroad

EmA: Emmanuel Association (religious)

EMA: Early Music America (musical)

EMB: Evangelical Mennonite Brethren (religious denomination)
EMBA: Elks Mutual Benefit Association (mutual benefit)
EMBA: Employees' Mutual Benefit Association (mutual benefit)
EMBAC: Executive MBA Council (education)
EMBC: Energy and Minerals Business Council (trade group)
EMC: Episcopal Missionary Church (religious denomination)
EMC: Ensworth Medical College (Missouri) (higher education)
EMC: Evangelical Methodist Church (religious denomination)
EMC: Evangelical Mennonite Church (religious denomination)
EMC: Evangelical Mennonite Conference (religious denomination)
EMC: Evangelical Missionary Church (religious denomination)
EMC: Excelsior Medical College (Massachusetts) (higher education)
EMC: Excelsior Medical College (New York) (higher education)
EMCI: Eclectic Medical College of Indiana (higher education)
EMCM: Eclectic Medical College of Maine (higher education)
EMHR: East Mahanoy and Hazelton Railroad
EMM: Eastern Mennonite Missions (religious)
EMM: Episcopal Migration Ministries (religious)
EMM: Enrolled Missouri Militia (military, Civil War)
EMMC: Evangelical Mennonite Mission Conference (religious denomination)
EMMF: Episcopal Medical Missions Foundation (religious)
EMRA: Eastern Motor Racing Association (motorsports)
EMRY: Eastern Maine Railway (railroad)
EMS: Eclectic Medical Society (trade group)
EMSR: Eastern Massachusetts Street Railway (railroad)
EN: Every Nation (religious denomination)
EN: Corps of Engineers (Army branch)
ENAEE: European Network for Accreditation of Engineering Education (education)
ENR: E & N Railway (railroad)
ENS: Episcopal Network for Stewardship (religious)
EOBD: Exalted Order of Big Dogs (fraternal)
EofA: Empire of Africa (ethnic)
EOGD: Esoteric Order of the Golden Dawn (mystical)
EOKA: National Organisation of Cypriot Fighters (guerilla organization)
EOMA: Empire Order of Mutual Aid (mutual benefit)
EORC: Engineer Officer Reserve Corps (military, World War I)

EOTS: Engineer Officer Training School (military, World War I)

EPA: Environmental Protection Agency (governmental)

EPA: Evangelical Press Association (trade group)

EPC: Evangelical Presbyterian Church (United States) (religious denomination)

EPF: Episcopal Preaching Foundation (religious)

EPHL: Eastern Professional Hockey League (sports)

EPM: English Presbyterian Mission (religious)

EPP: Epsilon Pi Phi (emergency management) (academic honorary)

ERB: Educational Records Bureau (education)

EPR: Popular Revolutionary Army (guerilla organization)

EPRY: East Penn Railway (railroad)

EPS: Evangelical Philosophical Society (religious, academic)

EPS: Exmoor Pony Society (equine)

EPT: Epsilon Pi Tau (technology) (academic honorary)

EPTC: East Portland Traction Company (railroad)

EQIS: European Quality Improvement System (education)

ER: Endowment Rank (mutual benefit)

ER-D: Episcopal Relief and Development (religious, civic)

ERA: Equitable Reserve Association (mutual benefit)

ERCC: Evangelical Reformed Church of Christ (religious denomination)

ERDA: Energy Research and Development Administration (governmental)

ERIC: Education Resources Information Center (governmental)

ERIE: Erie Railroad

ERPC: Evangelical Reformed Presbyterian Church (religious denomination)

ES: Eastern Star (fraternal, Masonic)

ES: Endocrine Society (professional)

ESA: Ecological Society of America (professional)

ESA: Entomological Society of America (academic)

ESA: Episcopal Synod of America (religious)

ESA: Economics and Statistics Administration (governmental)

ESA: Economic Stabilization Agency (governmental)

ESA: Entertainment Software Association (trade group)

ESAI: Epsilon Sigma Alpha International (fraternal, service)

ESBFA: Eastern Star Benevolent Fund of America (mutual benefit)

ESC: Episcopal Sisters of Charity (religious order)

ESC: Episcopal Service Corps (religious)

ESC: Evangelical Social Congress (religious)
ESD: Eta Sigma Delta (hospitality management) (academic honorary)
ESD: Episcopal School of Dallas (school)
ESG: Eta Sigma Gamma (health education) (academic honorary)
ESHR: Eastern Shore Railroad
ESLJ: East St. Louis Junction Railroad
ESM: Evangelical Sisterhood of Mary (religious order)
ESM: Episcopal Senior Ministries (religious)
ESOH: Exalted Society of Order Hounds (trade group – salesmen)
ESP: Eta Sigma Phi (classics) (academic honorary)
ESPN: Entertainment and Sports Programming Network (business)
ESSHC: European Social Science History Conference (learned)
ESSO: Standard Oil Company (business)
ESTA: Entertainment Services and Technology Association (trade group)
ESU: English Speaking Union (educational)
ESWU: Evangelical Slovak Women's Union (mutual benefit)
ETA: Basque Fatherland and Liberty (guerilla organization)
ETA: Employment and Training Administration (governmental)
ETC: East Texas Central Railroad
ETF: Episcopalians for Traditional Faith (religious)
ETHA: East Texas Historical Association (civic)
ETL: Essex Terminal Railway (railroad)
ETO: European Theater of Operations (military)
ETP: Epsilon Tau Pi (Eagle Scouts) (academic honorary)
ETRY: East Tennessee Railway (railroad)
ETSU: East Tennessee State University (higher education)
ETTF: European Tanker Task Force (military)
ETV&G: East Tennessee, Virginia & Georgia (railroad)
EU: Edinburg University (higher education)
EUA: Evelyn Underhill Association (religious)
EUB: Evangelical United Brethren (religious denomination)
EUBM: Eternal and Universal Brotherhood of Mystics (mystical, Rosicrucian)
EUCOM: U. S. European Command (military)
EURADA: European Association of Development Agencies (governmental, business)
EUROSEAS: European Association for South East Asian Studies (learned)

EV: Everett Railroad
EVRC: Fremont and Elkhorn Valley Railroad
EVT: Evansville Terminal (railroad)
EVWR: Evansville Western Railway (railroad)
EWBA: Electrical Workers Benefit Association (mutual benefit, labor)
EWK: European White Knights of the Ku Klux Klan (KKK)
EWR: Elkhart and Western Railroad
EWS: Episcopal Work Society (religious)
EWU: Electrical Workers Union (labor union)
EXO: Epsilon Chi Omicron (international business) (academic honorary)
EZLN: Zapatista Army of National Liberation (guerilla organization)

F

F: Federalist Party (political party)
F4J: Fathers 4 Justice (political)
F9: Frontier Airlines, Inc. (airline code)
F&AM: Free and Accepted Masons (sometimes FAM) (fraternal, Masonic)
F&M: Franklin & Marshall College (higher education)
FA: Field Artillery (Army branch)
FA: Female Association (religious)
FA: Fuel Administration (governmental, WWI)
FA: Food Administration (governmental, WWI)
FA&IU: Farmers Alliance & Industrial Union (labor union)
FAA: Free and Accepted Americans (also AB – American Brethren) (nativist)
FAA: Federal Aeronautics Administration (governmental)
FAA: Federal Aviation Administration (governmental)
FAA: Florida Air Academy (school)
FAA: Fraternal Aid Association (mutual benefit)
FAA: Fraternal Association of America (mutual benefit)
FAA: Federal Alcohol Administration (governmental)
FAAYM: Free And Accepted Ancient York Rite Masons (Masonic, ethnic)
FAC: Florida Agricultural College (higher education)
FACOTS: Field Artillery Central Officers Training School (military, World War I)
FACP: Free Apostolic Church of Pentecost (religious denomination)
FACT: Federation Against Copyright Theft (trade group)
FAGO: Fellow of the American Guild of Organists (music)
FAH: Federation of American Hospitals (trade group)
FAHL: Federal Amateur Hockey League (sports)
FALZW: Zarate Wilka Armed Forces of Liberation (guerilla group)
FAM: (less frequently seen abbreviation for Free and Accepted Masons – see F&AM) (fraternal, Masonic)
FannieMae: Federal National Mortgage Association, Inc. (also FNMA) (quasi-governmental business)
FAO: Food and Agriculture Organization (UN agency)
FAPR: Floydada and Plainview Railroad

FARC: Revolutionary Armed Forces of Colombia (guerilla organization)

FARD: Field Artillery Replacement Depot (military, World War I)

FARK: Kosovo Republic Armed Forces (guerilla organization)

FAS: Franciscan Apostolic Sisters (religious order)

FATAL: Fairest Among Ten Thousand Altogether Lovely (Eastern Star) (fraternal, Masonic)

FAU: Fraternal Aid Union (mutual benefit)

FAWCO: Federation of Women's Clubs Overseas (civic)

FB: Fenian Brotherhood (political, fraternal)

FB: Fraternal Brotherhood (mutual benefit)

FB: Freedmen's Bureau (governmental)

FBA: Federal Benefit Association (mutual benefit)

FBAA: Food and Beverage Association of America (trade group)

FBC: Free Will Baptist Church (also FWBC) (FBC) (religious denomination)

FBCS: First Baptist Christian School (also FAA - Florida City Christian) (school)

FBF: Farm Bureau Federation (agricultural)

FBF: Field Band Federation (musical)

FBFA: Fundamental Baptist Fellowship Association (religious denomination)

FBFA: Fundamental Baptist Fellowship of America (religious denomination)

FBG: Fellowship of Brethren Genealogists (hobby)

FBI: Federal Bureau of Investigation (governmental)

FBN: Federal Bureau of Narcotics (governmental)

FC: Brothers of Charity (religious order)

FC: Frederick College (Virginia) (higher education)

FC: Fredericksburg College (Virginia) (higher education)

FC: Fulton County Railroad

FC: Fecit Club (youth)

FC: Finance Corps (Army branch)

FCA: Farm Credit Administration (governmental)

FCB: "Friendship, Charity, and Benevolence" motto of Knights of Pythias (fraternal)

FCC: Federal City College (District of Columbia) (higher education)

FCC: Federal Communications Commission (governmental)

FCC: Florida City Christian (also FBCS – First Baptist Christian School) (school)

FCC: Federated Colored Catholics (religious)

FCCA: Florida Cracker Cattle Association (cattle)

FCCJS: First California Company of the Jamestowne Society (lineage)

FCCUS: Friends of Canterbury Cathedral in the United States (religious)

FCDA: Federal Civil Defense Authority/Administration (governmental)

FCE: Free Church of England (religious denomination)

FCEN: Florida Central Railroad

FCF: "Freedom, Charity, and Friendship" motto of Order of the Red Men (fraternal)

FCF: Firefighters' Charitable Foundation (civic)

FCFI: Faith Christian Fellowship International (religious denomination)

FCFP: First Command Financial Planning (military support)

FCHA: Florida Cracker Horse Association (equine)

FCII: Federated Council of Israel Institutions (religious, political)

FCIC: Federal Citizen Information Center (governmental)

FCIN: Frankfort and Cincinnati Railroad

FCJ: Faithful Companions of Jesus (religious order)

FCL: "Fraternity, Charity, Loyalty" (Masonic and union motto)

FCMC: First Congregational Methodist Church (religious denomination)

FCMS: Foreign Christian Missionary Society (religious)

FCNC: Fraternal Council of Negro Churches (political)

FCR: Fulton County Railway

FCRD: First Coast Railroad

FCRK: Falls Creek Railroad

FCS: Female Charitable Society (religious)

FCS: Female Cent Society (religious)

FCS: Free Catholic Church (religious denomination)

FCS: Free Church of Scotland (religious denomination)

FCS: Friends' Central School (Philadelphia) (school)

FCSC: Free Church of Scotland (Continuing) (religious denomination)

FCSC: Foreign Claims Settlement Commission (governmental)

FCSIC: Farm Credit System Insurance Corporation (governmental)

FCSLA: First Catholic Slovak Ladies Association (charitable, mutual benefit)

FCSLU: First Catholic Slovak Ladies Union (mutual benefit)

FCSP: Sisters of Providence (also SP) (religious order)
FCSU: First Catholic Slovak Union of the USA and Canada (mutual benefit)
FCUS: Fellowship of Catholic University Students (religious)
FCWC: Federation of Colored Women's Clubs
FDA: Food and Drug Administration (governmental)
FDC: Daughters of Diving Charity (religious order)
FdCC: Canossian Daughters of Charity (religious order)
FdCC: Canossian Sons of Charity (religious order)
FDDM: Fort Dodge, Des Moines and Southern Railway (railroad)
FDECUS: Fund for the Diaconate of the Episcopal Church in the United States (religious)
FDIC: Federal Deposit Insurance Corporation (governmental)
FDLC: Federation of Diocesan Liturgical Commissions (religious)
FDSB: Field Dog Stud Book (canine)
FDU: Fairleigh Dickinson University (higher education)
FDX: FedEx (airline code)
FEA: Florida Evangelistic Association (religious)
FEA: Foreign Economic Administration (governmental)
FEAF: Far East Air Forces (military)
FEBC: Fellowship of Evangelical Bible Churches (religious denomination)
FEBCC: Fellowship of Evangelical Baptist Churches in Canada (religious denomination)
FEC: Florida East Coast (railroad)
FEC: Free Evangelical Churches (religious denomination)
FEC: Federal Election Commission (governmental)
FedEx: FedEx Corporation (formerly Federal Express) (business)
FEI: Federation Equestrian Internationale (equestrian)
FEMA: Federal Emergency Management Agency (governmental)
FEMA: Fire Equipment Manufacturers' Association (trade group)
FEPC: French Evangelical Presbyterian Church (religious denomination)
FEPC: Fair Employment Practices Committee (political)
FERA: Federal Emergency Relief Administration (New Deal) (governmental)
FERC: Federal Energy Regulatory Commission (governmental)
FF: Friendly Few (fraternal)

FF: Tower Air (airline code)
FF: Farm Foundation (trade group)
FFA: Future Farmers of America (youth)
FFA: Faverolles Fanciers of America (poultry)
FFB: Federal Farm Board (governmental)
FFBC: Fellowship of Fundamental Bible Churches (religious denomination)
FFC: Faith and Freedom Coalition (political/religious)
FFF: Fraternity of Friendly Fellows (fraternal, mutual benefit)
FFG: First Families of Georgia (lineage)
FFI: French resistance group, WWII (military)
FFIEC: Federal Financial Institutions Examination Council (governmental)
FFMA: Friends' Foreign Mission Association (religious)
FFS: Foresters Friendly Society (mutual benefit)
FFV: First Families of Virginia (see also OFFV) (lineage)
FG: Friends of God (religious denomination)
FG: Fraternal Guild (mutual benefit)
FG: Full Gospel (religious denomination)
FGBC: Full Gospel Baptist Church (religious denomination)
FGBC: Fellowship of Grace Brethren Church (religious denomination)
FGC: Friends General Conference (religious denomination)
FGC: First Georgia Company (lineage)
FGCS: Federation of German Catholic Societies (religious, mutual benefit)
FGICP: Federation of Government Information Processing Councils (quasi-governmental)
FGLK: Finger Lakes Railway Corp (railroad)
FGS: Federation of Genealogical Societies (hobby)
FH: Farm House (college fraternity)
FHA: Federal Housing Administration (New Deal) (governmental)
FHA: Friesian Horse Association of North America (equine)
FHEO: Fair Housing and Equal Opportunity (governmental)
FHFB: Federal Housing Finance Board (governmental)
FHIS: Fraternal Home Insurance Society (mutual benefit)
FHLBB: Federal Home Loan Bank Board (governmental)
FHMA: Forest Hill Military Academy (school)
FHS: Friesian Horse Society (equine)
FHS: Forest History Society (learned)
FHT: Federated Hebrew Trades of NYC (union)
FI: Franciscans of the Immaculate (religious order)

FI: Family International (religious)

FIA: Futures Industry Association (trade group)

FIAF: International Federation of Film Archives (professional)

FIBAA: Foundation for International Business Administration Accreditation (education)

FIC: Fourth International Caucus (political)

FICPI: International Federation of Intellectual Property Attorneys (professional)

FIDF: Friends of the Israel Defense Forces (religious, military)

FIEC: Fellowship of Independent Evangelical Churches (religious denomination)

FiFNA: Forward in Faith, North America (religious)

FIN: Finnair Oyj (airline code)

FIR: Flats Industrial Railroad

FIRA: Financial Industry Regulatory Authority (trade group)

FISPA: Federation of Internet Solution Providers of the Americas (trade group)

FIT: Fashion Institute of Technology (New York) (higher education)

FIT: Florida Institute of Technology (Florida) (higher education)

FIU: Florida International University (higher education)

FJC: Friends of Jesus Christ (religious denomination)

FJG: Fonda, Johnstown and Gloversville Railroad

FL: Feminists for Life (political)

FL: Fraternal League (fraternal, mutual benefit)

FL: Fraternal Legion (mutual benefit)

FL: Farmer Labor Party (political party)

FL: AirTran Airways (airline code)

FLA: Fraternity Leadership Association (umbrella organization)

FLC: First Louisiana Company (lineage)

FLDS: Fundamentalist Church of Jesus Christ of Latter Day Saints (religious denomination)

FLE: Fraternity of Linemen and Wiremen (fraternal, charitable)

FLI: Friends of Labor Israel (religious)

FLIA: Federation Life Insurance of America (mutual benefit)

FLICC: Federal Library and Information Center Committee (governmental)

FLOC: Farm Labor Organizing Committee (labor union)

FLP: Farmer-Labor Party (political party)

FLRA: Federal Labor Relations Authority (governmental)

FLSB: Fair Labor Standards Board (governmental)

FLT: "Friendship, Love and Truth" – (probably) motto of Independent Order of Odd Fellows (see IOOF) (fraternal)

FMA: Daughters of Mary Help of Christians (Salesian Sisters) (religious order)

FMA: Salesian Sisters, Daughters of Mary, Help of Christians (religious order)

FMA: Salesian Sisters of St. John Bosco (religious order)

FMC: Fraternal Mystic Circle (mutual benefit)

FMC: Free Methodist Church (religious denomination)

FMC: Franklin Medical College (higher education)

FMC: Federal Maritime Commission (governmental)

FMCNA: Free Methodist Church in North America (religious denomination)

FMCS: Federal Mediation and Conciliation Service (governmental)

FMCSA: Federal Motor Carrier Safety Administration (governmental)

FMDM: Franciscan Missionaries of the Divine Motherhood (religious order)

FMF: Fleet Marine Force (military)

FMI: Daughters of Mary Immaculate (Marianist Sisters) (religious order)

FMID: Florida Midland Railroad

FML: Fraternal Mystic Legion (mutual benefit)

FMLM: Farabundo Marti National Liberation Front (guerilla organization)

FMM: Four Minute Men (governmental, WWI)

FMM: Franciscan Missionaries of Mary (religious order)

FMM: Brothers of Mercy of Our Lady of Perpetual Help (religious order)

FMS: Female Missionary Society of the Western District (religious)

FMS: Marist Brothers (religious order)

FMS: Fishburne Military School (school)

FMW: Federation of Masons of the World, Inc. (Masonic)

FMWA: Fraternity of Modern Woodmen of America (fraternal)

FNCB: First National City Bank (now Citibank) (business)

FNCC: First North Carolina Company (lineage)

FNCC: First National City Corporation (bank holding company)

FNDOZBTKC: "Fear Not Daughter of Zion Behold the King Cometh" (motto) (women, Masonic)

FNF: Friends of Negro Freedom (ethnic, charitable)

FNMA: Federal National Mortgage Association, Inc.(also FannieMae) (quasi-governmental business)

FNOR: Florida Northern Railroad

FOA: Foresters of America (mutual benefit)

FOA: Friends of Animals (civic, political)

FOAST: Fraternal Order of Alaskan State Troopers (labor union)

FOB: Fraternal Order of Bears (fraternal)

FOB: Fraternal Order of Beavers (fraternal)

FOB: First Boston Corporation (business)

FOC: Fraternal Order of Colonials (mutual benefit)

FOC: Fraternal Order of the Cross (KKK)

FOC: First Ohio Company (lineage)

FOCL: Fraternal Order of Clover Leaves (fraternal, secret)

FOE: Fraternal Order of Eagles (fraternal, mutual benefit)

FOF: Fraternal Order of Firefighters (labor union)

FOFGW: Fraternal Order of Flat Glass Workers (labor union)

FOGA: Fashion Originators' Guild of America (trade group)

FOH: Fraternal Order of Hawks (fraternal, ethnic)

FOLUSA: Friends of Libraries, USA (civic)

FOM: Fraternal Order of Moai (fraternal, Polynesian)

FOMA: Fraternal Order (of) Modern America (fraternal, mutual benefit)

FOMES: Fifth Order of Melchizedek and Egyptian Sphinx (fraternal)

FONC: Founders of the New Haven Colony (lineage)

FOO: Fraternal Order of Orioles (fraternal, service)

FOO: Fraternal Order of Owls (fraternal)

FOP: Fraternal Order of Police (mutual benefit)

FOP: Fraternal Order of Protectors (mutual benefit)

FOP: Fraternal Order of the Pineapple (fraternal)

FOR: Fraternal Order of Reindeer (mutual benefit)

FOR: Fore River Railroad (also FRY)

FOTLU: Federation of Organized Trades and Labor Unions (labor union)

FOW: Friends of the World (fraternal)

FP: Order of the Founders and Patriots of America (sometimes FPofA) (lineage)

FPofA: (see FP – Order of the Founders and Patriots of America) (lineage)

FPA: Forest Products Association (trade group)

FPA: Federation of Professional Athletes (labor union)

FPA: Fraternal Patriotic Americans (mutual benefit)

FPA: Family Protective Association (mutual benefit)
FPC: Free Presbyterian Church (religious denomination)
FPA: Financial Planning Association (professional)
FPA: Food Products Association (trade group)
FPC: Federal Power Commission (governmental)
FPCNA: Free Presbyterian Church of North America (religious denomination)
FPE: Fairport, Painesville & Eastern (railroad)
FPEC: Free Protestant Episcopal Church (religious denomination)
FPM: Presentation Brothers (religious order)
FPMR: Manuel Rodriguez Patriotic Front (guerilla group)
FPNY: Freedom Party of New York (political party)
FPOA: Fraternal Patriotic Order of Americans (?)
FPS: Federal Protective Service (governmental)
FPS: Fell Pony Society and Conservancy of the Americas (equine)
FPSA: Freemen's Protective Silver Association (political)
FPSF: Freemen's Protective Silver Federation (political)
FPSNA: Fell Pony Society of North America (equine)
FPWU: Federal Printing Workers Union (labor union)
FR: Ryanair, Inc. (airline code)
FRA: Fleet Reserve Association (military support)
FRA: Fraternal Reserve Association (mutual benefit)
FRA: Federal Reserve Association (mutual benefit)
FRA: Fraternitas Rosicruciana Antiqua (Rosicrucian, fraternal)
FRA: Federal Railroad Administration (governmental)
FRB: Federal Reserve Bank (governmental)
FRC: Fraternitas Rosae Crucis (Rosicrucian, fraternal, cult)
FRC: Federal Radio Commission (governmental)
FRC: Family Research Council (political)
FRCH: Federation of Reconstructionist Congregations and Havurot (religious)
FRCNA: Free Reformed Churches of North America (religious denomination)
FRDN: Ferdinand Railroad
FreddieMac: Federal Home Loan Mortgage Corporation (governmental)
FRETILIN: Revolutionary Front of Independent East Timor (guerilla group)
FRF: Free Russia Fund (political)
FRG: Family Readiness Group (military support)
FRISCO: St. Louis & San Francisco (also SLSF) (railroad)

FRSO: Freedom Road Socialist Organization (political)
FRP: Free and Regenerated Palladium (fraternal)
FRR: Falls Road Railroad Company (railroad)
FRRC: Fiscal Responsibility and Reform Commission (governmental)
FRTIB: Federal Retirement Thrift Investment Board (governmental)
FRV: Fox River Valley Railroad
FRVR: Fox Valley and Western (railroad)
FRVT: Fore River Transportation Company (railroad)
FRY: Fore River Railroad (also FOR)
FS: Federalist Society (political organization)
FS: Free Soil Party (political party)
FS: Fellowship of Scientists (religious)
FS: Freedom Station (military support)
FSA: Farm Security Administration (New Deal) (governmental)
FSA: Farm Service Agency (governmental)
FSA: Federal Security Administration (governmental)
FSAIC: Federal Student Aid Information Center (governmental)
FSC: Brothers of the Christian Schools (Christian Brothers/Lasallian Brothers) (religious order)
FSC: De La Salle Christian Brothers (religious order)
FSCJ: Comboni Missionaries of the Sacred Heart of Jesus, Verona Fathers (religious order)
FSCU: First Slovak Catholic Union (mutual benefit)
FSEEE: Forest Service Employees For Environmental Ethics (advocacy)
FSF: Daughters of St. Francis of Assisi (religious order)
FSF: Financial Services Forum (trade group)
FSH: Foundation for Shackleford Horses (equine)
FSI: Free Sons of Israel (see also IOFSI – Independent Order of the Free Sons of Israel) (Jewish, mutual benefit)
FSJ: Free Sons of Judah (mutual benefit)
FSJM: Society of the Franciscan Servants of Jesus and Mary (religious community)
FSL: Friends Schools League (sports)
FSL: Fraternitas Scintilla Legis (fraternal, service)
FSM: Franciscan Sisters of Mary (religious order)
FSMI: Franciscan Sisters of Mary Immaculate (religious order)
FSN: Sons and Daughters of the First Settlers of Newbury, MA (lineage)
FSOI: Free Sons of Israel (mutual benefit)
FSP: Daughters of St. Paul (religious order)

FSP: Free Soil Party (political party)
FSP: Freedom Socialist Party (political party)
FSP: Franciscan Sisters of Peace (religious order)
FSPA: Franciscan Sisters of Perpetual Adoration (religious order)
FSR: Fort Smith Railroad
FSR: Financial Services Roundtable (trade group)
FSS: Federated Slovak Societies (ethnic)
FSSP: Priestly Fraternity of St. Peter (religious order)
FSTA: Fantasy Sports Trade Association (trade group)
FSU: Florida State University (Florida) (higher education)
FSU: Framingham State University (Massachusetts) (higher education)
FSVB: Fort Smith and Van Buren Railroad
FT: Fraternal Tributes (mutual benefit)
FTA: Federal Transit Administration (governmental)
FTC: Federal Trade Commission (governmental)
FU: Fordham University (higher education)
FU: Furman University (higher education)
FUA: Fraternal Union of American (mutual benefit)
FUF: Fraternity of United Friars (fraternal)
FUM: Friends United Meeting (religious denomination)
FUMA: Fork Union Military Academy (school)
FURX: First Union Rail (railroad)
FVAP: Federal Voting Assistance Program (governmental)
FVRR: Fredonia Valley Railroad
FVS: Fountain Valley School of Colorado (school)
FVW: Fox Valley and Western (railroad)
FWA: Financial Women's Association (business)
FWA: Federal Works Administration (governmental)
FWB: Free Will Baptists (religious denomination)
FWBC: Free Will Baptist Church (also FBC) (religious denomination)
FWBI: Fort Wayne Bible Institute (religious)
FWC: Federation of Women's Clubs (umbrella organization)
FWCM: Fort Wayne College of Medicine (higher education)
FWCR: Florida West Coast Railroad
FWD: Fort Worth and Denver Railway (railroad)
FWDB: Fort Worth and Dallas Belt Railroad
FWDR: Fort Worth and Dallas Railroad
FWK: Fraternal White Knights (KKK)
FWMC: Fort Wayne Medical College (higher education)
FWP: Florida Whig Party (political party)

FWRY: Fillmore and Western Railroad
FWS: Fish and Wildlife Service (governmental)
FWU: Fort Worth University (Texas) (higher education)
FWWR: Fort Worth and Western Railroad
FX: FedEx (airline code)

G

G&W: Genesee & Wyoming (railroad)

GA: Georgia Railroad

GAB: General Association of Baptists (religious denomination)

GAB: Georgia Association of Broadcasters (trade group)

GAGB: General Association of General Baptists (religious denomination)

GAGBC: General Association of General Baptist Churches (religious denomination)

GAISF: General Association of International Sports Federations (sports)

GALSTPTR: German American league/Legion of St. Peter (Also GALStPt) (mutual benefit)

GAM: Gettysburg Academy of Miami (school)

GANO: Georgia Northern Railway (railroad)

GAO: General Accounting Office (governmental)

GAO: Government Accountability Office (governmental)

GAP: Group for the Advancement of Psychiatry (professional)

GAPP: German Academy of Psychiatric Physicians (higher education)

GAR: Grand Army of the Republic (US Civil War Union Army veterans) (veterans)

GARBC: General Association of Regular Baptist Churches (religious denomination)

GARRA: Grand American Road Racing Association (motorsports)

GAS&C: Georgia, Auburn, Sylvester & Camilla (railroad)

GASC: Georgia, Ashburn, Sylvester & Camilla Railroad

GASP: Group Against Smokers' Pollution (political)

GASPBC: General Association of Six Principle Baptist Churches (religious denomination)

GATF: Graphic Arts Technical Foundation (trade group)

GATX: General American Tank Car (business)

GB: Girls' Brigade (youth)

GBA: Gospel Baptist Association (religious denomination)

GBF: Grace Baptist Fellowship (denomination)

GBLA: German Baptist Life Association (mutual benefit)

GBOO: Grand Black Order of Orangemen (Northern Irish, political)

GBP: Gamma Beta Phi (honorary fraternity)
GBRE: General Board of Religious Education (of the
Protestant Episcopal Church) (religious)
GBRY: Gettysburg Railway (railroad)
GBS: God's Bible School (religious)
GBU: German Beneficial Union (mutual benefit)
GBUP: Greater Beneficial Union of Pittsburgh (mutual benefit)
GBW: Green Bay Western (railroad)
GC: Gooding College (Idaho) (higher education)
GC: Georgia Central (railroad)
GCA: Garden Club of America (civic)
GCAMD: Grand Council of Allied Masonic Degrees (Masonic)
GCAT: Guild of Colonial Artisans and Tradesmen (lineage)
GCAVOH: Grand Chapter of the Ancient and Venerable Order
of Harodim (Masonic)
GCC: Graphic Communications Conference (labor union)
GCCC: General Conference of the Congregational Church
(religious denomination)
GCD: Greenwich Country Day School (Connecticut) (school)
GCEBC: General Conference of the Evangelical Baptist Church
(religious denomination)
GCFX: Alston (railroad-related)
GCIU: Graphic Communications International Union (labor
union)
GCMO: German College of Medicine and Obstetrics (higher
education)
GCOC: Grand Court Order of Calanthe (Knights of Pythias)
(fraternal)
GCR: Grand College of Rites of the USA (Masonic)
GCSAA: Golf Course Superintendents Association of America
(trade group)
GCSF: Gulf, Colorado and Santa Fe Railroad
GCSR: Gulf, Colorado and San Saba Railway (railroad)
GCU: Greek Catholic Union of the USA (mutual benefit)
GCW: Garden City Western Railroad
GD: Hermetic Order of the Golden Dawn (mystical)
GDA: Grain Dealers Association (trade group)
GE: General Electric Company (business)
GEA: German Evangelical Association (religious denomination)
GEA: Geothermal Energy Association (trade group)
GEC: Greek Evangelical Church (religious denomination)
GEMS: Gotham Early Music Festival (musical)

GERC: German Evangelical Reformed Church (religious denomination)

GETY: Gettysburg Railroad

GEXR: Goderick-Exeter Railway (railroad)

GF: Georgia & Florida (railroad)

GF: Grand Fraternity (mutual benefit)

GFA: Guitar Foundation of America (musical)

GFC: Grand Falls Central Railroad

GFL: Globe Fraternal Legion (mutual benefit)

GFR: Frand Forks Railway (railroad)

GFS: Girls' Friendly Society (religious)

GFS: German Freedom Society (WWII, expatriate German)

GFS: Garrison Forest School (school)

GFWC: General Federation of Women's Clubs (umbrella organization)

GG: Girls' Guild (religious)

GGC: Girls of the Golden Court (Masonic, youth)

GGS: Georgia Great Southern Division of South Carolina Central Railroad

GHA: Georgia Holiness Association (religious)

GHA: Georgia Hospital Association (trade group)

GHBA: Galiceno Horse Breeders Association (equine)

GHH: Galveston, Houston and Henderson Railroad

GHMC: German Homeopathic Medical College (higher education)

GHQAF: General Headquarters Air Force (military)

GI: Goodwill Industries (civic)

GIAA: The Guild of Italian American Actors (labor union)

GIC: Grand Island College (Nebraska) (higher education)

GinnieMae: Government National Mortgage Association (also GNMA) (quasi-governmental corporation)

GIRN: GI Rights Network (military support)

GISNY: Guild of Independent Schools of New York (education)

GITM: Golden Isles Terminal Railroad

GJ: Greenwich and Johnsonville Railroad

GJ&S: Gainesville, Jefferson & Southern (railroad)

GJR: Guelph Junction Railway (railroad)

GJR: George Junior Republic (religious, youth)

GKA: Gamma Kappa Alpha (Italian) (academic honorary)

GKHS: Golden Key Honour Society (academic honorary)

GL: Guardians of Liberty (political, anti-Catholic)

GL: Granite League (mutual benefits)

GLAAD: Gay and Lesbian Alliance Against Defamation (political)
GLAS: German Ladies Aid Association (civic, charitable)
GLAUM: Grand Lodge Ancient Order of Mysteries (Masonic)
GLC: Great Lakes Central Railroad
GLDS: Grand Lodge, Daughters of Scotia (fraternal)
GLE: Grand Lodge of England Freemasonry (Masonic)
GLF: Grange League Federation (farmers' cooperative)
GLGT: Grand Lodge of Good Templars (fraternal)
GLIS: The Gleaners Life Insurance Society (mutual benefit)
GLMA: Gay and Lesbian Medical Association (professional)
Glmy: Glenmary Home Missioners (religious order)
GLO: General Land Office (governmental)
GLR: Guild of the Living Rosary of Our Lady and St. Dominic (religious)
GLSR: Gloster Southern Railroad
GM: Grail Movement (religious)
GM: Gainesville Midland (railroad)
GM: General Motors (business)
GM&O: Gulf, Mobile & Ohio (also GMO) (railroad)
GMA: Gateway Military Academy (school)
GMA: Game Manufacturers Association (trade group)
GMA: Grocery Manufacturers Association (trade group)
GMAC: General Motors Acceptance Corporation (business)
GMC: God's Missionary Church (religious denomination)
GMC: German Medical College (higher education)
GMMNA: Conference of Grand Masters of Masons in North America (fraternal, Masonic)
GMO: Gulf, Mobile and Ohio Railroad (also GM&O)
GMP: Glass, Molders, Pottery, Plastics and Allied Workers International Union (labor union)
GMC: German Methodist Church (religious denomination)
GMRC: Green Mountain (also GMRR) (railroad)
GMRR: Green Mountain Railroad (also GMRC)
GMRY: Great Miami and Scioto Railway (railroad)
GMS: Genesee Missionary Society (religious)
GMSR: Gulf & Mississippi Railroad
GMU: George Mason University (higher education)
GN: Great Northern (railroad)
GNA: Grottoes of North America (fraternal)
GNA: Graysonia, Nashville and Ashdown Railroad
GNCTU: Grand National Consolidated Trade Union (labor union)

GNE: Gamma Nu Eta (information technology) (academic honorary)
GNMA: Government National Mortgage Association (also GinnieMae) (quasi-governmental corporation)
GNRR: Georgia Northeastern Railroad
GNSH: Grey Nuns of the Sacred Heart (religious order)
GNWR: Genesee and Wyoming Railroad
GOA: Gun Owners of American (lobby)
GOGF: Grand Order of Galilean Fishermen (fraternal, mutual benefit)
GOH: German Order of Harugari (fraternal)
GOLS: Grand Orange Lodge of Scotland (militant Protestant)
GON: Grand Order of Nazarites (mutual benefit)
GONX: RailBox/RailGon (also ABOX and RBOX) (rail car leasing company)
GOP: "Grand Old Party" (a/k/a Republican Party) (political party)
GOT: Greater Toronto Transit Authority (railroad)
GOWR: Grand Order of Water Rats (British, fraternal, service)
GP: Greenback Party (political party)
GPCSSUCBS: General Protestant Episcopal Sunday School Union and Church Book Society (religious)
GPI: Glass Packaging Institute (trade group)
GPO: Government Printing Office (governmental)
GPO: Government Publishing Office (governmental)
GR: Grand Rapids Eastern Railroad
GR&I: Grand Rapids & Indiana Railroad
GRA: German Reading Association (Deutsche Lesegesellschaft) (educational)
GRA: Golden Rule Alliance (mutual benefit)
Grange: (not an abbreviation) Order of the Patrons of Husbandry (fraternal, mutual benefit)
GRA: Green Restaurant Association (advocacy)
GRC: Gendarmerie Royale du Canada (governmental)
GRCKStG: German Roman Catholic Knights of St. George (mutual benefit)
GRIV: Gauley River Railroad
GRLW: Greenville & Western Railway (railroad)
GRMC: Grand Rapids Medical College (Michigan) (higher education)
GRN: Greenville and Northern Railroad
GRNR: Grand River Railway (railroad)
GRNW: Great Northwest Railroad

GROTTO: Grand Order of Veiled Prophets of the Enchanted Realm (Masonic)
GRR: Georgetown Railroad
GRWR: Great Walton Railroad
GRYR: Grenada Railway (railroad)
GS: Girl Scouts (youth)
GS: Gideon Society (religious)
GS: Gaelic Society (hereditary?)
GSA: Girl Scouts of America (youth)
GSA: Gamma Sigma Alpha (honorary fraternity)
GSA: Genetics Society of America (learned)
GSA: Geological Society of America (learned)
GSA: Gerontological Society of America (professional)
GSA: General Services Administration (governmental)
GSAS: Golden Seal Assurance Society (mutual benefit)
GSC: George R. Smith College (Missouri) (higher education)
GSCW: General Society of Colonial Wars (lineage)
GSD: Gamma Sigma Delta (agriculture) (academic honorary)
GSE: Gamma Sigma Epsilon (chemistry) (academic honorary)
GSF: Golden Star Fraternity (mutual benefit)
GSF: Georgia Southern and Florida (railroad)
GSIS: Geoscience Information Society (professional)
GSLIC: Guarantee Security Life Insurance Company (business)
GSM: Great Smoky Mountains Railroad
GSMC: Gold Star Mothers Club (military support)
GSPB: General Six-Principle Baptists (religious denomination)
GSU: Georgia State University (higher education)
GSU: Grambling State University (higher education)
GSUSA: Girl Scouts of the United States of America (youth)
GSW: Great Southwest Railroad
GSWA: Gold Star Wives of America (military support)
GT: Grand Trunk (railroad)
GT: Georgia Institute of Technology (higher education)
GTE: Gamma Tau Epsilon (high school sorority)
GTER: Grafton Terminal Railroad
GTP: Grand Trunk Pacific Railroad
GTR: Great River Railroad
GTRA: Golden Triangle Railroad
GTU: General Trades Union (labor union)
GTU: Gamma Theta Upsilon (geography) (honorary fraternity)
GTW: Grand Trunk Western (railroad)
GU: Grafton & Upton (railroad)

GUG: Gegenseite Unterstutzungsgeselshaft Germania (mutual benefit)

GUOISDP: Grand United Order Independent Sons and Daughters of Purity (mutual benefit)

GUOOF: Grand United Order of Odd Fellows (also GUOofOF) (fraternal, ethnic)

GUOofGF: Grand United Order of Galilean Fishermen (ethnic, mutual benefit)

GUOof OF: Grand United Order of Odd Fellows (of America) (also GUOOF) (fraternal, ethnic)

GUOTR: Grand United Order of True Reformers (fraternal, ethnic)

GVLC: Golden Valley Lutheran College (Minnesota) (higher education)

GVS: Giuseppe Verdi Society (fraternal)

GVSR: Galveston Railroad

GUOTR: Grand United Order of True Reformers (ethnic)

GWC: Gospel Workers Church (religious denomination)

GWER: Gateway Eastern Railway (railroad)

GWMNMA: George Washington Masonic National Memorial Association (Masonic)

GWRR: Genesee & Wyoming Railroad

GWI: Genesee & Wyoming Railroad

GWMNMA: George Washington Masonic National Memorial Association (Masonic)

GWR: Great Western Railway of Colorado (railroad)

GWRC: Georgia Woodlands Railroad

GWS: Gospel Workers Society (religious)

GWTU: General Workers' Trade Union (labor union)

GWU: George Washington University (District of Columbia) (higher education)

GWWE: Gateway Eastern Railroad

GWWR: Gateway Western Railroad

GZP: Gazpromavia Aviation Company, Ltd. (airline code)

H

H: The Homesteaders (fraternal, mutual benefit)
H: The Hunters (political, Canadian)
H: Home Circle (the H appears in a circle) (mutual benefit)
HA: Heavy Artillery (military, World War I)
HA: House of Aaron (religious denomination)
HA: Hawaiian Airlines (airline code)
HAC: Historians of American Communism (academic)
HAC: Historical Advisory Committee (of the Atomic Energy Commission) (governmental)
HAL: Hawaiian Airlines (airline code)
HARDI: Heating, Air conditioning & Refrigeration Distributors International (trade group)
HAS: Holy Angels Sodality (religious)
HAU: Hebrew Actors' Union, Inc. (labor union)
HB: Hampton and Branchville Railroad
HBA: Holiness Baptist Association (religious denomination)
HBA: Healthcare Businesswomen's Association (professional)
HBA: Home Benefit Association (mutual benefit)
HBL: Harbor Belt Line (railroad)
HBL: Hermetic Brotherhood of Luxor (occult)
HBR: Hudson Bay Railway (railroad)
HBRY: Hudson Bay Railway (railroad)
HBT: Houston Belt and Terminal Railroad
HC: Hillsong Church (religious denomination)
HC: Home Circle (fraternal, mutual benefit)
HC: Holiness Church (religious denomination)
HC: Huron College (South Dakota) (higher education)
HC: Henry College (Texas) (higher education)
HCA: Heavy Coast Artillery (military, World War I)
HCA: Horse Cavalry Association (veterans)
HCA: Holy Childhood Association (religious)
HCC: Holiness Christian Church (religious denomination)
HCC: Holiness Church of Christ (religious denomination)
HCC: Horrible Conspiration Club (Masonic)
HCC: Hamburg Canal College (New York) (higher education)
HCC-WR: Holy Catholic Church – Western Rite (religious denomination)
HCRC: Hillsdale County Railway (railroad)

HCRR: Honey Creek Railroad
HCRS: Heritage Conservation and Recreation Service (governmental)
HCRY: Huron Central Railway (railroad)
HCYR: Huron County Railroad
HD: Society of Daughters of Holland Dames (lineage)
HD: House of David (various organizations including a commune and a travelling basketball team)
HDM: Hudson and Manhattan (the Hudson Tubes) (railroad)
HDNA: Habonim-Dror North America (religious, youth)
HE: Hollis and Eastern Railroad
HEI: Health Effects Institute (research)
HELM: HELM Leasing (railroad car leasing company)
HERE: Hotel Employees and Restaurant Employees Union (labor union)
HES: History of Education Society (academic)
HESR: Huron and Eastern Railroad
HF: Hermetic Fraternity (occult)
HFA: Heavy Field Artillery (military, World War I)
HFAA: Hardanger Fiddle Association of America (musical)
HFBS: Home Forum Benefit Society (mutual benefit)
HFES: Human Factors and Ergonomics Society (professional)
HHB: Hard Hat Brotherhood (fraternal)
HHFA: Housing and Home Finance Agency (governmental)
HHS: Department of Health and Human Services (governmental)
HFBO: Home Forum Benevolent (or Benefit) Order (mutual benefit)
HFBS: Home Fraternal Beneficiary Society (mutual benefit)
HFI: Hepatitis Foundation International (medical research)
HFIAW: Heat and Insulators and Asbestos Workers (labor union)
HFMA: Hepzibath Faith Missionary Association (religious)
HFSA: Heart Failure Society of America (professional)
HGA: Home Guards of America (mutual benefit)
HHA: Hackley Horse Affiliates (equine)
HHCA: Heartland Highland Cattle Association (cattle)
HHHH: "Head, Heart, Hands, Health" (see also 4H) (youth)
HHN: Healing Heroes Network (military support)
HHS: Health and Human Services Department (governmental)
HI: Holton Interurban Railway (railroad)
HI: Heifer International (charity)
HIA: Hemp Industries Association (trade group)

HIAS: Hebrew Immigrant Aid Society (migration)[1]
HIP: Hawaii Independence Party (political party)
HJ: Heroines of Jericho (also HOJ) (fraternal, Masonic)
HJC: Heroines of Jericho Courts (ethnic, fraternal)
HL: Hygienic Library, the (health care, WWI)
HL: Heralds of Liberty (fraternal, mutual benefit)
HL: Hunters' Lodge (political, Canadian)
HLA: Homesteaders Life Association (mutual benefit)
HLC: Homesteaders Life Company (mutual benefit)
HLC: Higher Learning Commission (education, accrediting)
HLI: Human Life International (religious, political)
HLMD: Hooded Ladies of the Mystic Den (women, KKK)
HLNE: Hillsboro and North Eastern (railroad)
HLSC: Hampton Railway (railroad)
HM: Haymakers (fraternal)
HM: Sisters of the Humility of Mary (religious order)
HMA: Hargrave Military Academy (school)
HMA: Howe Military Academy (school)
HMC: Holiness Movement Church (religious denomination)
HMC: Harvey Medical College (higher education)
HMC: Hering Medical College (higher education)
HMC: Harvey Mudd College (higher education)
HMCR: Huntsville and Madison County Railroad
HMS: Hampshire Missionary Society (religious)
HMS: Homeopathic Medical Society (professional)
HMS: High Mowing School (school)
HN: Hutchinson and Northern Railroad
HN: Highland Nobles (mutual benefit)
HNS: Holy Name Society (religious)
HoA: Horse of the Americas (equine)
HOAC: Historians of American Communism (learned)
HOBGI: Ancient and Honorable Order of the Blue Goose (see also AHOBG) (fraternal, service, insurance industry)
HOFFM: Hereditary Order of the First Families of Massachusetts (lineage)
HOG: Heart of Georgia Railroad
HOGD: Hermetic Order of the Golden Dawn (Rosicrucian, fraternal)
HOJ: Heroines of Jericho (also HJ) (fraternal, Masonic)
HOKBHC: Holy Order of Knights Beneficent of the Holy City (Masonic)

---

[1] Thanks to Marc Shulman

HOLC: Home Owners Loan Corporation (New Deal) (governmental)
HOO-HOO: International Order of Hoo-Hoo, also Concatenated Order of Hoo-Hoo (mutual benefit)
HOS: Hoosier Southern Railroad
HOSC: Indiana and Eastern Railroad (a/k/a The Hoosier Connection)
HP: Home Palladium (mutual benefit)
HP: Hewlett-Packard Corporation (business)
HP: America West Airlines (airline code)
HPB: Handmaids of the Precious Blood (religious order)
HPBA: Hearth, Patio & Barbecue Association (trade group)
HPC: Highland Park College (Iowa) (higher education)
HPTD: High Point, Thomasville and Denton Railroad
HPTR: Houston Port Terminal Railroad
HR: Household of Ruth (ethnic, fraternal)
HRA: Horse Rangers Association (equestrian)
HRC: Heritage Reformed Congregations (religious denomination)
HRDL: Hudson River Day Line (maritime excursion company)
HRFA: Hungarian Reformed Federation of America (mutual benefit)
HRMA: Human Resources Management Association (professional)
HRRC: Housatonic Railroad Co. (railroad)
HRS: Hollidaysburg and Roaring Spring Railroad
HRS: Historical Records Survey (New Deal – Works Progress Administration) (governmental)
HRS: Heart Rhythm Society (professional)
HRSA: Health Resources and Services Administration (governmental)
HRT: Hartwell Railroad
HS: Holland Society (lineage)
HS: Hartford & Slocomb (railroad)
HS: Housatonic Southern Railroad
HS: Hampshire Southern Railroad
HSA: Huguenot Society of America (lineage)
HSBC: The Hong Kong and Shanghai Banking Corporation (business)
HSC: Hiram Scott College (Nebraska) (higher education)
HSC: Center for Studying Health System Change (policy research)
HSCRS: Historic Stock Car Racing Series (motorsports)

HSFM: Huguenot Society of the Founders of Manakin in the Colony of Virginia (lineage)

HSMA: High School of Music and Art (school)

HSPA: High School of Performing Arts (school)

HSRR: Hardin Southern Railroad

HSTC: Hyannis State Teachers College (Massachusetts) (higher learning)

HSUS: Humane Society of the United States (charity, political)

HSW: Helena Southwestern Railroad

HTI: High Twelve International (fraternal, Masonic)

HTNG: Hotel Technology Next Generation (trade group)

HTW: Hoosac Tunnel and Wilmington Railroad

HTWSSTKS: Initialization for Bible verse used by Royal Arch Masons ("Hiram the Widow's Son Sent to King Solomon") (fraternal)

HUAC: House Un-American Activities Committee (political, governmental)

HUBA: Hudson Bay Railroad

HUD: Department of Housing and Urban Development (governmental)

HZ: Haro Zero (or Zaro) (fraternal)

I

I: Independent (political party)
IA-ECOSOC: Inter-American Economic and Social Council (political)
IAAP: International Association of Administrative Professionals (professional)
IAAPA: International Association of Amusement Parks and Attractions (trade group)
IABA: International Association of Black Actuaries (professional)
IABC: International Association of Business Communicators (trade group)
IABM: International Association of Broadcasting Manufacturers (trade group)
IABSOIWA: International Association of Bridge, Structural, and Ornamental Iron Workers of America (labor union)
IACA: InterAmerican Christian Academy (school)
IACBE: International Assembly for Collegiate Business Education (education, accrediting)
IACCS: Independent Anglican Church Canada Synod (religious denomination)
IACHI: International Association of Certified Home Inspectors (professional)
IACK: International Alliance of Catholic Knights (lay society)
IAEA: International Atomic Energy Agency (UN agency)
IAEC: International Association of Elevator Consultants (trade group)
IAEKM: International Association of Electronic Keyboard Manufacturers (trade group)
IAF: International Association of Fire Fighters (labor union)
IAFF: International Association of Fire Fighters (labor union)
IAG: Independent Assemblies of God (religious denomination)
IAHS: International Association for Human Singing (music)
I-AHS: Irish-American Historical Society (lineage)
IAHA: International Association of Historians of Asia (learned)
IAHU: International Apostolic Holiness Union (religious denomination)
IAIRA: International Association of Independent Recording Artists (professional)

IAIS: Iowa Interstate Railroad
IAJVS: International Association of Jewish Vocational Services (religious)
IAM: International Association of Machinists and Aerospace Workers (labor union)
IAMTA: International Art Materials Trade Association (trade group)
IANA: Internet Assigned Numbers Authority (international)
IANR: Iowa Northern Railroad
IANU: Italo-American National Union (ethnic, mutual benefit)
IAofM: International Association of Machinists (labor union)
IAOP: International Association of Operative Millers (trade group)
IAP: Independent American Party (political party)
IAPD: International Association of Plastics Distributors (trade group)
IAPMO: International Association of Plumbing and Mechanical Officials (professional)
IARA: International Association Rebekah Assemblies (fraternal)
IARU: International Amateur Radio Union (hobby)
IARW: International Association of Refrigerated Warehouses (trade group)
IASSIST: Association for Social Science Information Service and Technology (professional)
IASTMP: International Association of Scientific, Technical, and Medical Publishers (trade group)
IAT: Iowa Terminal Railroad
IATA: International Air Transport Association (trade group)
IATAN: International Association of Travel Agents Network (trade group)
IATR: Iowa Traction Railroad
IATSE: International Alliance of Theatrical Stage Employees (labor union)
IAYO: Italian-American Youth Organization (youth)
IB: Independent Baptist (religious denomination)
IB: Iberia (airline code)
IBA: Independent Business Alliance (trade group)
IBA: Industrial Benefit Association (mutual benefit)
IBB: International Brotherhood of Bookbinders (labor union)
IBB: International Brotherhood of Boilermakers, Iron Ship Builders, Blacksmiths, Forgers and Helpers (labor union)
IBBH: International Brotherhood of Blacksmiths and Helpers (labor union)

153

IBC: International Baptist Convention (religious denomination)
IBCA: Independent Baptist Church of America (religious denomination)
IBCC: Iowa Blue Chicken Club (poultry)
IBEW: International Brotherhood of Electrical Workers (also IB of EW) (labor union)
IBF: Independent Baptist Fellowship (religious denomination)
IBFI: Independent Baptist Fellowship International (religious denomination)
IBFNA: Independent Baptist Fellowship of North America (religious denomination)
IBM: International Brotherhood of Magicians (trade union)
IBM: International Business Machines Corporation, Inc. (business)
IBMA: International Bluegrass Music Association (music)
IBN: International Baptist Network (religious denomination)
IBO: Industrial Benefit Order (mutual benefit)
IBOB: International Brotherhood of Old Bastards (fraternal)
IBofEW: International Brotherhood of Electrical Workers (also IBEW) (labor union)
IBofT: International Brotherhood of Teamsters, Chauffeurs, Warehousemen, and Helpers of America (also IBT) (labor union)
IBPA: Independent Book Publishers Association (trade group)
IBPOE: Improved Benevolent Protective Order of Elks (see IBPOW) (fraternal, ethnic)
IBPOM: Independent Benevolent and Protective Order of Moose (fraternal, ethnic)
IBPOW: Improved Benevolent Protective Order of Elks (see IBPOE) (fraternal, ethnic)
IBRD: International Bank for Reconstruction and Development (UN agency)
IBRM: Institute of Boiler and Radiator Manufacturers (trade group)
IBS: International Bible Society (religious)
IBT: International Brotherhood of Teamsters (also IBofT) (labor union)
IBU: International Bakers Union (labor union)
IBVM: Institute of the Blessed Virgin Mary (Loreto Sisters) (religious order)
IBWA: International Bottled Water Association (trade group)
IBYU: Tuscola and Saginaw Bay Railroad
IC: Institute of Charity (Rosminians) (religious order)

IC: Instruction Center (military, World War I)
IC: Illinois Central (railroad)
IC: Invincible Club (political, Irish-American)
IC: Iroquois Club (political)
IC3: Internet Crime Complaint Center (governmental)
ICA: International Clarinet Association (musical)
ICA: International Communication Association (professional)
ICA: International Council on Archives (professional)
ICA: International Clarinet Association (musical)
ICAF: Industrial College of the Armed Forces (governmental)
ICAN: International Commission for Air Navigation
(International organization)
ICAO: International Civil Aviation Organization (UN Agency)
ICBA: Independent Community Bankers of America (trade group)
ICBU: Irish Catholic Benefit (or Benevolent) Union (religious, mutual benefit)
ICC: Interstate Commerce Commission (governmental)
ICC: Influenza Citizens' Committee (health care, WWI)
ICC: Independent Christian Churches (Churches of Christ)
(religious denomination)
ICC: International Christian Church (religious denomination)
ICE: Iowa, Chicago & Eastern (railroad)
ICE: Immigration and Customs Enforcement (governmental)
ICF: International Coach Federation (professional)
ICFA: International Cemetery and Funeral Association (trade group)
ICG: The Intercontinental Church of God (religious denomination)
ICG: Illinois Central Gulf (railroad)
ICHSEA: International Conference on the History of Science in East Asia (learned)
ICI: Investment Company Institute (trade group)
ICJ: International Commission of Jurists (political front)
ICJL: Institute for Computers in Jewish Life (religious, education)
ICL International Communist League (Fourth International) (political)
ICM: International Christian Mission (religious)
ICMA: International Card Manufacturers Association (trade group)
ICMJE: International Committee of Medical Journal Editors (professional)

155

ICMM: Indiana College of Medicine and Midwifery (higher education)

ICMM: International Council on Mining and Metals (trade group)

ICOC: International Churches of Christ (religious denomination)

ICOHH: International Concatenated Order of the Hoo-Hoo (business, social)

ICOTS: Infantry Central Officers Training School (military, WWI)

ICRF: Israel Cancer Research Fund (religious)

ICRK: Indian Creek Railroad

ICROJOY: International Coalition for the Revival of the Jews of Yemen (religious)

ICRSS: Institute of Christ the King Sovereign Priest (religious order)

ICS: Imperial Court System (fraternal, service)

ICS: International College of Surgeons (professional)

ICSC: International Council of Shopping Centers (trade group)

ICSC: International Civil Service Commission (UN activity)

ICSCC: International Conference of Sports Car Clubs (motorsports)

ICSOM: International Conference of Symphony and Opera Musicians (professional)

ICTP: International Centre for Theoretical Physics (UN activity)

ICU: International Communist Union (political)

ID: Independent Democrat (political party)

IDA: International Development Association (US agency)

IDDBA: International Dairy-Deli-Bakery Association (trade group)

IDEA: International District Energy Association (advocacy)

IDES: Brotherhood of the Divine Holy Spirit (fraternal)

IDF: Israeli Defense Forces (military)

IDGR: International Dairy Goat Registry (goats)

IDHS: Irish Draught Horse Society of North America (equine)

IDRS: International Double Reed Society (musical)

IDS: Imago Dei Society (religious)

IDSA: Infectious Disease Society of America (professional)

IE: Office of International Evangelism of the Presbyterian Church (religious)

IEA: Interscholastic Equestrian Association (equestrian)

IEC: Independent Electrical Contractors (trade group)

IEEE: Institute of Electrical and Electronics Engineers (professional)

IEEE-SA: Institute of Electrical and Electronics Engineers Standards Association (professional)

IEMC: Indiana Eclectic Medical College (high education)

IERG: International Executive Resources Group (trade group)

IES: Institute of Education Sciences (governmental)

IETA: International Electrical Testing Association (trade group)

IFA: International Fraternal Alliance (mutual benefit)

IFAD: International Fund for Agricultural Development (UN agency)

IFBC: International Fellowship of Bible Churches (religious)

IFC: Interfraternity Conference (umbrella organization)

IFC: International Finance Corporation (UN agency)

IFCA: International Fellowship of Christian Assemblies (religious denomination)

IFDA: International Foodservice Distributors Association (trade group)

IFEA: International Festivals and Events Association (trade group)

IFES: International Federation for Equestrian Sports (equestrian)

IFGA: International Fainting Goat Association (goats)

IFIP: International Federation for Information Processing (professional)

IFLAI: International Federation of Library Associations and Institutions (umbrella organization)

IFLMBA: Interstate & Foreign Landmark Missionary Baptists Association (religious)

IFLWU: International Fur and Leather Workers Union (Furriers) (labor union)

IFP: Interns for Peace (religious)

IFPI: International Federation of the Phonographic Industry (trade group)

IFPTE: International Federation of Professional and Technical Engineers (labor union)

IFR: International Fellowship of Rotarians (civic)

IFSC: International Firefighters Square Club (mutual benefit)

IFT: Institute of Food Technologists (professional)

IFTA: Independent Film & Television Association (trade group)

IFWBA: Independent Free Will Baptist Associations (religious denomination)

IG: Internationalist Group (League for the Fourth International) (political)
IG: Inspector General (governmental)
IGA: Independent Grocers Association (trade group)
IGA: International Geneva Association (think tank)
IGA: International Geneva Association (mutual benefit, for hotel and catering trades)
IGBC: Imperial Grand Black Chapter of the British Commonwealth (fraternal, Northern Irish)
IGCRAM: International Grand Chapter of Royal Arch Masons (Masonic)
IGCCRSM: International General Grand Council of Royal & Select Masons (Masonic)
IGM: Immanuel General Mission (religious)
IGUA: International Guards Union of America (labor union)
IH: Iron Hall (Order of Iron Hall) (mutual benefit)
IHA: Illinois (or Iowa) Holiness Association (religious denomination)
IHA: International Hydropower Association (advocacy)
IHA: International Housewares Association (trade group)
IHEU: International Humanist and Ethical Union (religious denomination)
IHB: Indiana Harbor Belt (railroad)
IHC: Inter-Church Holiness Convention (religious denomination)
IHI: Institute for Healthcare Improvement (professional)
IHL: International Hockey League (sports)
IHM: Congregation of the Sisters, Servants of the Immaculate Heart of Mary (religious order)
IHM: International Holiness Mission (religious denomination)
IHMO: International Health Ministries (religious)
IHOP: International House of Pancakes (business)
IHR: Indiana Hi-Rail (railroad)
IHRA: International Hot Rod Association (motorsports)
IHS: International Horn Society (musical)
IHSSM: In Hoc Signo Spes Mea – White Shrine of Jerusalem (fraternal, charitable)
IHU: Illinois Health University (higher education)
IHSV: "In Hoc Signo Vinces" Masonic and Military Order of the Red Cross of Constantine (Masonic)
IIA: Institute for International Affairs (religious)
IIABA: Independent Insurance Agents and Brokers of America (lobby)

IICS: International Interactive Communications Society (trade group)

IIDA: Iowa Implement Dealers Association (trade group)

IIFC: Islamic International Foundation of Cooperation (religious)

IIHF: International Ice Hockey Federation (sports)

III: Iota Iota Iota (women/gender studies) (academic honorary)

IIIA: International Imaging Industry Association (trade group)

IIOO: independent International Order of Owls (fraternal)

IIPA: International Intellectual Property Alliance (trade group)

IIPRC: Interstate Insurance Product Regulation Commission (governmental)

IIRC: Indiana Interstate Railway (railroad)

IIS: Institute for International Sport (sports)

IIT: Illinois Institute of Technology (higher education)

IIUG: International Informix Users Group (trade group)

IIW: Institute of the Incarnate Word (religious order)

IJ: Infant Jesus Sisters (religious order)

IJA: Imperial Japanese Army (military)

IJN: Imperial Japanese Navy (military)

IKA: Imperial Klans of America   (KKK)

IKEA: Ingvar Kamprad Elmtaryd Agunnaryd – name of founder, town, and farm (business)

IKK: International Keystone Knights (KKK)

IKKKK: International Knights of the Ku Klux Klan (KKK)

IL: Imperial Legion (mutual benefit)

ILA: International Longshoremen's Association (labor union)

ILA: Iowa Legion of Honor (usually ILH) (mutual benefit)

ILBA: Independent Landmark Baptist Associations (religious denomination)

ILC: Immanuel Lutheran College (North Carolina) (higher education)

ILGWU: International Ladies' Garment Workers' Union (labor union)

ILID: Intercollegiate League for Industrial Democracy (political, 1930s)

ILEOSC: International Law Enforcement Officers Square Club (mutual benefit)

ILH: Iowa Legion of Honor (also ILA) (mutual benefit)

ILM: Illinois Lumber Merchants (trade group)

ILO: International Labour Organization (UN agency)

ILS: International Libertarian Solidarity (political)

ILW: Illinois Western Railroad

ILWU: International Longshore and Warehouse Union (labor union)

IM: Interseminary Movement (political, 1930s)

IM: Identity Movement (cult)

IMA: Institute of Management Accountants (professional)

IMB: International Mission Board (religious)

IMBCA: Institutional Missionary Baptist Conference of America (religious denomination)

IMC: Illinois Medical College (higher education)

IMC: Independent Medical College (higher education)

IMC: Indiana Medical College (higher education)

IMCA: International Motor Contest Association (motorsports)

IMCUSA: Institute of Management Consultants of the USA (professional)

IMF: International Monetary Fund (UN agency)

IMFW: International Moulders and Foundry Workers Union of North America (labor union)

IMGA: International Mounted Games Association (equestrian)

IMGS: International Medical Graduates Section (professional)

IMI: International Marketing Institute (political front)

IMJA: International Messianic Jewish Alliance (religious denomination)

IML: Imperial Mystic Legion (fraternal, mutual benefit)

IMLS: Institute of Museum and Library Services (governmental)

IMO: International Maritime Organization (UN agency)

IMPI: International Microwave Power Institute (professional)

IMRL: Illinois &Missouri Rail Link (railroad)

IMRO: Irish Music Rights Organization (trade group)

IMRR: Illinois and Midland Railroad

IMOSC: International Military Order of the Southern Cross (lineage)

IMS: Indian Mountain School (Connecticut) (school)

IMSA: International Motor Sports Association (motorsports)

IMU: Iron Molders' Union (labor union)

IN: Infantry (Army branch)

INC: Irish National Caucus (lobby)

IND: Independent Subway System (railroad)

IND: Immigration and Nationality Directorate (government – UK)

IND: Independent News Distributors (company)

IND: Institute of Notre Dame (educational)

IND: Interplanetary Network Directorate (governmental)

IND: Iota Nu Delta (college fraternity)

InHC: International Holiness Church (religious denomination)
INDEX: Independent School Data Exchange (education)
INLA: Irish National Liberation Army (guerilla organization)
INOF: Irish National Order of Foresters (mutual benefit)
INOH: Indiana and Ohio Railroad
INPR: Idaho Northern and Pacific Railroad
INRD: Indiana Railroad
INS: Immigration and Naturalization Service (governmental)
INSCOM: US Army Intelligence and Security Command
(military)
INT: Interstate Railroad
Interpol: International Criminal Police Organization
(governmental)
IO: Indiana and Ohio (railroad)
IO12: International Order of Twelve Knights and Daughters of
Tabor (fraternal, ethnic)
IOA: International Order of the Alhambra (social side of KofC)
(religious, charitable)
IOA: Industrial Order of America (fraternal, mutual benefit)
IOAI: Independent Order of American Israelites (ethnic,
mutual benefit)
IOBA: Independent Order of B'rith Abraham (ethnic, mutual
benefit)
IOBB: Independent Order of B'nai B'rith (fraternal, mutual
benefit)
IOBB: Improved Order of B'nai B'rith (fraternal, mutual
benefit)
IOBS: Independent Order of B'rith Sholom (religious, mutual
benefit)
IOC: International Olympic Committee (sports)
IOC: International Order of Characters (fraternal, service)
IOCF: Independent Order of Chosen Friends (mutual benefit)
IOCR: Indiana and Ohio Central Railroad
IOCY: International Association of Old Catholic Youth
(church, youth)
IOD: Improved Order of Deer (fraternal)
IODE: Independent Order, Daughters of the Empire (became
National Society Daughters of the British Empire) (lineage)
IOF: Independent Order of Foresters (mutual benefit)
IOFI: Independent Order of Foresters of Illinois (mutual
benefit)
IOFSI: Independent Order Free Sons of Israel (also IOFSofI,
FSI) (Jewish, mutual benefit)

IOFSofI: Independent Order Free Sons of Israel (also IOFSI, FSI) (Jewish, mutual benefit)
IOGS: Independent Order of Good Samaritans (also IOGSDS) (fraternal, ethnic, mutual benefit, educational)
IOGSDS: Independent Order of Good Samaritans & Daughters of Samaria (also IOGS) (fraternal, ethnic, mutual benefit, educational)
IOGT: Independent Order of Good Templars (also IOofGT) (fraternal, service)
IOH: Improved Order of Heptasophs: Seven Wise Men (mutual benefit)
IOHH: International Order of Hoo-Hoo (business, social)
IOI: Independent Order of Immaculates of the United States of America (also IOIUSA) (fraternal, ethnic)
IOIUSA: IOI: Independent Order of Immaculates of the United States of America (also IOI) (fraternal, ethnic)
IOJD: International (or Independent) Order of Job's Daughters (youth)
IOKD: Independent Order of King David (fraternal)
IOKDS: International Order of the King's Daughters and Sons (religious)
IOKP: Independent Order of Knights of Pythias (fraternal, mutual benefit)
IOKP: Improved Order of Knights of Pythias (fraternal, mutual benefit)
IOKSB: Independent Order of Kescher Schel Brazel (mutual benefit)
IOLofV: Independent Order Ladies of Vikings (lineage)
IOM: Independent Order of Mechanics (mutual benefit)
IOM: Imperial Order of Muscovites (related to IOOF) (fraternal)
IOM: Institute of Medicine (professional)
IOMA: Illinois Order of Mutual Aid (mutual benefit)
IOMB: Independent Order of Mystic Brothers (see also MB – Mystic Brothers) (fraternal, mutual benefit)
IOO: Independent Order of Owls (fraternal)
IOO: Independent Orange Order (militant Protestant)
IOOB: International Order of Old Bastards (bar owners, trade)[2]
IOOF: Independent Order of Odd Fellows (fraternal, mutual benefit)

---

[2] Special thanks to the Liberty NY Internet Group for this one.

IOOF-PM: Independent Order of Odd Fellows, Patriarchs Militant (may also refer to Past Master) (fraternal)

IOofGT: Independent Order of Good Templars (also IOGT) (fraternal)

IOofV: Independent Order of Vikings (lineage)

IOOT: International Order of Templars (fraternal)

IOof RM: Improved Order of Red Men (also IORM) (fraternal, mutual benefit)

IOP: Independent Order of Puritans (mutual benefit)

IOR: Independent Order of Rebekahs (fraternal)

IOR: Independent Order of Rechabites (mutual benefit)

IORG: International Order of Rainbow (for) Girls (youth, Masonic)

IORM: Improved Order of Red Men (a/k/a Sons of Liberty) (also IOofRM) (fraternal, mutual benefit)

IORM: Independent Order of Red Men (fraternal, service)

IOS: Independent Order of Shepherds (mutual benefit)

IOS: International Order of Scichioh (Svithiod) (fraternal, mutual benefit)

IOSA: Independent Order Sons of Abraham (mutual benefit)

IOSB: Independent Order of the Sons of Benjamin (also SB: Sons of Benjamin) (Jewish, fraternal)

IOSH: Institution of Occupational Safety & Health (advocacy)

IOStL: Independent Order of St. Luke (mutual benefit, ethnic)

IOTC: Infantry Officers Training Center (military, World War I)

IOUF: Independent Order of United Friends (see also OUF – Order of United Friends) (fraternal)

IOV: International Order of Vikings (fraternal, mutual benefit)

IOV: Independent Order of Vikings (fraternal, service)

IOYD: Improved order of Yellow Dogs (fraternal)

IP: Independence Party (a/k/a Independence League) (political party)

IPA: Independence Party of America (see also IPOA) (political party)

IPA: Independent Pilots Association (labor union)

IPA: International Progressive Association (political)

IPA: Institute for Public Affairs (religious, political)

IPA: International Polka Association (musical, ethnic)

IPA: Inland Press Association (trade group)

IPA: Irish Protestant Association (political)

IPAB: International Polygraph Accreditation Board (professional)

IPAMS: Independent Petroleum Association of Mountain States (trade group)

IPAY: International Performing Arts for Youth (arts)

IPCC: International Pentecostal Church of Christ (religious denomination)

IPF: Israel Policy Forum (religious, political)

IPFW: Indiana University Purdue University at Fort Wayne (higher education)

IPhA: Illinois Pharmaceutical Association (professional)

IPHC: International Pentecostal Holiness Church (religious denomination)

IPNY: Independence Party of New York (political party)

IPOA: Independence Party of America (see also IPA) (political party)

IPOA: International Peace Operations Association (trade group)

IPPA: Indo-Pacific Prehistory Association (learned)

IPPS: Integrated Physician Practice Section (professional)

IR: Independent Republican (political party)

IR: Iran Air (airline code)

IRA: Iran Air (airline code)

IRA: Irish Republican Army (political/guerilla organization)

IRB: Irish Republican Brotherhood (political)

IRC: International Rescue Committee (humanitarian)

IRC: Intercolonial Railway of Canada (railroad)

IRC: International Race of Champions (motorsports)

IRC: Innocenti Research Centre – International Child Development Centre (UN activity)

IRD: Infantry Replacement Depot (military, World War I)

IRD: Institute for Religion on Democracy (religious)

IREA: International Renewable Energy Alliance (trade group)

IRL: Indian Republican League (fraternal)

IRL: Indy Racing League (motorsports)

IRLDS: Independent RLDS (see RLDS) (religious denomination)

IRMC: Information Resource Management College (governmental)

IRN: Ironton Railroad

IRRC: Iowa Railroad

IRS: Internal Revenue Service (government)

IRS: Independent Research Service (political front)

IRT: Interboro Rapid Transit (railroad)

IS&SA: Illinois Soldiers and Sailors Association (veterans)

ISA: International Seabed Authority (international organization)
ISACS: Independent School Association of the Central States (education)
ISAR: Institute for the Study of American Religion (learned)
ISASS: International Society for the Advancement of Spine Surgery (professional)
ISB: International Society of Bassists (musical)
ISBC: International Small Business Congress (business)
ISC: Intercollegiate Student Council (political, 1930s)
ISC: International Student Conference (political, front)
ISCWM: International Supreme Council of World Masons (Masonic, possibly bogus)
ISDA: Italian Sons & Daughters of America Fraternal Association (also ISDAFA) (ethnic, mutual benefit)
ISDAFA: Italian Sons & Daughters of America Fraternal Association (also ISDA) (ethnic, mutual benefit)
ISDC: International Society of Descendents of Charlemagne (lineage)
ISDUP: International Society, Daughters of Utah Pioneers (lineage)
ISEE: International Society for Environmental Epidemiology (learned)
ISEE: International Society of Explosive Engineers (learned)
ISEE: International Society for Enhancement of Eyesight (learned)
ISEEN: Independent School Experiential Education Network (education)
ISES: International Solar Energy Society (advocacy)
ISF: International Snowboarding Federation (sports)
ISH: Independent Sons of Honor (temperance)
ISHRS: International Society of Hair Restoration Surgery (professional)
ISIE: International Society for Industrial Ecology (advocacy)
ISKC: International Society for Krishna Consciousness (religious cult)
ISLA: International Securities Lending Association (trade group)
ISM: Incorporated Society of Musicians (labor union)
ISM: Institute for Supply Management (trade group)
ISO: International Socialist Organization (political)
ISPi: Iota Sigma Pi (chemistry) (honorary fraternity)
ISPI: International Society for Performance Improvement (professional)

ISR: Iowa Southern Railroad
ISR: Independent Sisters of Rebecca (fraternal)
ISRI: Institute of Scrap Recycling Industries (trade group)
ISRR: Indiana Southern Railroad
ISS: International Sunshine Society (care for disabled children)
ISSCB: International Association of Sand Castle Builders (hobby)
ISSF: International School Sports Federation (sports)
ISU: Independent Steelworkers Union (labor union)
ISU: Iowa State University (Iowa) (higher education)
ISU: Indiana State University (higher education)
ISW: Indiana Southwestern Railway (railroad)
ISWA: International Solid Waste Association (trade group)
ITA: International Trombone Association (musical)
ITA: International Trade Administration (governmental)
ITAA: Information Technology Association of America (trade group)
ITC: Illinois Terminal Company (railroad)
ITC: International Trade Commission (governmental)
ITE: Institute of Transportation Engineers (professional)
ITEA: International Tuba Euphonium Association (musical)
ITG: International Trumpet Guild (musical)
ITPF: International Tent Pegging Federation (equestrian)
ITS: International Thespian Society (theatre) (high school, honorary)
ITU: International Telecommunications Union (UN agency)
ITUC: International Trade Union Confederation (labor union)
IUAPPA: International Union of Air Pollution Prevention & Environmental Protection Associations (umbrella organization)
IUB: International Union of Bricklayers and Allied Craftworkers (labor union)
IUB: Indiana University – Bloomington (higher education)
IUC: Intermountain Union College (Montana) (higher education)
IUE: International Union of Electrical, Radio and Machine Workers (labor union)
IUEC: International Union of Elevator Constructors (labor union)
IUGM: International Union of Gospel Missions (religious denomination)
IUJAT: International Union of Journeymen and Allied Trades (labor union)

IUJHAT: International Union of Journeymen Horseshoers and Allied Trades (labor union)
IUMMSW: International Union of Mine, Mill, and Smelter Workers (labor union)
IUOE: International Union of Operating Engineers (labor union)
IUOM: Independent United Order of Mechanics (labor union)
IUPA: International Union of Police Associations (labor union)
IUPAT: International Union of Painters and Allied Trades (labor union)
IUS: International Union of Students (political front)
IUSADS: Inter-University Seminar on Armed Forces and Society (academic)
IUSPFPA: International Union Security, Police, Fire Professionals of America (labor union)
IW: International Association of Bridge, Structural, Ornamental and Reinforcing Iron Workers (labor union)
IWA: International Workers Association (labor union)
IWA: International Water Association (professional)
IWA: International Webmasters Association (trade group)
IWA: Independent Workmen of America (mutual benefit)
IWBA: International Waterfowl Breeders Association (poultry)
IWBC: International Women's Brass Conference (musical)
IWC: Independent Workmen's Circle (mutual benefit)
IWG: Internationalist Workers' Group (political)
IWK: Imperial White Knights (KKK)
IWSO: Independent Western Star Order (or Union) (ethnic, mutual benefit)
IWW: Industrial Workers of the World (labor union)
IWW: International Workers of the World (labor union)
IYM: Ireland Yearly Meeting (religious denomination)
IYOB: International Order of Job's Daughters (youth)
IYOB FILIAE: (see Job's Daughters, IYOB) (youth)

J

J: Jacksonian (political party)

J4J: Jews for Jesus (also JFJ) (religious denomination)

JA: Junior Achievement (youth)

JA: Jesus Army (religious denomination)

JACL: Japanese American Citizens League (political)

JAG: Judge Advocate General's Corps (Army branch)

JAGD: Judge Advocate General's Department (military, World War I)

JAHA: Junior Amateur Hockey Association (sports)

JAI: Jet Airways (India) Limited (airline code)

JAL: Japan Airlines International Co., Ltd. (airline code)

JAOUW: Junior Order, Ancient Order of United Workmen (also JOAOUW) (mutual benefit)

JAPA: Junior American Protective Association (nationalist, anti-Catholic)

JAS: Jewish Agricultural Society (mutual benefit)[3]

JASRAC: Japanese Society for Rights of Authors, Composers and Publishers (trade group)

Jaycees: (see Junior Chamber of Commerce) (JCC) (civic)

JBA: Java Breeders of America (poultry)

JBAP: Junior Brotherhood of Andrew and Philip (religious, youth)

JBFCS: Jewish Board of Family and Children's Services (religious)

JBI: Jewish Braille Institute of America (religious)

JBIU: Journeymen Barbers' International Union (labor union)

JBP: Junior Brotherhood for Presbyterians (religious, youth)

JBS: John Birch Society (political)

JBStA: Junior Bortherhood of St. Andrew (religious, youth)

JC: Jolly Corks (fraternal)

JCAHO: Joint Commission on Accreditation of Healthcare Organizations (medical)

JCAN: Jewish Children's Adoption Network (religious)

JCBA: Jewish Conciliation Board of America (religious)

JCC: Junior Chamber of Commerce (Jaycees) (civic)

JCC: Jewish Chaplains Council (religious, military)

---

[3] Thanks to Marc Shulman

JCC: Jockey Club of Canada (equestrian)
JCCA: Jewish Community Centers Association of North America (religious)
JCD: Jatiotabadi Chatra Dal (Bangladeshi student, political)
JCDA: Junior Catholic Daughters of the Americas (religious)
JCE: Junior Christian Endeavor (religious)
JCI: Junior Chamber International (Jaycees) (civic)
JCI: Junior Civitan International (civic)
JCS: John Carroll Society (religious)
JCS: Jewish Chautauqua Society, Inc. (religious, education)
JCSA: Jewish Communal Service Association of North America (Jewish, civic)
JD: Job's Daughters (teenage, female, Masonic)
JDRF: Juvenile Diabetes Research Foundation (medical research, advocacy)
JE: Jerseyville and Eastern (railroad)
JE: Junior Endeavor Society (also JES) (religious, youth)
JEB: Japanese Evangelistic Band (religious)
JEDEC: Joint Electron Device Engineering Council (now JEDEC Solid State Technology Association) (trade group)
JEFW: Jefferson Warrior Railroad
JEL: Junior Epworth League, Methodist Episcopal Church (religious)
JEM: Jewish Education in Media (religious)
JES: Junior Endeavor Society (also JE) (religious, youth)
JESNA: Jewish Education Service of North America (religious, education)
JF: Juniors of the Forest (fraternal, youth)
JFA: Junior Foresters of America (fraternal)
JFCPA: Jewish Family and Children's Professionals Association (religious)
JFJ: Jews for Jesus (also J4J) (religious denomination)
JG: Jockeys' Guild (labor union)
JGA: Jersey Giants of America (poultry)
JHU: Journeymen Horseshoers' Union (labor union)
JIAS: Jewish Immigrant Aid Services of Canada (religious)
JINSA: Jewish Institute for National Security Affairs (religious, political)
JIOA: Joint Intelligence Objectives Agency (governmental)
JJRD: J & J Railroad
JKFM: Junior Knights of Father Mathew (youth, temperance, religious)
JL: Junior League (fraternal, women)

169

JL: Junior Lodge (IOOF, youth)
JL: Japan Airlines International Co., Ltd. (airline code)
JLB: Jewish Labor Bund (socialist, labor, Jewish)
JLC: Jewish Labor Committee (union, ethnic)
JM: Air Jamaica (airline code)
JMC: Jenner Medical College (higher education)
JMU: James Madison University (higher education)
JNFA: Jewish National Fund of America (religious)
JNWA: Jewish National Workers Alliance (mutual benefit)
JOAM: Junior Order of American Mechanics (anti-Catholic, mutual benefit)
JOAOUW: Junior Order, Ancient Order of United Workmen (also seen as JAOUW (fraternal, mutual benefit)
JOC: Jewish Occupational Council (religious)
JOKP: Junior Order, Knights of Pythias (youth)
JON: Jewish Online Network (religious)
JOOI: Junior Optimist Octagon International (civic)
JOPS: Junior Order of the Princes of Syracuse (boys, Knights of Pythias)
JOUAM: Junior Order of United American Mechanics (also, Junior Order, Order of United American Mechanics) (fraternal, nativist, mutual benefit)
JP: Justice Party (political party)
JPA: Juice Products Association (trade group)
JPF: Jewish Peace Fellowship (religious)
JPFO: Jews for the Preservation of Firearm Ownership (lobby)
JPMA: Juvenile Products Manufacturers Association (trade group)
JPO: Jewish Progressive Order (ethnic, mutual benefit)
JR: Jackson Republicans (political party)
JR: Junior Republic (school)
JRC: Junior Red Cross (civic)
JRCERT: Joint Review Committee on Education Programs in Radiologic Technology (accrediting)
JRCNMT: Joint Review Committee on Educational Programs in Nuclear Medicine Technology (accrediting)
JRF: Jewish Reconstructionist Federation (religious)
JRHS: Julia Richman High School (school)
JROTC: Junior Reserve Officer Training Corps (education, military)
JRTCA: Jack Russell Terrier Club of America (canine)
JS: Jamestowne Society (lineage)
JSA: Junior Statesmen of America (youth)

JSAA: Japanese Studies Association of Australia (learned)
JSRC: Jackson and Southern Railroad
JSRW: Jersey Southern Railway (railroad)
JSU: Jackson State University (Mississippi) (higher education)
JT: Juvenile Templars (fraternal, youth)
JTA: Jewish Teachers Association-Morim (religious, education)
JTS: Jewish Theological Seminary (higher education)
JTST: Jamaica Training School for Teachers (New York)
(higher education)
JTU: Journeymen Tailors' Union (labor union)
JVRR: Juniata Valley Railroad
JVW: Jewish War Veterans of the USA (veterans)
JWA: Jewish Welfare Association (religious, civic)
JWB: Jewish Welfare Board (religious, military)
JWC: Jenny Wren Club (not an organization: actually a line of
sewing patterns)
JWJ: Jobs With Justice (labor union)
JWV: Jewish War Veterans of the USA (religious, veterans)
JY: Jesus Youth (religious)

K

K&LofI: Knights and Ladies of Industry (fraternal)
K&LofH: Knights and Ladies of Honor (also KLH) (mutual benefit)
K&LofS: Knights & Ladies of Security (also KLS) (mutual benefit)
K&M: Kanawha and Michigan Railway (railroad)
K&WV: Kanawha and West Virginia Railroad
K-N: Know-Nothings (political party)
KA: Kappa Alpha (college fraternity)
KA: Knights of the Altar (several organizations) (former altar boys, Roman Catholic)
KA: Knights of the Apocalypse (secret, Roman Catholic)
KAA: Kendall Acres Academy (school)
KAB: Kansas Association of Broadcasters (trade group)
KAC: Kuwait Airways (airline code)
KAEO: Knights of the Ancient Essenic Order (mutual benefit)
KAL: Korean Air Lines Co. Ltd. (airline code)
KAMELIA: Women's auxiliary of the KKK
KAOMC: Knights of the Ancient Order of the Mystic Chain (mutual benefit)
KAPi: Kappa Alpha Pi (high school fraternity)
KASB: Knights of Ak-Sar-Ben (fraternal)
KAT: Kappa Alpha Theta (college sorority)
KATY: Missouri-Kansas-Texas (also MKT) (railroad)
KBCW: Knights of the Blue Cross of the World (mutual benefit)
KBD: Kappa Beta Delta (business) (academic honorary)
KBHC: Knights Beneficent of the Holy City (Masonic)
KBS: Kankakee, Beaverville and Southern (railroad)
KBSR: Kankakee, Beaverville and Southern (railroad)
KC: Knights of Columbus (also Kof C) (fraternal, religious, mutual benefit)
KC: Kanawha Central Railway (railroad)
KC: Knights of the Cross (Knights of the Cross with the Red Star) (religious order)
KC: Knights of the Cross (Teutonic Knights) (Order of Brothers of the German House of Saint Mary in Jerusalem) (religious order)

KC: Knights of the Cork (fraternal, secret)
KC: Knothole Club (Rotary) (civic)
KCDC: Kansas City Dental College (Missouri) (higher education)
KCI: Kiwanis Club International (fraternal)
KCLS: Kansas City School of Law (Missouri) (higher education)
KCNW: Kelly's Creek and Northwestern Railroad
KCS: Kansas City Southern (railroad)
KCT: Kansas City Terminal Railway (railroad)
KCU: Kansas City University (Kansas) (higher education)
KCVC: Kansas City Veterinary College (Missouri) (higher education)
KD: International Order of the King's Daughters and Sons (religious)
KD: Kappa Delta (sorority)
KD: Knights of Donamis (Boy Scouts)
KD: King's Daughters (perhaps Daughters of the King?) (religious)
KDE: Kappa Delta Epsilon (education) (academic honorary)
KDG: Knights of Da Gama (fraternal)
KDPi: Kappa Delta Pi (education) (academic honorary)
KDR: Kappa Delta Rho (fraternity)
KE: Kansas Eastern Railroad
KE: Knights of Equity (religious)
KE: Korean Air Lines Co. Ltd. (airline code)
KENN: Kennecott Railroad
KEWH: Kewash Railroad
KF: Knights of Friendship (fraternal, ethnic, mutual benefit)
KFC: Kentucky Fried Chicken (business)
KFM: Knights of Father Matthew (also KofFM) (temperance, religious, mutual benefit)
KFR: Kettle Falls International Railroad
KG: Knights of St. George (also KStG) (chivalry, honorific)
KG: Knights of the Globe (mutual benefit)
KG: Keystone Guard (military, Civil War)
KG: Keystone Guard (mutual benefit)
KGC: Knights of the Golden Chain (mutual benefit)
KGC: Knights of the Golden Circle (Civil War Southern sympathizers)
KGE: Knights of the Golden Eagle (fraternal)
KGL: Knight Grand Legion (French, honorific)
KGL: Knights of the Gallant Leaders (high school sorority)
KGL: Knights of the Gallant Leaders (high school fraternity)

173

KGLW: Knights of the Golden Links of the World (mutual benefit)
KGPi: Kappa Gamma Pi (leadership, Catholic colleges) (academic honorary)
KGR: Knights of the Golden Rule (mutual benefit)
KH: Knights of Honor (also KofH) (fraternal, mutual benefit)
KHC: Knights of the Holy Cross (religious order)
KHG: Knights of the Holy Grail (religious, inter-denominational)
KHS: Knights of the Holy Sepulchre (honorific chivalric order)
KHW: Knights of Honor of the World (mutual benefit)
KI: Kiwanis International (fraternal)
KI: Knights of the Immaculata (religious)
KICK: Knights of the Invisible Colored Kingdom (ethnic, charitable)
KIE: Knights of the Invisible Empire (KKK-related)
KIE: Kennedy Institute of Ethics (research)
KIGY: Klansman I Greet You or Klan Interests Guide You (KKK-related)
KJ: Knights of Jericho (also KofJ) (fraternal)
KJ: Knights of Jubilation (also KofJ) (Masonic)
KJR: Kiski Junction Railroad
KJRY: Keokuk Junction Railway (railroad)
KJZT: Catholic Women's Fraternal of Texas (Slovak, mutual benefit)
KK: Knights of Khorasan (also KofK) (Knights of Pythias)
KKA: Knights of King Arthur (religious, interdenominational)
KKG: Kappa Kappa Gamma (sorority)
KKK: Ku-Klux Klan (also, Knights of the Ku-Klux Klan)
KKK: Ku Klos Knights (KKK)
KKK: TriKappa Fraternity (now Delta Kappa Theta) (fraternity)
KKKK: Knights of Ku Klux Klan (KKK)
KKKR: Ku Klux Klan Radio (KKK)
KKKT: Ku Klux Klan of Texas (KKK)
KKKTV: Ku Klux Klan Television (KKK)
KKR: Kohlberg, Kravis and Roberts (company)
KKRR: Knox and Kane Railroad
KKP: Kappa Kappa Psi (music) (academic honorary)
KL: Knights of Labor (also KOL, KofL) (labor union)
KL: Knights of Liberty (also KofL) (KKK)
KL: Knights of Lithuania (also KofL) (ethnic, mutual benefit)
KL: Knights of Loyola (also KofL) (religious, mutual benefit)

KL: Knights of Luther (also KofL) (religious, mutual benefit)
KL: Kuhn, Loeb & Co. (business)
KL: KLM Royal Dutch Airlines (airline code)
KLA: Kosovo Liberation Army (guerilla organization)
KLA: Knights and Ladies of Azar (fraternal)
KLA: Knights and Ladies of America (mutual benefit)
KLD: Knights and Ladies of David (mutual benefit)
KLF: Knights and Ladies of the Fireside (mutual benefit)
KLG: Knights of the Loyal Guard (mutual benefit)
KLGP: Knights and Ladies of the Golden Precept (mutual benefit)
KLGR: Knights and Ladies of the Golden Rule (mutual benefit)
KLGS: Knights and Ladies of the Golden Star (mutual benefit)
KLH: Knights and Ladies of Honor (also K&LofH) (mutual benefit)
KLK: Knights and Ladies of Kaleva (musical, ethnic)
KLM: KLM Royal Dutch Airlines (airline code)
KLOC: Knights and Ladies of the Cross (mutual benefit)
KLPC: Knights and Ladies of Peter Claver (religious)
KLRT: Knights and Ladies of the Round Table (mutual benefit)
KLS: Knights and Ladies of Security (also K&LofS) (mutual benefit)
KLSC: Kalamazoo, Lake Shore and Chicago Railway (railroad)
KM: Knights of the Maccabees (also KofM and KOTM) (fraternal, mutual benefit)
KM: Knights of Malta (Masonic)
KM: Knights Militant (of the KKK)
KM: Kansas and Missouri Railroad
KM: Knights of Methodism (religious, youth)
KMA: Kemper Military Academy (Missouri) (education)
KMC: Knights of the Mystic Chain (also AOKMC) (fraternal)
KMC: Keokuk Medical College (Iowa) (higher education)
KMCE: The Knights of the Militia Crucifera Evangelica (fraternal, Rosicrucian)
KME: Kappa Mu Epsilon (mathematics) (honorary fraternity)
KMHA: Kentucky Mountain Holiness Association (religious denomination)
KMNOG: Society of Descendants of Knights of the Most Noble Order of the Garter (lineage)
K-N: Know Nothings (see also KNP) (political)
KNOR: Klamath Northern Railway (railroad)
KNP: Know-Nothing Party (see also K-N) (political)
KO: Kansas & Oklahoma Railroad

KofC: Knights of Columbus (see also KC) (religious, fraternal, mutual benefit)

KofE: Knights of Equity (ethnic, mutual benefit)

KofFM: Knights of Father Matthew (also KFM) (also "and Ladies") (mutual benefit)

KofGE: Knights of the Golden Eagle (also KGE) (fraternal)

KofGF: Knights of the Green Forest (KKK-related)

KofH: Knights of Honor (also KH) (fraternal)

KofJ: Knights of St. John (mutual benefit)

KofJ: Knights of Jericho (also KJ) (fraternal)

KofJ: Knights of Jubilation (also KJ) (Masonic)

KofK: Knights of Khorasan (also KK) (Knights of Pythias)

KofL: Knights of Labor (also KL, also KOL) (labor union)

KofL: Knights of Liberty (also KL) (KKK)

KofL: Knights of Lithuania (also KL) (mutual benefit)

KofL: Knights of Loyola (also KL) (religious, mutual benefit)

KofL: Knights of Luther (also KL) (religious, mutual benefit)

KofM: Knights of the Maccabees (also KM and KOTM) (fraternal, mutual benefit)

KofM: Knights of Malta (also LM) (Masonic)

KofP: Knights of Pythias (also KP) (fraternal, mutual benefit)

KofSJ: Knights of St. John (see KofJ) (mutual benefit)

KofSJM: Knights of St. John and Malta (religious, fraternal)

KofSTP: Knights of St. Patrick (Irish-American)

KofSTW: Knights of St. Wenceslas (Czech royal order)

KofT: Knights of Tabor (also KT) (ethnic, fraternal)

KofT: Knights of Temperance (self improvement)

KofTM: Knights of the Maccabees (see KM and KofM) (fraternal, mutual benefit)

KOG: Kansas, Oklahoma and Gulf Railroad

KoGC: Knights of the Golden Circle (fantasy, fraternal)

KOGEL: Knights of the Golden Eagle (fraternal)

KoH: Knights of Honor (also KH) (fraternal)

KoH: Knights of St. John (Knights Hospitaller) (religious, fraternal)

KOL: Knights of Labor (also KL, KofL) (labor union)

KON: Kappa Omicron Nu (human sciences) (academic honorary)

KOS: Knights of the Sword (fantasy)

KOTGR: Knights of the Golden Rule (fraternal, yellow fever epidemic survivors)

KOTM: Knights of the Maccabees (see KM) (fraternal)

KP: Knights of Pythias (see also KofP) (fraternal, mutual benefit)
KP: Knights of Pythias of North and South America (see also CKP: Colored Knights of Pythias) (fraternal, mutual benefit, ethnic)
KP: Knights Party (KKK)
KP: Kappa Psi (pharmacy) (honorary)
KPC: Knights of Peter Claver (fraternal, ethnic, religious)
KPi: Kappa Pi (art) (academic honorary)
KPR: Kelowna Pacific Railway (railroad)
KPRR: Kodak Park Railroad
KPVL: Knights Party Veterans League (KKK)
KR: Knights of Reciprocity (fraternal, mutual benefit)
KR: Knight Riders (KKK)
KR: Knghts of Rizal (fraternal)
KRA: Knights of the Royal Arch (fraternal, mutual benefit)
KRC: Knights of the Red Cross (mutual benefit)
KRCC: Knights of the Red Cross of Constantine (fraternal – Masonic)
KRL: Kasgro Rail Lines (railroad)
KRR: Kiamichi Railroad
KRT: Knights of the Round Table (legendary)
KS: Kappa Sigma (college fraternity)
KSA: Knights of St. Andrew (see KStA) (Scottish Rite Masonic)
KSB: Kesher Shel Barzel (mutual benefit)
KSC: Knights of St. Columbkille (Irish-American)
KSC: Knights of the Southern Cross (Catholic, fraternal, Australia)
KSC: Knights of St. Columba (fraternal)
KSF: Knights of Sherwood Forest (fraternal)
KSFI: Knights of Sobriety, Fidelity, and Integrity (mutual benefit)
KSJ: Knights of St. Joseph (religious)
KSL: Knights of St. Lawrence (Catholic, fraternal)
KSM: Knights of St. Mulumba (fraternal)
KSRY: Kosciusko and Southwestern Railway (railroad)
KStA: Knights of St. Andrew (see KSA) (Scottish Rite Masonic)
KStG: Knights of St. George (see KG, also KSTG, KStG) (chivalry)
KSTG: Knights of St. George (see KG, also KSTG, KStG) (chivalry)
KSTI: Knights of St. Ignatius (religious)
KSTJ: Knights of St. John (fraternal)

KSTJ: Knights of St. Joseph (Catholic, fraternal)
KSTM: Knights of St. Martin (Catholic, fraternal)
KSTP: Knights of St. Paul (Masonic)
KSTP: Knights of St. Peter (Catholic, fraternal)
KSTT: Knights of St. Thomas (Hospitallers of St Thomas of Canterbury at Acre) (Christian military order))
KSU: Kansas State University (Kansas) (higher education)
KSU: Kent State University (higher education)
KSW: Kansas and Oklahoma Railroad
KT: Knights Templar (Sovereign Military Order of the Temple of Jerusalem) (Masonic)
KT: Knights of Tabor (also KofT) (ethnic, fraternal)
KT: Kentucky and Tennessee Railroad
KT: Knights of the Thistle (Scottish)
KTA: Kappa Tau Alpha (journalist) (academic honorary)
KTE: Kappa Theta Epsilon (academic honorary)
KTR: Kendallville Terminal Railway (railroad)
KU: Kuwait Airways (airline code)
KU: University of Kansas (higher education)
KVR: Kern Valley Railroad
KW: King's Workers (religious)
KWAKH: Kurdish Women Against Honor Killings (political)
KWM: Knights of Wise Men (ethnic, mutual benefit)
KXHR: Knoxville and Holston River Railroad
KYCH: Knights of the York Cross of Honor (Masonic)
KYLE: Kyle Railroad

L

L8: International Air Cargo Company (LoadAir) (airline code)
L&A: Louisiana & Arkansas (also LA) (railroad)
L&N: Louisville & Nashville (also LN) (railroad)
LA: Louisiana and Arkansas (also L&A) (railroad)
LA: Lambda Alpha (anthropology) (honorary fraternity)
LA: Light of the Ages (mutual benefit)
LA: Lan (Chile) Airlines (airline code)
LAA: Lithuanian Alliance of America (mutual benefit, political, cultural)
LAB: League of American Bicyclists (sports)
LABA: Loyal Additional Benefit Association (mutual benefit)
LACP: League of American Communications Professionals (professional)
LAFF: Luso-American Fraternal Federation (mutual benefit)
LAGF: League of American German Friends (mutual benefit)
LAJ: Los Angeles Junction Railway (railroad)
LAL: Livonia, Avon & Lakeville Railroad Corp. (railroad)
LAL: Ladies of Abraham Lincoln (fraternal)
LAL: Lithuanian Airlines (business)
LAL: Ladies American League (mutual benefit)
LAL: Loyal American Legion (mutual benefit)
LALA: Loyal American Life Association (mutual benefit)
LALIS: Luso-American Life Insurance Society (mutual benefit)
LAMP: Lutheran Association of Missionaries and Pilots (religious)
LAN: Lan (Chile) Airlines (airline code)
LANA: Lipizzan Association of North America (equine)
LANO: Lancaster Northern Railway (railroad)
LAO: League of American Orchestras (umbrella organization)
LAOH: Ladies of the Ancient Order of Hibernians (fraternal)
LAPC: Los Angeles Pacific College (California) (higher education)
LAPM: Ladies Auxiliary, Patriarchs Militant (women, IOOF)
LAS: Ladies' Aid Society, Methodist Episcopal Church (religious)
LAS: Ladies' Aid Society, Protestant Episcopal Church (religious)
LASB: Lackawaxen and Stourbridge Railroad

LASofSV: Ladies Aid Society of the Sons of Veterans (lineage)
LAVFW: Ladies Auxiliary Veterans of Foreign Wars (lineage)
LAW: League of American Wheelmen (sports)
LB: Lutheran Brotherhood (religious denomination)
LB: Lutheran Brotherhood (mutual benefit)
LB: Landmark Baptists (religious denomination)
LBA: Lutheran Brotherhood of America (mutual benefit)
LBA: Luxembourg Brotherhood of America (lineage)
LBA: Latin Businessmen's Association (business)
LBAS-IGLKMPBLU: Loyal Black Association of Scotland, the
Imperial Grand Lodge of Knights of Malta and Parent Black
Lodge of the Universe (fraternal, political)
LBBU: Lager Beer Brewers' Union (labor union)
LBC: Landmark Baptist Church (religious denomination)
LBF: Little Brothers of Francis (religious community)
LBF: Liberty Baptist Fellowship (religious denomination)
LBP: Looking Back Party (political party)
LBR: Lowville & Beaver River Railroad Co. (railroad)
LC: Louisiana Colonials (lineage)
LC: Legion of Christ (religious order)
LC: Lancaster & Chester (railroad)
LC: Library of Congress (governmental)
LC: Lambuth College (Tennessee) (higher education)
LC: Ladies' Circle (fraternal)
LC: Loyal Circle (mutual benefit)
LCA: Lutheran Church of Australia (religious denomination)
LCA: Lithuanian Catholic Alliance (cultural, mutual benefit)
LCBA: Ladies' Catholic Benevolent Association (mutual
benefit)
LCBA: Loyal Christian Benefit Association (mutual benefit)
LCC: Liberal Catholic Church (religious denomination)
LCC: Lutheran Church of China (religious denomination)
LCC: Leander Clark College (Iowa) (higher education)
LCF: Lutheran Community Foundation (religious)
LCFMS: Litchfield County (CT) Foreign Mission Society
(religious)
LCG: Living Church of God (religious denomination)
LCI: Lions Clubs International (civic)
LCLAA: Labor Council for Latin American Advancement
(labor union)
LCM: Little Company of Mary (religious order)
LCM: Little Company of Mary (Australia) (religious order)

LCMC: Lutheran Congregations in Mission for Christ (religious denomination)
LCMS: Lutheran Church, Missouri Synod (religious denomination)
LCP: Library of Congress Preservation (civic)
LPC: Library of Congress Police (governmental)
LCR: Lake County Railroad
LCRC: Lenawee County Railroad
LCRR: Lincoln Central Railroad
LCS: Loomis Chafee School (school)
LCUSA: Lutheran Council in the United States of America (religious)
LDG: Independent Order of Foresters (fraternal, mutual benefit)
LDRR: Louisiana and Delta Railroad
LDRT: Lake Front Dock and Railroad Terminal (railroad)
LDS: Church of Jesus Christ of the Latter Day Saints. (Mormons) (religious denomination)
LDU: Livery Drivers Union (labor union)
LE: Lady Elks (fraternal)
LE: Louisiana Eastern Railroad
LEAA: Law Enforcement Alliance of America (political)
LEAA: Law Enforcement Assistance Administration (governmental)
LEAC: Lay Episcopalians for the Anglican Communion (religious)
LEE: Lake Erie and Eastern Railroad
LEF: Lake Erie, Franklin and Clarion Railroad
LELCA: Latvian Evangelical Lutheran Church in America (religious denomination)
LEML: Locomotive Engineers Mutual Life (mutual benefit)
LEN: Lake Erie and Northern Railway (railroad)
LEP: Lorraine, Eastern and Pacific Railroad
LEPC: Lutheran Evangelical Protestant Church (religious denomination)
LER: Logansport and Eel River Short Line (railroad)
LF: Legion of Frontiersmen (fraternal)
LFC: Latino Fraternal Council (umbrella organization)
LFC: Latino Fraternal Caucus (umbrella organization)
LFMOS: League of Friendship of the Mechanical Order of the Sun (became the Ancient Order of United Workmen) (fraternal)
LFU: Lincoln Fraternal Union (mutual benefit)
LGAR: Ladies of the Grand Army of the Republic (lineage)

LGE: Ladies of the Golden Eagle (fraternal)
LH: Legion of Honor (French Foreign Legion-related)
LH: Deutsche Lufthansa AG (airline code)
LHC: Lutheran Historical Conference (religious)
LHI: Local Heroes, Incorporated (military support)
LHM: Lutheran Hour Ministries (religious)
LHMS: Linton Hall Military School (school)
LHR: Lehigh and Hudson River (railroad)
LHR: League for Human Rights (religious)
LHRR: Longhorn Railroad
LHS: Litchfield Historical Society
LI: Lions International (fraternal)
LI: Long Island Railroad (also LIRR)
LI MTA: Long Island Railroad (as part of the MTA, see LIRR) (railroad)
LID: League for Industrial Democracy (political)
LIFE: stands of Liberty, Integrity, Fraternity, and Equality (Fraternal Order of Orioles) (fraternal)
LIL: FlyLAL – Lithuanian Airlines (airline code)
LINC: Louis and Clark Railroad
LIOR: Ladies Independent Order of Reindeer (fraternal)
LIRC: Louisville and Indiana Railroad
LIRR: Lapeer Industrial Railroad
LIRR: Long Island Rail Road (see also LI MTA and LI) (railroad)
LIRS: Lutheran Immigration and Refugee Service (religious)
LISA: Life Insurance Settlement Association (trade group)
LIT: Lambda Iota Tau (literature) (honorary fraternity)
LITA: Library and Information Technology Association (professional)
LIU: Long Island University (New York) (higher education)
LIU: Laborers' International Union of North America (also LIUNA) (labor union)
LIUNA: Laborers' International Union of North America (also LIU) (labor union)
LJC: Luther Junior College (Nebraska) (higher education)
LJW: League of Jewish Women (UK) (women)
LKA: Loyal Knights of America (also LKofA) (fraternal)
LKC: Lime Kiln Club (fraternal)
LKL: Loyal Knights and Ladies (fraternal, mutual benefit)
LKofA: Loyal Knights of America (also LKA) (fraternal)
LKL: Loyal Knights and Ladies (also LK&L) (ethnic, fraternal, mutual benefit)

LK&L: Loyal Knights and Ladies (also LKL) (ethnic, fraternal)
LKRR: Little Kanawha River Rail, Inc. (railroad)
LKRT: Loyal Knights of the Round Table
LKWR: Lackland Western Railroad
LL: Lincoln League (political)
LL: Loyal Leagues (political, Civil War)
LL: Poplar River Mine Railroad
LL: Luther League (religious)
LLA: Ladies of Liberty Alliance (lobby)
LLC: Liberty Loan Committee (patriotic)
LLC: National Lay Leadership Committee (religious, education)
LLISC: Lutheran Life Insurance Society of Canada (mutual benefit)
LLL: Loyal Ladies' League (lineage)
LLL: Lutheran Laymen's League (religious)
LLL: Live and Let Live (fraternal)
LLLL: Loyal Legion of Lumbermen and Loggers (labor union, mutual benefit)
LLOI: Ladies Loyal Orange Institution of the USA (political, Northern Irish)
LLRA: Loyal Ladies of the Royal Arcanum (fraternal)
LLS: Litchfield Law School (educational)
LM: Ladies of the Maccabees (also LofM) (fraternal, mutual benefit)
LM: Labor Militant (political party)
LM: Litchfield and Madison Railroad
LM: Legion of Mary (religious)
LMAA: Ladies Militant Auxiliary Association (fraternal)
LMBA: Lippitt Morgan Breeders' Association (equine)
LMBAQ: Landmark Missionary Baptist Association of Quebec (religious, Canadian)
LMC: Louisville Municipal College (Kentucky) (higher education)
LMC: Louisville Medical College (Kentucky) (higher education)
LMHR: Lippitt Morgan Horse Registry (equine)
LMIC: Lake Michigan and Indiana Railroad
LMLA: Loyal Mystic Legion of America (mutual benefit)
LMM: Lady Missionaries of Mary (religious order)
LMS: London Missionary Society (religious)
LMS: Lutheran Ministerium and Synod (religious denomination)
LMW: Ladies of the Maccabees of the World (fraternal, mutual benefit)
LN: Louisville & Nashville (also L&N) (railroad)

183

LN: Labor Notes (labor reform group)
LNAC: Louisville, New Albany and Corydon Railroad
LNE: Lehigh and New England (railroad)
LNO: Laona and Northern Railway (railroad)
LNVT: Landisville Terminal and Transfer (railroad)
LNW: Louisiana and North West Railroad
LO: Lot Polish Airlines (airline code)
LOA: Loyal Orange Association (also known as Orangemen) (political, Northern Irish)
LoadAir: International Air Cargo Company (business)
LOAM: Louisiana Midland Railroad
LOAS: Loyal Order of Ancient Shepherds (mutual benefit)
LOAW: League of American Wheelmen (sports)
LOBA: Ladies Orange Benevolent Association (mutual benefit)
LOBB: Loyal Order of Beer Buffalo (fraternal)
LOC: Latvian Orthodox Church (religious denomination)
LOC: Library of Congress (governmental)
LOG: Legion of Honor (Masonic)
LOI: Loyal Orange Institution (Northern Irish)
LofM: Ladies of the Maccabees (also LM) (fraternal, mutual benefit)
LOL: Loyal Orange Legion (Northern Irish)
LOL: Loyal Order Orange Lodge (The Orange Order, Orange Men, The Orange Lodge) (Northern Irish)
LOM: Legion of the Moose (fraternal, mutual benefit)
LOM: Loyal Order of Moose (see LOOM) (fraternal, mutual benefit)
LOOB: Loyal Order of Buffaloes (fraternal)
LOOM: Loyal Order of (the) Moose (see LOM) (fraternal, mutual benefit)
LOS: Loyal Order of Sparrows (fraternal?)
LOS: League of the South (KKK)
LOSNA: Ladies Oriental Shrine of North America (Masonic)
LOT: Loyal Order of Tecumseh (fraternal, ethnic)
LOT: Lot Polish Airlines (airline code)
LOTIE: Lady (or Ladies) of the Klan (KKK)
LOTM: Ladies of the Maccabees (fraternal)
LOVUS: Legion of Valor of the United States (military honorary)
LOYB: Loyal Order of Young Britons (political)
LP: Labor Party (political party)
LP: Liberty Party (political party)
LP: Lincoln Pacific Railway (railroad)

LP200: Los Pobladores 200 (lineage)
LPE: Lambda Pi Eta (communications) (academic honorary)
LPF: Lutheran Peace Fellowship (religious)
LPG: Los Pinoy Gang (high school sorority)
LPN: Longview, Portland and Northern Railway (railroad)
LPNY: Liberal Party of New York (political party)
LPP: Liverpool Protestant Party (militant Protestant)
LPRR: Lincoln Pacific Railway (railroad)
LPS: Loyal Publications Society (political)
LPSCU: Ladies Pennsylvanian Slovak Catholic Union (mutual benefit)
LPSG: Live Oak, Perry and South Georgia Railroad
LPT: Les Petite Terpsichore (high school sorority)
LR: Liberal Republican (political party)
LRA: Lord's Resistance Army (guerilla organization)
LRC: Ladies Relief Corps (affiliate of GAR, women, charitable)
LRC: Legion of the Red Cross (fraternal, mutual benefit)
LRCAA: Lithuanian Roman Catholic Alliance of America (cultural, charitable)
LREI: Little Red School House & Elisabeth Irwin High School (New York) (school)
LRNA: League of Revolutionaries for a New America (political)
LRP: League for the Revolutionary Party (political)
LRP: Liberal Republican Party (political party)
LRPA: Little Rock Point Railroad
LRS: Laurinburg and Southern Railroad
LRUP: La Raza Unida Party (political party)
LRWN: Little Rock and Western Railroad
LRWY: Lackawanna Railway (railroad)
LS: Luzerne Susquehanna Railway (railroad)
LS: Lambda Sigma (academic honorary)
LSA: Loyal Sons of America (mutual benefit)
LSA: Lute Society of America (musical)
LSA: Lutheran Services in America (religious)
LSA: Linguistic Society of America (scholarly)
LSBC: LaSalle and Bureau County Railroad
LSI: Lake Superior and Ishpeming Railroad
LSJ: Little Sisters of Jesus (religious order)
LSO: London Symphony Orchestra (musical)
LSO: Louisiana Southern Railway (railroad)
LSP: Little Sisters of the Poor (religious order)
LSRC: Lake State Railway (railroad)
LSRR: Lone Star Railroad

LSTT: Lake Superior Terminal and Transfer Railway (railroad)
LSU: Louisiana State University (Louisiana) (higher education)
LSUW: Ladies' Society of United Workers (religious)
LSV: Secret honor society for women at University of Missouri
LT: Lake Terminal Railroad
LT: Lex Talionis (fraternal)
LTA: Les Trente Amies (high school sorority)
LTB: Loyal True Blue (apparently Orange Order affiliate) (political)
LTTE: Liberation Tigers of Tamil Eelam (Tamil Tigers) (guerilla organization)
LU: Livingston University (New Jersey) (higher education)
LUC: Loyola University – Chicago (higher education)
LULAC: League of United Latin American Citizens (political)
LUM: Lutheran United Mission (religious)
LUN: Ludington and Northern Railway (railroad)
LURD: Liberians United for Reconciliation and Democracy (guerilla organization)
LV: Legion of Valor (of the United States of America) (lineage)
LV: Lehigh Valley (railroad)
LVA: Lao Veterans of America (lobby, veterans)
LVAL: Lackawanna Valley Railroad
LVRC: Lamoille Valley Railroad
LVRR: Lycoming Valley Railroad
LW: Louisville and Wadley Railway (railroad)
LWAL: Loyal Women of American Liberty (nativist, anti-Catholic)
LWC: Lutheran Women's Caucus (religious)
LWF: Lutheran World Federation (religious)
LWIU: Laundry Workers International Union (labor union)
LWK: Loyal White Knights (KKK)
LWMA: Lyman Ward Military Academy (school)
LWR: Lakeland and Waterways Railway (railroad)
LWR: Lutheran World Relief (religious)
LWV: League of Women Voters (civic)
LWV: Lackawanna & Wyoming Valley Railroad
LXA: Lambda Chi Alpha (college fraternity)
LXOH: Lexington and Ohio Railroad
LXVR: Luxapalila Valley Railroad
LY: El Al Israel Airlines (airline code)
LZAC: Labour Zionist Alliance of Canada (political, religious)

M

M-19: 19th of April Movement (guerilla group)
M&CL: Medford & Crater Lake (railroad)
M&H: Mohawk & Hudson Railroad
M&K: Morgantown and Kingwood Railroad
M&W: Morgantown and Wheeling Railway (railroad)
MA: Monticello Association (lineage)
MA: Modern Aztecs (mutual benefit)
MAA: Miami Aerospace Academy (school)
MAA: Magma Arizona Railroad
MAA: Medieval Academy of America (learned)
MAAF: Military Association of Atheists and Freethinkers
(military support)
MAB: Mississippi Aryan Brotherhood (KKK)
MAC: Mount Angel College (Oregon) (higher education)
MACTE: Montessori Accreditation Council for Teacher
Education (accrediting)
MACV: Military Assistance Command Vietnam (military)
MADD: Mothers Against Drunk Driving (civic, political)
MAESA: Mid-Atlantic Episcopal Schools Association
(education, religious)
MAF: Move America Forward (military support)
MAFO: Modern American Fraternal Order (mutual benefit)
MAHF-F&AM: Most Ancient and Honorable Fraternity of Free
and Accepted Masons (Masonic, ethnic)
MALC: Mexican-American Legislative Caucus (political)
MAP: Medieval Association of the Pacific (learned)
MARAC: Mid-Atlantic Regional Archives Conference
(professional)
MARAD: Maritime Administration (governmental)
MARCENT: Marine Corps Central Command (military)
MARCORSYSCOM: Marine Corps Systems Command
(military)
MARFORRES: Marine Forces Reserve (military)
MARSOC: Marine Corps Forces Special Operations Command
(military)
MAS: Malaysia Airline System Berhad (airline code)
MAS: Minority Affairs Section (professional)
MASCS: Mid-America Stock Car Series (motorsports)

MAT: Mu Alpha Theta (mathematics) (academic honorary)
MATS: Military Air Transport Service (military)
MAW: Marine Aircraft Wing (or Marine Air Wing) (military)
MAX: Alpha Chi/Men of Alpha Chi (high school fraternity)
MAYC: Methodist Association of Youth Clubs (religious)
MAYO: Mexican American Youth Organization (political)
MB: Mystic Brothers (see also: IOMB: Independent Order of Mystic Brothers) (fraternal)
MB: Muslim Brotherhood (fraternal)
MB: Meridian and Bigbee Railroad
MB: Mortar Board (honorary, leadership)
MBA: Military Benefit Association (mutual benefit)
MBA: Modern Brotherhood of America (mutual benefit)
MBA: Minnesota Baptist Association (religious denomination)
MBA: Music Business Association (trade group)
MBA: Mortgage Bankers Association (trade group)
MBARTE: Mutual Benefit Association of Rail Transportation Employees, Inc. (mutual benefit)
MBAS: Mutual Benefit and Aid Society (mutual benefit)
MBBA: Metropolitan Black Bar Association (professional)
MBC: Minnesota Baptist Conference (religious denomination)
MBC: Manipur Baptist Convention (religious denomination)
MBC: Myanmar Baptist Convention (religious denomination)
MBC: Mennonite Brethren Churches (religious denomination)
MBF: Medical Benevolence Foundation (religious)
MBH: The Melanesian Brotherhood (religious community)
MBIC: Mennonite Brotherhood in Christ (religious denomination)
MBLIC: Mutual Benefit Life Insurance Company (business)
MBMA: Metal Building Manufacturers Association (trade group)
MBN: Mainstream Baptist Network (religious denomination)
MBP: Mu Beta Psi (music) (academic honorary)
MBS: Mutual Benefit Society (mutual benefit – generic term, also a specific organization by this name)
MBSCC: Maine Boys Sweet Corn Club (youth, agricultural)
MBT: Marianna and Blountstown Railroad
MBTA: Massachusetts Bay Transportation Authority (railroad)
MBWM: Macedonia Baptist World Missions (religious)
MC: Military Coalition (generic)
MC: Missionaries of Charity (religious order)
MC: Moravian Church (religious denomination)
MC: Montezuma College (New Mexico) (higher education)

MC: Michigan Central Railroad
MC: Massachusetts Coastal Railroad
MC: Methodist Church (religious denomination)
MC: Morristown College (Tennessee) (higher education)
MC: Murphy College (Tennessee) (higher education)
MC: Missionary Church (religious denomination)
MC: Medical Corps (Army branch)
MCA: Marine Corps Association (military)
MCA: Mueller Christian Academy (school)
MCA: Metropolitan Church Association (religious denomination)
MCA: Music Corporation of America, Inc. (business)
MCA: Mohair Council of America (goats)
MCA: Metal Construction Association (trade group)
MCAA: Mason Contractors Association of America (trade group)
MCBA: Master Car Builders Association (trade group)
MCC: Mennonite Central Committee (religious denomination)
MCC: Medico-Chirurgical College (Pennsylvania) (higher education)
MCC: Mennonite Church Canada (religious denomination)
MCC: Ministry of Christ Church (cult)
MCCJ: Comboni Missionaries of the Sacred Heart of Jesus, Verona Fathers (religious order)
MCCS: Marine Corps Community Services (military)
MCDB: National Society, Magna Charta Dames and Barons (lineage)
MCE: Medical College of Evansville (higher education)
MCEITS: Marine Corps Enterprise Information Technology Service (military)
MCEN: Marine Corps Enterprise Network (military)
MCER: Massachusetts Central Railroad
MCFA: Michigan Cock Fanciers Association (sports)
MCFW: Medical College of Fort Wayne (higher education)
MCGB: Methodist Church of Great Britain (religious denomination)
MCHS: Mother Cabrini High School (school)
MCI: Medical College of Indiana (higher education)
MCL: Marine Corps League (military)
MCLA: Marine Corps League Auxiliary (military, women)
MCLA: Massachusetts College of Liberal Arts (Massachusetts) (higher education)
MCLR: McLaughlin Line Railroad

MCMS: Middlesex College of Medicine and Surgery (Massachusetts) (higher education)
MCN: Military Counseling Network (military support)
MCO: Massachusetts College of Osteopathy (higher education)
MCOF: Massachusetts Catholic Order of Foresters (mutual benefit)
MCPS: Mechanical Copyright Protection Society (trade group)
MCR: Maine Central (railroad)
MCR: McCloud River Railroad
MCRR: Monongahela Connecting Railroad
MCRR: Michigan Central Railroad
MCRY: Mid Continent Railroad
MCSA: Moscow, Camden and San Augustine Railroad
MCTA: Minnesota Central Railroad
MCUSA: Mennonite Church USA (religious denomination)
MDA: Memorial Day Association (patriotic)
MDA: Music Distributors Association (trade group)
MDA: Missile Defense Agency (governmental)
MDC: Movement for Democratic Change (political)
MDDE: Maryland and Delaware Railroad
MDR: Kansas City Southern Railway (railroad)
MDRA: Motorcycle Drag Racing Association (motorsports)
MDRT: Million Dollar Round Table (trade group)
MDYC: Million Dollar Yeoman Club (mutual benefit)
MDS: Miss Dana's School for Young Ladies (school)
MDS: Meridian Southern Railway (railroad)
MDV: Moldavian Airlines (airline code)
MDW: Minnesota, Dakota and Western Railway (railroad)
ME: Methodist Episcopal (former name of the Methodist Church) (religious denomination)
ME: Morristown & Erie Railway, Inc. (railroad)
MEANA: Malayalee Engineers Association in North America (professional)
MEB: Club Excello (high school fraternity)
MEBA: Marine Engineers Beneficial Association (labor union)
MEC: Maine Central (railroad)
MEC: Methodist Episcopal Church (religious denomination)
MECS: Methodist Episcopal Church, South (religious denomination)
MEDSERVE: Medical Service Corps (Army branch)
MEF: Marine Expeditionary Force (military)
MEFB: Methodist Episcopal Foreign Board (religious)

MENC: The National Association for Music Education (musical)
MENC: Music Educators National Conference (musical)
MENG: Marketing Executives Network Group (professional)
MENSA: (actual name of society; acronym from Latin words meaning Mind, Table, and Month) (other)
MEP: Missions Etrangeres de Paris (Paris Foreign Missions Society) (religious order)
MEP: Midwest Airlines Inc. (airline code)
MERC: Medical Enlisted Reserve Corps (military, World War I)
MERR: Maine Eastern Railroad
MES: Methodist Episcopal Church, South (religious denomination)
MESA: Mining Enforcement and Safety Administration (governmental)
MET: Modesto and Empire Traction (railroad)
MetLife: Metropolitan Life Insurance Company (business)
METRA: Chicago Area Transportation Authority (railroad)
MF: Middle Fork Railroad
MFA: Maritime Fiddlers Association (musical)
MFA: Managed Funds Association (lobby)
MFC: Masonic Fraternal Congress (fraternal)
MFDP: Mississippi Freedom Democratic Party (political party)
MFG: Mission of Full Gospel (religious denomination)
MFH: Master of Foxhounds (sports)
MFHA: Masters of Foxhounds Association (sports)
MG: Machine Gun (military, World War I)
MG: Mobile and Gulf Railroad
MG: Mutual Guild (Masonic)
MGA: Mounted Games Association (equestrian)
MGA: Monongahela Railway (also MRY) (railroad)
MGAA: Mounted Games Across America, Inc. (equestrian)
MGAGB: Mounted Games Association of Great Britain (equestrian)
MGC: Mennonite General Conference (religious denomination)
MGCOTS: Machine Gun Officers' Training School (military, World War I)
MGGS: Mutual Guild of Grand Secretaries (fraternal)
MGR: Myotonic Goat Registry (goats)
MH: Mount Hood Railroad
MH: Malaysia Airline System Berhad (airline code)
MHA: Masonic Hall Association (Masonic)
MHA: Mormon History Association (religious, learned)

MHC: Mountain Home College (Arkansas) (higher education)
MHCO: Marquette and Huron Mountain Railroad
MHL: Medal of Honor Legion (veterans)
MHM: Mount Hope Mineral Railroad
MHMS: Massachusetts Home Missionary Society (religious)
MHMS: Missouri Home Missionary Society (religious)
MHP: Mississippi Highway Patrol (governmental)
MHS: Marine Hospital Service (military, WWI)
MHS: Masonic Historical Society (fraternal – Masonic)
MHT: Manufacturers Hanover Trust Company (bank)
MHWA: Mohawk Adirondack & Northern Railroad Co. (railroad)
MI: Military Intelligence (Army branch)
MI: Missouri-Illinois Railroad
MIA: Messianic Israel Alliance (religious denomination)
MIAFA: My Interests Are For America (Ku Klux Klan)
MIC: Congregation of Marians of the Immaculate Conception (Marian Fathers) (religious order)
MIC: Mississippi Industrial College (higher education)
MIC: Motorcycle Industry Council (trade group)
MiCA: Missionary Church Association (religious)
MICOM: U. S. Army Missile Command (military)
MID: Midway Railroad
MID: Military Information Division (governmental)
MILF: Moro Islamic Liberation Front (guerrilla movement)
MIDH: Middletown and Hummelstown Railroad
MIDL: Midland Railway (railroad)
MIGN: Michigan Northern Railway (railroad)
MII: Mineral Information Institute (trade group)
MILW: Chicago, Milwaukee, St. Paul and Pacific (railroad)
MINE: Minneapolis Eastern Railway (railroad)
MIOB: Magnanimous and Invincible Order of Blackmen (Protestant Irish) (ethnic)
MIR: Minneapolis Industrial Railway (railroad)
MIS: Mississippi Central Railroad
MISS: Mississippian Railway Cooperative (railroad)
MIT: Massachusetts Institute of Technology (Massachusetts) (higher education)
MITA: Musical Instruments Technicians Association (labor union)
MJ: Manufacturers' Junction Railway (railroad)
MJAA: Messianic Jewish Alliance of America (religious denomination)

MJC: Monett Junior College (Missouri) (higher education)
MK: Militant Knights (of the KKK) (KKK)
MK: Maryknoll (religious order)
MKBO: Mystic Knights of the Blue Ox (social, conservation)
MKC: McKeesport Connecting Railroad
MKFL: Modern Knights Fidelity League (mutual benefit)
MKNR: Mackenzie Northern Railroad
MKSP: Modern Knights of St. Paul (youth, religious, inter-denominational)
MKT: Missouri – Kansas – Texas Railroad (also KATY) (railroad)
MKT: Mu Kappa Tau (marketing) (academic honorary)
MKW: Militant Knights and Women (KKK)
ML: Marquette League (religious)
MLA: Masonic Life Association (mutual benefit)
MLA: Modern Language Association (learned)
MLA: Music Library Association (music)
MLA: Medical Library Association (professional)
MLBPA: Major League Baseball Players Association (labor union)
MLCA: Miami Lakes Christian Academy (school)
MLD: Midland Railway Company of Manitoba (railroad)
MLD: Air Moldova (airline code)
MLSPU: Major League Soccer Players Union (labor union)
MLU: Masons' Laborers' Union (labor union)
MM: Molly Maguires (labor union, ethnic)
MM: Catholic Foreign Mission Society of America (Maryknoll) (religious order)
MM: Mothers Mission (women, religious)
MM: Marymount (New York City) (school)
MM: Marymount Manhattan (higher education)
MM: Moral Majority (political/religious)
MM: Maryknoll Sisters – Catholic Foreign Mission Society of America (religious order)
MMA: Methodist Ministers Association (religious)
MMA: Massanutten Military Academy (school)
MMA: General Douglas MacArthur Military Academy (school)
MMA: Marine Military Academy (school)
MMA: Marion Military Academy (school)
MMA: Missouri Military Academy (school)
MMA: Miami Military Academy (school)
MMA: Mennonite Mutual Aid (see also MMAA – Mennonite Mutual Aid Association) (mutual benefit)

MMA: Montreal, Maine and Atlantic Railroad (also MMAC)

MMA: MIDI Manufacturers Association (trade group)

MMAA: Mennonite Mutual Aid Association (also MMA) (mutual benefit)

MMAC: Montreal, Maine and Atlantic Railroad (also MMA)

MM&P: International Organization of Masters, Mates & Pilots (labor union)

MMAS: Messenian Mutual Aid Society (mutual benefit)

MMC: Mount Morris College (Illinois) (higher education)

MMC: Milwaukee Medical College (Wisconsin) (higher education)

MMC: Miami Medical College (Ohio) (higher education)

MMC: Massachusetts Metaphysical College (higher education)

MMC: Maryland Medical College (higher education)

MMC: Metropolitan Medical College (New York) (higher education)

MMC: Michigan Medical College (Michigan) (higher education)

MMC: Mohawk Medical College (New York) (higher education)

MMC: Marine Mammals Commission (governmental)

MMID: Maryland Midland Railway (railroad)

MMLA: Masonic Mutual Life Association (mutual benefit)

MMM: Ossian Everett Mills Music Mission (musical)

MMMU: Fesco Pacific Lines (railroad)

MMRR: Mid-Michigan Railroad

MMS: Methodist Missionary Society (religious)

MMS: Massachusetts Missionary Society (religious)

MMS: Maine Missionary Society (religious)

MMSA: Mill (or Mineral) Mine & Smelters Association (trade group)

MNA: Missouri Northern Arkansas (railroad)

MMBR: M and B Railroad

MNC: Missouri North Central Railroad

MNCR: Metro-North Commuter Railroad (also MNCW)

MNCW: Metro-North Commuter Railroad (also MNCR)

MNJ: Middletown & New Jersey (railroad)

MNLF: Moro National Liberation Front (guerilla organization)

MNN: Minnesota Northern Railroad

MNNR: Minnesota Commercial Railroad

MNO: Military and Naval Order of the United States (lineage)

MNS: Minneapolis, Northfield and Southern Railway (railroad)

MoA: Maids of Athens (sometimes Maids of Athena) (Greek) (ethnic, youth)

MOAA: Military Officer Association of America (military support)

MOC: Military Order of the Cootie (VFW honor designation) (veterans)

MOC: Military Order of the Carabao (military support)

MOC: Military Order of the Crusades (lineage)

MOC: Modern Order of Chaldeans (fraternal, mutual benefit)

MOC: Missouri Central Railroad

MOC: Master Order of Craftsmen (mutual benefit)

MOC: Modern Order of Craftsmen (mutual benefit)

MOD: Missouri Pacific Railroad

MOD: Military Order of the Dragon (military support)

MOFW: Military Order of Foreign Wars (of the United States) (lineage)

MOHG: Ministries Of His Glory (religious denomination)

MoHo: Mount Holyoke College (higher education)

MOLA: Major Orchestra Librarians' Association (music)

MOLLUS: Military Order of the Loyal Legion of the United States (lineage)

MON: Monon Railroad

MOOSE: Loyal Order of the Moose (see LOM and LOOM) (fraternal)

MOP: Missionaries of the Poor (religious order)

MOP: Modern Order of the Praetorians (mutual benefit)

MOPH: Military Order of the Purple Heart (veterans)

MORC: Medical Officers' Reserve Corps (military, World War I)

MOS: Mechanical Order of the Sun (mutual benefit)

MOS: Military Order of the Serpent (veterans, Spanish-American War, fraternal)

MOSB: Military Order of the Stars and Bars (also MOS&B) (lineage)

MOS&B: (see MOSB – Military Order of the Stars and Bars) (lineage)

MOSC: Military Officers' Spouses Club (military support)

MOT: Marine Oil Transport (railroad)

MOTC: Medical Officers' Training Camp (military, World War I)

MOVPER: Mystic Order of Veiled Prophets of the Enchanted (sometimes Mystic) Realm (a/k/a Grotto) (fraternal, Masonic, charitable)

MOWC: Military Officers' Wives Club (military support)

MOWW: Military Order of the World Wars (lineage)

MOXV: Moxahala Valley Railway (railroad)
MP: Military Police (Army branch)
MP: Missouri Pacific (railroad)
MPA: Miner's Protective Association (business union)
MPA: Modern Pentathlon Association (sports)
MPA: Music Publishers Association (trade group)
MPA: Master Plumbers' Association (labor union)
MPA: Maryland & Pennsylvania (railroad)
MPA: Meeting Professionals International (professional)
MPAA: Motion Picture Association of America (trade group)
MPC: Methodist Protestant Church (religious denomination)
MPE: Mu Phi Epsilon (music) (academic honorary)
MPHA: Mountain Pleasure Horse Association (equine)
MPIT: Missouri Pacific Railroad
MPLA: Popular Movement for the Liberation of Angola
(political)
MPLI: Minnesota Prairie Line (railroad)
MPLZ: Missouri Pacific Railroad
MPMO: (see MPMOU – Motion Picture Machine Operators'
Union) (labor union)
MPMOU: Motion Picture Machine Operators' Union (also
MPMO) (labor union)
MPPM: Missouri Paw Paw Militia (military, Civil War)
MPSA: Midwest Political Science Association (professional)
MPT: Master Piano Technicians (trade group)
MPTA: Minnesota Public Television Association (trade group)
MPU: Missouri Pacific Railroad
MPZ: Missouri Pacific Railroad
MQT: Marquette Rail (railroad)
MR: McCloud River Railroad (also McLeod Railway) (railroad)
MR: Modern Romans (mutual benefit)
MR-A: Moral Re-Armament (political)
MRA: Men's Rights Agency (political)
MRA: Royal Arcanum (fraternal)
MRA: Masonic Relief Association (Masonic, mutual benefit)
MRA: Marketing Research Association (trade group)
MRFF: Military Religious Freedom Foundation (military
support)
MRHS: Midland Railway (railroad)
MRI: Mohall Railroad
MRL: Montana Rail Link (railroad)
MRP: Marijuana Reform Party (political party)

MRPA: Modification and Replacement Parts Association (trade group)

MRR: Mid Atlantic Railroad

MRS: Manufacturers Railway (railroad)

MRTA: Tupac Araru Revolutionary Movement (guerilla group)

MRY: Monongahela Railway (also MGA) (railroad)

MS: Missionaries of our Lady of LaSalette (religious order)

MS: Modern Samaritans (mutual benefit)

MS: Mystical Seven (college fraternity)

MS: Mystic Star (see also OMS: Order of the Mystic Star) (fraternal)

MS: Michigan Shore Railroad

MS: EgyptAir (airline code)

MSA: Masonic Service Association (Masonic, charitable)

MSA: Mutual Security Agency (governmental)

MSA: Mineralogical Society of America (learned)

MSA: Mycological Society of America (learned)

MSACS: Middle States Association of Colleges and Schools (education)

MSBA: Merino Sheep Breeders Association (trade, Vermont)

MSBF: Mountain States Baptist Fellowship (religious denomination)

MSBT: Missionary Cenacle Family (also ST) (religious order)

MSBT: Missionary Servants of the Most Blessed Trinity – Missionary Servants of the Most Holy Trinity (also MSSST) (religious order)

MSC: Missionary Society of Connecticut (religious)

MSC: Missionaries of the Sacred Heart (religious order)

MSC: Daughters of Our Lady of the Sacred Heart (religious order)

MSC: Mount Senario College (Wisconsin) (higher education)

MSC: Mississippi Central (railroad)

MSC: Medical Specialist Corps (Army branch)

MSC-D: Massachusetts State College, Devens (higher education)

MSCAS: Middle States Council for the Social Studies (education)

MSE: Mississippi Export (railroad)

MSF: Medicins Sans Frontiers (Doctors Without Borders) (humanitarian)

MSFS: Missionaries of St. Francis de Sales (Fransalians) (religious order)

MSI: Military Service Institution of the United States (military support)

MSIC: Missionary Sisters of the Immaculate Conception (religious order)

MSHA: Mine Safety and Health Administration (governmental)

MSL: Montgomery Short Line (railroad)

MSLC: Minnesota Short Lines (railroad)

MSM: Medical School of Maine (higher education)

MSM: Missouri State Militia (military, Civil War)

MSMC: Marion Sims-Beaumont Medical College (Missouri) (higher education)

MSMV: Medical Society of the Missouri Valley (professional)

MSN: Meeker Southern Railroad

MSO: Michigan Southern Railroad

MSOLA: Missionary Sisters of Our Lady of Africa (religious order)

MSR: Mu Sigma Rho (statistics) (honorary fraternity)

MSR: Egyptair (airline code)

MSRC: MidSouth Railcorp (railroad)

MSRW: Mississippian Railway Cooperative (railroad)

MSS: Medical Student Section (professional, student)

MSSA: Mid-South Sociological Association (professional)

MSSCC: Missionaries of the Sacred Hearts of Jesus and Mary (religious order)

MSSST: Missionary Servants of the Most Holy Trinity (also MSBT) (religious order)

MSTL: Minneapolis & St. Louis (railroad)

MSTR: Massena Terminal Railroad Co. (railroad)

MSTU: Middle Tennessee State University (higher education)

MSU: Morehead State University (higher education)

MSU: Montclair State University (higher education)

MSV: Mississippi and Skuna Valley Railroad

MSWY: Minnesota Southern Railway (railroad)

MT: Mississippi and Tennessee Railnet (railroad)

MTA: Mosaic Templars of America (fraternal, ethnic)

MTA: Metropolitan Transit Authority (most frequently associated with Boston, MA)

MTAC: Music Teachers Association of California (labor union)

MTC: Military Training Camp (military, World War I)

MTC: Miner Teachers College (District of Columbia) (higher education)

MTCC: Mosaic Templars Cultural Center (fraternal)

MTFR: Minnesota Transfer Railway (railroad)

MTMS: Median Temple of the Mystic Shrine (Masonic)

MTNA: Music Teachers National Association (music)

MTO: Mediterranean Theater of Operations (military)

MTP: Minnesota Territorial Pioneers (lineage)

MTR: Montour Railroad

MTRA: Money Transmitter Regulators Association (trade group)

MTV: Music Television (company)

MTW: Mannette, Tomahawk and Western Railroad

MU: Mailers' Union (labor union)

MUNA: Manchester Unity of North America (Also MUofNA) (IOOF, British)

MUofNA: (see MUNA) – Manchester Unity of North America (IOOF, British)

MUTA: Mechanics Union Trade Association (labor union)

MUUSA: Mothers' Union USA (religious)

MV: Midland Valley Railroad

MVA: Mexican Veterans Association (veterans, now lineage)

MVA: Masonic Veterans Association (Masonic)

MVCC: Mohawk Valley Community College (New York) (higher education)

MVDF: Verbum Dei Missionary Fraternity (religious order)

MVLA: Mount Vernon Ladies' Association (women, historical)

MVP: Missouri and Valley Park Railroad

MVRY: Mahoning Valley Railway (railroad)

MWA: Modern Woodmen of America (fraternal, mutual benefit)

MWAF: Modern Woodmen of American Foresters (mutual benefit)

MWB: Ministries Without Borders (religious denomination)

MWC: Montana Wesleyan College (Montana) (higher education)

MWC: Missouri Wesleyan College (higher education)

MWCX: MidWest Car Company (railroad car lessors)

MWF: Modern Woodmen Foresters (see also MWFA – Modern Woodmen Foresters of America) (fraternal, mutual benefit)

MWFA: Modern Woodmen Foresters of America (see also MWF – Modern Woodmen Foresters) (fraternal, mutual benefit)

MWK: Militant White Knights (KKK)

MWMC: Markham-Waterloo Mennonite Conference (religious denomination)

MWP: Modern Whig Party (political party)

MWR: Muncie and Western Railroad

MWRC: Mount Washington Railway (railroad)

MWRL: Molalla Western Railroad
MWRR: Montana Western Railway (railroad)
MWRX: Midwest Rail (railroad)
MWW: Modern Woodmen of the World (mutual benefit)
MWW: Mystic Workers of the World (fraternal, mutual benefit)
MYF: Methodist Youth Fellowship (religious)

N

N: Nullifier (political party)

N&W: Norfolk & Western (also NW) (railroad)

NA: Naval Aviation (military, World War I)

NA: Naval Air (military, World War II and later)

NAA: National Aeronautic Association (trade group)

NAA: Newspaper Association of America (trade group)

NAA: National Algae Association (trade group)

NAA: National Apartment Association (trade group)

NAA: National Auctioneers Association (trade group)

NAAA: National Academic Advising Association (education, professional)

NAAB: National Architectural Accrediting Board (education)

NAAC: National Accreditation and Assessment Council (education)

NAAC: National Albanian American Council (lobby)

NAACLS: National Accrediting Agency for Clinical Laboratory Sciences (accrediting)

NAACP: National Association for the Advancement of Colored People (political)

NAAEE: North American Association of Environmental Education (professional)

NAAHL: National Association of Affordable Housing Lenders (trade group)

NAASE: North American Association of Synagogue Executives (religious, professional)

NAASE: North American Association of Sports Economists (professional)

NAB: National Association of Broadcasters (trade group)

NABA: North American Benefit Association (mutual benefit)

NABA: National Association of Black Accountants (professional)

NABC: North American Baptist Conference (religious denomination)

NABCJ: National Association of Blacks in Criminal Justice (professional)

NABF: North American Baptist Fellowship (religious denomination)

NABGG: National Association of Black Geologists and Geophysicists (professional)

Nabisco: National Biscuit Company (noted as the first business in the US to trademark a shortened form of its name – 1901) (business)

NABJ: National Association of Black Journalists (professional)

NABO: North American Basque Organizations (umbrella organization)

NABT: National Association of Biology Teachers (professional)

NABV: National Association for Black Veterans (veterans)

NAC: New Apostolic Church (religious denomination)

NAC: Northwest Accreditation Commission (education)

NAC: National Association of Counties (trade group)

NACA: National Association for Campus Activities (education)

NACA: National Advisory Committee for Aeronautics (governmental)

NACAA: National Association of Clean Air Agencies (umbrella organization)

NACB: National Association of College Broadcasters (trade group)

NACC: National Association of Catholic Chaplains (religious)

NACCC: National Association of Congregational Christian Churches (religious denomination)

NACCD: National Advisory Commission on Civil Disorders (Kerner Commission) (governmental)

NACCHO: National Association of County and City Health Officials (professional)

NACCS: National Association of Chicana and Chicano Studies (education)

NACF: National Association of Catholic Families (religious)

NACFLM: National Association of Catholic Families Life Ministers (religious)

NACHA: North American Clearing House Association (trade group)

NACM: National Association of Credit Management (trade group)

NACP: National Association of Church Personnel (religious)

NACR: Nashville and Ashland City Railroad

NACS: North American Caspian Society (equine)

NACS: Nordic Association for China Studies (learned)

NACS: National Association of Convenience Stores (trade group)

NACST: National Association of Catholic School Teachers (labor union)

NACWC: National Association of Colored Women's Clubs (civic)

NADA: National Automobile Dealers Association (trade group)

NADD: National Association of Diaconate Directors (religious)

NADO: National Association of Development Organizations (advocacy)

NAE: National Association of Evangelicals (religious)

NAEA: National Art Education Association (education)

NAEA: National Association of Enrolled Agents (professional)

NAECC: National Associate of Episcopal Christian Communities (religious)

NAED: National Association of Electrical Distributors (trade group)

NAEM: National Association for Environmental Health Management (professional)

NAEP: National Association of Environmental Professionals (professional)

NAES: National Association of Episcopal Schools (education, religious)

NAEYC: National Association for the Education of Young Children (education)

NAF: National Abortion Federation (political)

NAF: National Amputation Foundation, Inc. (self-help)

NAFCU: National Association of Federal Credit Unions (trade group)

NAFS: National Association of Fraternal Societies (umbrella organization)

NAFTY: North American Federation of Temple Youth (religious, youth)

NAFWB: National Association of Free Will Baptists (religious denomination)

NAG: National Association of Grocers (trade group)

NAGA: National Altar Guild Association (religious)

NAGARA: National Association of Government Archives and Records Administrators (professional)

NAGC: National Asian Greek Council (umbrella organization)

NAGC: National Association of Government Contractors (trade group)

NAGE: National Association of Government Employees (labor union)

NAGR: National Association for Gun Rights (lobby)

NAH: National Association of Haymakers (mutual benefit)

NAHB: National Association of Home Builders (trade group)

NAHC: National Association of Holiness Churches (religious denomination)

NAHDSA: National Association of Hebrew Day School Administrators (religious, education)

NAHRO: National Association of Housing and Redevelopment Officials (professional)

NAHS: National Art Honor Society (academic honorary)

NAHU: National Association of Health Underwriters (trade group)

NAIC: North American Interfraternity Conference (umbrella organization)

NAIC: National Association of Insurance Commissioners (professional)

NAIP: New American Independent Party (political party)

NAIS: National Association of Independent Schools (education)

NAIS: Northwest Association of Independent Schools (education)

NAJAKS: Nordic Association for Japanese and Korean Studies (learned)

NAJL: National Association of Jewish Legislators (religious, political)

NAJSA: North American Jewish Students Appeal (religious, youth)

NAKCS: North American Kerry Cattle Association (cattle)

NALC: National Association of Letter Carriers (labor union)

NALCO: National Aluminate Corporation (company)

NALEAO: National Association of Latino Elected and Appointed Officials (professional)

NALFO: National Association of Latino Fraternal Organizations (umbrella organization)

NALM: National Association for Lay Ministry (religious)

NALRA: North American Lincoln Red Association (cattle)

NAM: National Academy of Music (civic)

NAM: National Association of Manufacturers (trade group)

NAMA: North American Manx Association (lineage)

NAMA: National Agri-Marketing Association (trade group)

NAMA: National Automatic Merchandising Association (trade group)

NAMAD: National Association of Minority Auto Dealers (trade group)

NAMB: National Association of Mortgage Brokers (trade group)

NAME: National Association for Music Education (music)

NAME: National Association of Medical Examiners (professional)

NAMI: National Alliance on Mental Illness (community)

NAMIC: National Association of Mutual Insurance Companies (trade group)

NAMM: National Association of Music Merchants (trade group)

NAMPA: North American Meat Processors Association (trade group)

NAMSS: National Association (for) Medical Staff Services (professional)

NANBPWC: National Association of Negro Business and Professional Women's Clubs (civic)

NANV: National Association of Naval Veterans (veterans)

NAOH: National Ancient Order of Hibernians (religious, fraternal, mutual benefit)

NAON: National Association of Orthopedic Nurses (professional)

NAP: New Alliance Party (political party)

NAP: Narragansett Pier Railroad

NAPA: National Asian Pacific Islander American Panhellenic Association (umbrella organization)

NAPCIS: National Association of Private Catholic and Independent Schools (religious, education)

NAPHIA: North American Pet Health Insurance Association (trade group)

NAPHP: National Association for Public Health Policy (professional)

NAPM: National Association of Pastoral Musicians (professional, musical)

NAPM: National Association of Presort Mailers (trade group)

NAPO: National Association of Police Organizations (lobby)

NAPO: National Association of Professional Organizers (trade group)

NAPR: National Association of Physician Recruiters (professional)

NAPW: National Association of Professional Women (professional)

NAR: Northern Alberta Railway (railroad)

NAR: National Association of Realtors (trade group)

NARA: National Archives and Records Administration (governmental)

NARAL: National Abortion Rights League (lobby)

NARAS: National Academy of Recording Arts and Sciences (professional)

NARC: National Association of Regional Councils (umbrella organization)

NARC: National Advertising Review Council (trade group)

NARF: Native American Rights Fund (political)

NARHA: North American Riding for the Handicapped Association (equestrian)

NARM: National Association of Recording Merchandisers (trade group)

NARUC: National Association of Regulatory Utility Commissioners (advocacy)

NAS: National Academy of Sciences (learned)

NAS: National Audubon Society (nature)

NASA: National Aeronautics and Space Administration (governmental)

NASA: North American Swiss Alliance (fraternal, mutual benefit)

NASA: Norwegian American Seamen's Association (labor union, mutual benefit)

NASA: National Auto Sport Association (motorsports)

NASA: Nordic Association for South Asian Studies (learned)

NASAD: National Association of Schools of Art and Design (education)

NASAP: North American Society of Adlerian Psychology (professional)

NASC: National Association of Sports Commissioners (professional)

NASCAR: National Association for Stock Car Auto Racing (business)

NASD: National Association of Securities Dealers (trade group)

NASDAQ: National Association of Security Dealers and Automated Quotation (trade group)

NASE: National Association of Stationary Engineers (labor union)

NASE: National Association for the Self-Employed (trade group)

NASED: National Association of State Election Directors (professional)

NASF: North American Sports Federation (sports)

NASFT: National Association for the Specialty Food Trade (trade group)
NASHP: National Academy for State Health Policy (research)
NASLIN: North American Sport Library Network (umbrella organization)
NASM: National Association of Schools of Music (education)
NASPD: National Association of State Park Directors (professional)
NASS: North American Spine Society (professional)
NASSC: National Association of Sewer Service Companies (trade group)
NASSH: North American Society for Sports History (learned)
NASW: National Association of Social Workers (professional)
NATA: National Association of Temple Administrators (religious, professional)
NATA: National Air Transportation Association (trade group)
NATB: National Association of Tunnerbunds (German, mutual benefit)
NATCA: National Air Traffic Controllers Association (labor union)
NATD: National Army Training Detachment (military, World War I)
NATO: North American Treaty Organization (military)
NATO: National Association of Theatre Owners (trade group)
NATOA: National Association of Telecommunications Officers and Advisors (trade group)
NATP: National Association of Tax Professionals (professional)
NATS: National Association of Teachers of Singing (musical)
NATSA: North American Taiwan Studies Association (learned)
NATSO: National Association of Truck Stop Owners (trade group)
NAU: North American Union (mutual benefit)
NAUG: Naugatuck Railroad Company (railroad)
NAVAIR: Naval Air Systems Command (military)
NAVCENT: Naval Forces Central Command (military)
NAW: New Age Workers (Russian) (worker training)
NAW: National Association of Wholesalers-Distributors (trade group)
NAWBO: National Association of Women Business Owners (interest)
NAWG: National Association of Wheat Growers (trade group)
NAWSA: National American Woman Suffrage Association (political)

NAYO: National Association of Youth Orchestras (musical)
NB: Northampton and Bath Railroad
NBA: National Bar Association (professional)
NBA: National Basketball Association (sports)
NBA: National Bankers Association (trade group)
NBB: National Biodiesel Board (trade group)
NBC: Needle and Bobbin Club (social)
NBC: Northern Baptist Convention (religious denomination)
NBC: National Broadcasting Company (business)
NBC: National Beta Club (academic honorary)
NBC: National Brotherhood of Consumers (mutual benefit)
NBCA: National Baptist Convention of America (religious denomination)
NBCC: National Black Catholic Congress (religious)
NBCC: National Black Chamber of Commerce (civic)
NBCC: National Board of Certified Counselors (professional)
NBCL: National Birth Control League (civic)
NBCUSA: National Baptist Convention of the USA (religious denomination)
NBEA: National Business Education Association (trade group)
NBEC: New Brunswick East Coast Railway (railroad)
NBER: National Bureau for Economic Research (scholarly)
NBER: Nittany and Bald Eagle Railroad
NBF: New Battlefront Foundation (military support)
NBFA: National Black Farmers Association (trade group)
NBLSA: National Black Law Students Association (student)
NBMBAA: National Black MBA Association (student)
NBNA: National Black Nurses Association (professional)
NBNR: Nicolet Badger Northern Railroad
NBPA: National Basketball Players Association (labor union)
NBPA: National Black Police Association (law enforcement)
NBR: Northern & Bergen Railroad
NBS: National Benefit Society (mutual benefit)
NBS: National Benevolent Society (mutual benefit)
NBSR: New Brunswick Southern Railway (railroad)
NBTC: National Building Trades Council (trade group)
NBWA: National Beer Wholesalers Association (trade group)
NC: Nestorian Church (religious denomination)
NC: Nashville and Chattanooga Railroad
NCA: National Christian Association (religious, political)
NCA: National Cemetery Administration (governmental)
NCA: Nankin Club of America (poultry)
NCA: National Communication Association (professional)

NCA: National Coffee Association (trade group)
NCA: National Confectioners Association (trade group)
NCA: North Central Association of Colleges and Schools (education, accrediting)
NCA&T: North Carolina A&T State University (higher education)
NCAA: National Collegiate Athletic Association (sports)
NCAAA: National Commission for Academic Accreditation and Assessment (education)
NCAC: National Council of Acoustical Consultants (trade group)
NCACE: National Council on Accreditation of Coaching Education (education)
NCACS: North Central Association of Colleges and Schools (education)
NCADD: National Council on Alcoholism and Drug Dependence, Inc. (political)
NCAI: National Congress of American Indians (political)
NCAN: National Coalition of American Nuns (political/religious)
NCATE: National Council for Accreditation of Teacher Education (education)
NCBA: National Cattlemen's Beef Association (trade group)
NCBE: National Centre for Business Education (business)
NCBL: National Conference of Black Lawyers (professional)
NCC: Nebraska Central College (Nebraska) (higher education)
NCC: National Chicken Council (trade group)
NCCB: National Conference of Catholic Bishops (religious)
NCCC: New Christian Crusade Church (cult)
NCCC: National Council of Congregational Churches (religious)
NCCC: National Catholic Cemetery Conference (religious)
NCCC: National Council of Churches of Christ (in the US) (religious)
NCCHM: National Catholic Council for Hispanic Ministry (religious)
NCCL: National Conference for Catechetical Leaders (religious)
NCCRE: National Council Committee on Religious Education (Congregational) (religious)
NCCU: Northwest Commission on Colleges and Universities (education)
NCD: National Council on Disability (governmental)

NCEA: National Catholic Education Association (religious, education)

NCEM: National Centre for Early Music (music)

NCER: National Council on Educational Research (governmental)

NCES: National Compensating Emancipation Society (religious)

NCGA: National Cooperative Grocers Association (trade group)

NCGE: National Council for Geographic Education (education)

NCGS: National Coalition of Girls Schools (education)

NCHA: National Cutting Horse Association (equestrian)

NCHV: National Coalition for Homeless Veterans (veterans)

NCI: National Cancer Institute (governmental)

NCIP: National Commission for Employment Policy (governmental)

NCIR: New Castle Industrial Railroad

NCIS: Naval Criminal Investigative Service (military)

NCIS: National Cannabis Industry Association (trade group)

NCJW: National Council of Jewish Women (religious, civic)

NCL: National Civic League (civic)

NCL: National Consumers League (civic)

NCLC: National Child Labor Committee (civic)

NCM: National Congress of Mothers (civic – antecedent of P-TA)

NCM: Nazarene Compassionate Ministries (religious denomination)

NCMY: National Council of Methodist Youth (political, 1930s; religious)

NCOA: Non-Commissioned Officers Association (military)

NCOFG: National Christian Order of Frederick the Great (WWII, Nazi-Masonic)

NCOK: North Central Oklahoma Railway (railroad)

NCPC: National Capitol Planning Commission (governmental)

NCPOA: National Chief Petty Officers' Association (military support)

NCPSA: National Council for Private School Accreditation (education)

NCPSSM: National Committee to Preserve Social Security and Medicare (lobby)

NCPT: National Congress of Parents and Teachers (P-TA antecedent)

NCQDIS: National Coalition for Quality Diagnostic Imaging Services (trade group)
NCR: National Cash Register (company)
NCRA: National Court Reporters Association (professional)
NCRC: Nebraska Central Railroad
NCRC: Nantucket Central Railroad Company (railroad)
NCRPM: National Council on Radiation Protection and Measurement (professional)
NCRR: North Carolina Railroad
NCRR: Niles Canyon Railway (railroad)
NCRY: Northern Central Railway (railroad)
NCS: National Cymmrodorion Society (Welch language and culture)
NCS: National Croatian Society (mutual benefit)
NCSA: National Christian Science Association (religious denomination, cult)
NCSF: National Catholic Society of Foresters (fraternal, religious, mutual benefit)
NCSG: National Chimney Sweep Guild (trade group)
NCSJ: National Conference on Soviet Jewry (political, religious)
NCSP: National Conference of State Parks (professional)
NCSS: National Council for the Social Studies (education)
NCSU: North Carolina State University (higher education)
NCSY: National Conference of Synagogue Youth (religious, youth)
NCTA: National Cable & Telecommunications Association (trade group)
NCTA: National Christmas Tree Association (trade group)
NCTE: National Council of Teachers of English (professional)
NCUA: National Credit Union Administration (governmental)
NCVA: North Carolina and Virginia Railroad
NCWA: National Council of Women of Australia (women)
NCYR: Nash County Railroad
ND: National Defenders (charitable, mutual benefit)
ND: Notre Dame Sisters (religious order)
NDA: National Dental Association (professional)
NDGW: Native Daughters of the Golden West (lineage)
NDIA: National Defense Industrial Association (trade group)
NDIC: National Drug Intelligence Center (governmental)
NDMB: National Defense Mediation Board (governmental)
NDP: National Democratic Party (a/k/a Gold Democrats) (political party)
NDRC: National Defense Research Committee (governmental)

NDU: National Defense University (governmental)

NEA: National Education Association (education)

NEA: New Era Association (mutual benefit)

NEA: National Endowment for the Arts (governmental)

NEAAS: New England Conference of the Association for Asian Studies (learned)

NEAC: National Episcopal AIDS Coalition (religious, civic)

NEASC: New England Association of Schools and Colleges (education)

NEASC-CIHE: NEASC Commission on Institutions of Higher Education (education, accrediting)

NEASC-CTCI: NEASC Commission on Technical and Career Institutions (education, accrediting)

NEBB: National Environmental Balancing Bureau (professional)

NEC: National Economic Council (governmental)

NECA: Network of Episcopal Clergy Organizations (religious, umbrella organization)

NECA: National Electrical Contractors Association (trade group)

NECA: National Exchange Carrier Association (trade group)

Necco: New England Confectionery Company (business)

NECR: New England Central Railroad

NEDCC: Northeast Document Conservation Center (history)

NEEBF: New England Evangelical Baptist Fellowship (religious denomination)

NECR: New England Central Railroad

NED: National Endowment for Democracy (political)

NEDA: National Electronics Distributors Association (trade group)

NEEF: National Environmental Education Foundation (political)

NEFMC: New England Fat Men's Club (social)

NEGS: New England Southern Railroad

NEH: National Endowment for the Humanities (governmental)

NEHA: National Episcopal Historians and Archivists (religious)

NEHA: New England Historical Association (learned)

NEHGS: New England Historic Genealogical Society (academic)

NEHM: National Episcopal Health Ministries (religious)

NEHS: National Elementary Honor Society (academic honorary)

NEHS: National English Honor Society (academic honorary)

NEHTA: New England History Teachers' Association (professional)

NEI: Nuclear Energy Institute (trade group)

NELA: National Electric Light Association (trade group)

NELPS: New England Loyal Publications Society (Civil War, patriotic)

NEMA: New England Museum Association (trade group)

NEMA: National Electrical Manufacturers Association (trade group)

NEMSA: National Emergency Medical Services Association (labor union)

NENE: Nebraska Northeastern Railway (railroad)

NEOP: New England Order of Protection (mutual benefit)

NEPA: New England Parks Association (professional)

NEProvRegt: New England Provisional Regiment (military, World War I)

NERR: Nashville and Eastern Railroad

NERR: New England Railroad

NES: New England Society (lineage)

NESA: National Episcopal Scouters Association (religious)

NEW: New England Women (lineage)

NEZP: Nez Perce Railroad

NF: National Fraternity (mutual benefit)

NFA: National Flute Association (musical)

NFA: National Futures Association (trade group)

NFAA: National First Aid Association (youth, civic)

NFB: National Federation of the Blind (interest group)

NFC: National Federated Craft (fraternal – Masonic)

NFCA: National Fraternal Council (or Congress) of America (umbrella organization)

NFCYM: National Federation for Catholic Youth Ministry (religious)

NFD: Norfolk, Franklin and Danville Railroad

NFF: New Foundation Fellowship (religious denomination)

NFI: National Fisheries Institute (trade group)

NFIB: National Federation of Independent Business (lobby)

NFIP: National Flood Insurance Program (governmental)

NFIU: National Federation of Independent Unions (labor union)

NFL: National Football League (sports)

NFL: National Fraternal League (mutual benefit)

NFL: Nationwide Festival of Light (political/religious)

NFL: National Forensic League (academic honorary)

NFLPA: National Football League Players Association (labor union)
NFPA: National Fire Protection Association (trade group)
NFPA: National Fluid Power Association (trade group)
NFPC: National Federation of Priests' Councils (religious)
NFPF: National Film Preservation Foundation (history)
NFRC: National Fathers' Resource Center (political)
NFRFA: National Frozen & Refrigerated Foods Association (trade group)
NFRO: National First Responders Association (professional)
NFSD: National Fraternal Society of (for) the Deaf (mutual benefit)
NFTB: National Federation of Temple Brotherhoods (religious)
NFU: National Farmers Union (labor union)
NFU: National Fraternal Union (mutual benefit)
NG: National Guard (military)
NG: National Grange (see OPH) (fraternal)
NGA: National Guard Association of the United States (military support)
NGA: Needlework Guild of America (labor union)
NGA: National Glass Association (trade group)
NGAUS: National Guard Association of the US (see NGA) (military support)
NGCAE: National Guild for Community Arts Organizations (umbrella organization)
NGDA: National Grain Dealers Association (trade group)
NGS: National Genealogical Society (hobby)
NGSNY: National Guard of the State of New York (military)
NGWA: National Ground Water Association (professional)
NH: New York, New Haven & Hartford (railroad)
NH: All Nippon Airways (airline code)
NHA: National Holiness Association (religious denomination)
NHA: National Haymakers Association, Patrons of Husbandry (fraternal)
NHA: National Hay Association (trade group)
NHA: National Hockey Association (sports)
NHA: National Healthcareer Association (professional)
NHA: Nutritional Health Alliance (lobby)
NHA: National Hydrogen Association (trade group)
NHA: National Hydropower Association (trade group)
NHA: Naval Helicopter Association (military support)
NH&W: New River, Holston and Western Railroad
NHBC: National Honorary Beta Club (academic honorary)

NHBCA: New Hampshire Breeders Club of America (poultry)
NHCR: New Hampshire Central Railroad
NHD: Naval History Division (military)
NHDSC: National Hot Dog and Sausage Council (trade group)
NHEA: National Household Economics Association (civic)
NHG: National Horse Guards (paramilitary)
NHG: National Home Guard (mutual benefit)
NHIC: National Health Information Center (governmental)
NHJBC: National Honorary Junior Beta Club (academic honorary)
NHL: National Hockey League (sports)
NHLPA: National Hockey League Players Association (labor union)
NHMS: New Hampshire Missionary Society (religious)
NHMS: National Holiness Missionary Society (religious denomination)
NHRA: National Hot Rod Association (motorsports)
NHRR: New Hope and Ivyland (railroad)
NHS: National Honor Society (academic honorary)
NHS: National Huguenot Society (lineage)
NHSDA: National Honor Society for Dance Arts (academic honorary)
NHTSA: National Highway Traffic Safety Administration (governmental)
NHVT: New Hampshire and Vermont Railroad
NIA: National Infantry Association (military)
NIA: National Insurance Association (professional)
NIAJ: Niagara Junction Railway (railroad)
NIBS: Northwest Indian Bible School (school)
NIBS: Network of International Business Schools (education)
NIBS: National Institute of Building Sciences (professional)
NIC: National Interfraternity Conference (umbrella organization)
NIC: National Inventors Council (governmental)
NICD: South Shore Line (railroad)
NICUFO: National Investigations Committee on UFOs (uncategorized)
NIGP: National Institute of Government Purchasing (professional)
NIH: National Institutes of Health (governmental)
NIMH: National Institute of Mental Health (governmental)
NISP: National Institute of Sports Professionals (sports)
NISR: National Institute for Sports Reform (sports)

NISO: National Information Standards Organization (standards)
NIST: National Institute of Standards and Technology (governmental)
NIU: National Intelligence University (governmental)
NIWP: Nationalism and Identity for White People (KKK)
NJ: Niagara Junction (railroad)
NJCLF: National Jewish Children's Leukemia Fund (religious, civic)
NJCRAC: National Jewish Community Relations Advisory Council (religious, political)
NJCS: National Jewish Committee on Scouting (religious, youth)
NJDC: National Jewish Democratic Council (lobby)
NJDOT: New Jersey Transit (railroad)
NJGC: National Jersey Giant Club (poultry)
NJGSC: National Jewish Girl Scout Committee (religious, youth)
NJHS: National Junior Honor Society (academic honorary)
NJII: New Jersey, Indiana and Illinois (railroad)
NJT: New Jersey Transit Rail Operations, Inc. (railroad)
NJTR: New Jersey Transit (railroad)
NK: National Knights (KKK)
NKBA: National Kitchen & Bath Association (trade group)
NKCR: Nebraska, Kansas and Colorado Railnet (railroad)
NKF: National Kidney Foundation (professional)
NKP: New York, Chicago and St. Louis (railroad)
NL: National League (sports)
NL: Navy League (also USNL) (military)
NL: Navy Liberty (military support)
NLA: National Liberation Army (guerilla organization)
NLC: News and Letters Committees (political)
NLC: New Life Churches (religious denomination)
NLC: National Lanshan Club (poultry)
NLF: National Liberation Front (guerilla organization)
NLFA: New Life Fellowship Association (religious denomination)
NLG: North Louisiana and Gulf (railroad)
NLGR: National League for Good Roads (civic, cyclists)
NLH: Northwestern Legion of Honor (mutual benefit)
NLM: National League of Musicians (labor union)
NLM: National Library of Medicine (archival)
NLMC: National League of Masonic Clubs (Masonic)

NLN: National League for Nursing (education)
NLP: Natural Law Party (political party)
NLPCW: National League for the Protection of Colored Women (civic)
NLR: Northern Lines (railroad)
NLRB: National Labor Relations Board (governmental)
NLU: National Labor Union (labor union)
NMA: National Medical Association (professional)
NMA: National Meat Association (trade group)
NMA: National Mining Association (trade group)
NMB: National Mutual Benefit (mutual benefit)
NMBCA: National Missionary Baptist Convention of America (religious denomination)
NMD: National Ministries Division of the Presbyterian Church (religious)
NMDA: National Miniature Donkey Association (livestock)
NMEA: National Marine Educators Association (professional)
NMFA: National Military Family Association (military support)
NMFS: National Marine Fisheries Service (governmental)
NMFTA: National Motor Freight Traffic Association (trade group)
NMGR: New Mexico Gateway (railroad)
NMH: Northfield Mount Hermon (school)
NML: National Municipal League (civic)
NMMA: New Mexico Military Academy (school)
NMOR: Northern Missouri (railroad)
NMPA: National Music Publishers Association (trade group)
NMRA: National Model Railroads Association (hobby)
NMS: Ancient Order, Nobles of the Mystic Shrine (fraternal)
NMSU: New Mexico State University (higher education)
NMTA: National Money Transmitters Association (trade group)
NMU: National Maritime Union (labor union)
NMU: National Medical University (higher education)
NMWMA: National Mary Washington Memorial Association (civic, historic preservation)
NN: Nevada Northern (railroad)
NNBA: National Negro Bar Association (professional)
NNBL: National Negro Business League (professional)
NNFA: National Nutritional Foods Association (trade group)
NNN: Newspaper National Network (trade group)
NNOA: National Naval Officers' Association (military support)
NNOC: National Nurses Organizing Committee (labor union)

NNPA: National Newspaper Publishers Association (trade group)

NNPCW: National Network of Presbyterian College Women (religious)

NNSX: Newport News Shipbuilding & Dry Dock Company (railroad)

NNV: National Naval Volunteers (military, World War I)

NNW: Nebraska Northwestern (railroad)

NOA: National Order of America (mutual benefit, fraudulent)

NOA: National Opera Association (musical)

NOAA: National Oceanic and Atmospheric Administration (governmental)

NOAC: National Organization of Alley Cats (fraternal)

NOBG: National Order of the Blue and Gray (lineage)

NOBWLE: National Organization of Black Women in Law Enforcement (law enforcement)

NOCR: National Order of Cowboy Rangers (fraternal, mutual benefit)

NODOI: National Order of the Daughters of Isabella (religious)

NOEL: National Organization of Episcopalians for Life (religious)

NOFJ: New Orange Four Junction (railroad)

NOGC: New Orleans and Gulf Coast (railroad)

NOHA: Northern Ontario Hockey Association (sports)

NOK: New Order (of) Knights (of the Ku Klux Klan)

NOKL: Northwestern Oklahoma (railroad)

NOM: National Organization for Marriage (lobby)

NOMMA: National Ornamental & Miscellaneous Metals Association (trade group)

NORAD: North American Aerospace Defense Command (military)

NORCOM: Northern Command (military)

NORML: National Organization for Reform of Marijuana Laws (civic)

NOSM: New Orleans School of Medicine (Louisiana) (higher education)

NOU: New Orleans University (Louisiana) (higher education)

NOUS: Naval Order of the United States (lineage)

NOV: National Order of Videttes (fraternal)

NOW: National Organization for Women (civic)

NOW: Neighbors of Woodcraft (mutual benefit)

NOW: Northern Ohio and Western (railroad)

NP: Northern Pacific Railway (railroad)
NP: New Party (political party)
NP: Nullifier Party (political party)
NPA: New People's Army of the Philippines (guerilla organization)
NPA: National Production Authority (governmental)
NPA: National Pasta Association (trade group)
NPA: Natural Products Association (trade group)
NPB: Norfolk and Portsmouth Belt Line (railroad)
NPB&EA: National Poultry, Butter, and Egg Association (trade group)
NPBC: National Primitive Baptist Convention (of the USA) (religious denomination)
NPC: National Panhellenic Conference (umbrella organization)
NPCA: National Peace Corps Association (civic)
NPDC: North Pacific Dental College (Oregon) (higher education)
NPDF: National Police Defense Foundation (mutual aid)
NPES: National Printing Equipment Association (trade group)
NPF: National Psoriasis Foundation (self-help)
NPGA: National Propane Gas Association (trade group)
NPIC: National Passport Information Center (governmental)
NPL: Non-Partisan League (political party)
NPL: National Protective Legion (mutual benefit)
NPL: National Protective League (mutual benefit)
NPLA: National Protective Life Association (mutual benefit?)
NPLA: North Pacific Longliners Association (trade group)
NPLRC: National Pro-Life Religious Council (political/religious)
NPM: National Association of Pastoral Musicians (religious)
NPMA: National Pest Management Association (trade group)
NPMHU: National Postal Mail Handlers Union (labor union)
NPPC: Northwest Power Planning Council (governmental)
NPR: Northern Plains (railroad)
NPS: Normandy Preparatory School (school)
NPS: National Parks Service (governmental)
NPS: Newfoundland Pony Society (equine)
NPT: Portland Terminal (railroad)
NPTC: National Private Truck Council (trade group)
NPU: National Provident Union (mutual benefit)
NPWL: Network of Presbyterian Women in Leadership (religious)
NR: National Republican (political party)

NRA: National Recovery Administration (New Deal) (governmental)
NRA: National Recreation Association (professional)
NRA: National Reserve Association (mutual benefit)
NRA: National Rifle Association (lobby)
NRA: National Restaurant Association (trade group)
NRB: National Religious Broadcasters (trade group)
NRC: National Research Council (medical research)
NRC: National Railway of Canada (railroad)
NRC: Nuclear Regulatory Commission (governmental)
NRCA: National Roofing Contractors Association (trade group)
NRCC: National Republican Congressional Committee (political)
NRCS: Natural Resources Conservation Services (governmental)
NREP: National Registry of Environmental Professionals (professional)
NRECA: National Rural Electric Cooperative Association (trade group)
NREX: National Railway Equipment Co. (rail car lessor)
NRF: National Retail Federation (trade group)
NRHA: National Reining Horse Association (equestrian)
NRHA: National Rural Health Association (professional)
NRHH: National Residence Hall Honorary (honorary, leadership)
NRHS: National Railway Historical Society (hobby)
NRLCA: National Rural Letter Carriers Association (labor union)
NRMC: Naval Records Management Center (military)
NRMLA: National Reverse Mortgage Lenders Association (trade group)
NRNY: Northern Railroad (New York) (railroad)
NRP: National Republican Party (political party)
NRP: Nu Rho Psi (neuroscience) (academic honorary)
NRPA: National Recreation and Park Association (professional)
NRPC: National Railroad Passenger Corporation (Amtrak) (governmental)
NRR: Nantucket Rail Road (railroad)
NRWA: National Rural Water Association (trade group)
NS: Netherlands Society (lineage)
NS: National Sojourners, Inc. (also NSI) (Masonic)
NS: Norfolk & Southern (railroad)
NSA: National Student Association (political)

NSA: National Security Agency (government)
NSA: National Secretaries Association (trade group)
NSA: National Spiritualist Association (cult)
NSA: National Speakers Association (professional)
NSA: National Sheriffs' Association (trade group)
NSAA: Norwegian Singers Association of American (professional)
NSAC: National Spiritualist Association of Churches (cult)
NSAR: National Sons of the American Revolution (see SAR) (lineage)
NSARD: National Society Americans of Royal Descent (lineage)
NSAWFM: National Socialist American Workers Freedom Movement (political party)
NSBA: National Snaffle Bit Association (equestrian)
NSBA: North Star Benefit Association (mutual benefit)
NSBE: National Society of Black Engineers (professional)
NSC: National Society of Celts (lineage)
NSCAC: National Society Children of the American Colonists (lineage)
NSCAR: National Society Children of the American Revolution (see CAR) (lineage)
NSCD: National Society Colonial Dames XVII Century (lineage)
NSCDA: National Society of Colonial Dames in America (also CDA) (lineage)
NSCDSC: National Society Colonial Daughters of the Seventeenth Century (lineage)
NSCHBC: National Society of Certified Healthcare Business Consultants (professional)
NSCRA: National Stock Car Racing Association (motorsports)
NSCS: National Society of Collegiate Scholars (honorary fraternity)
NSCT: Niagara, St. Catherines, and Toronto (railroad)
NSDAC: National Society, Daughters of the American Colonists (lineage)
NSDAR: National Society, Daughters of the American Revolution (see also DAR) (lineage)
NSDBE: National Society Daughters of the British Empire in the USA (lineage)
NSDBR: National Society Daughters of the Barons of Runnemede (lineage)

NSDCH: National Society of the Dames of the Court of Honor
(lineage)
NSDCW: National Society Daughters of Colonial Wars
(lineage)
NSDFPA: National Society Daughters of Founders and Patriots
of America (lineage)
NSDU: National Society Daughters of the Union 1861 – 1865,
Inc. (lineage)
NSF: National Sports Foundation (sports)
NSF: National Science Foundation (governmental)
NSFA: National Student Federation of America (political,
1930s)
NSFFD: National Society of First Families of Delmarva
(lineage)
NSFFM: National Society of First Families of Minnesota
(lineage)
NSGA: National Sporting Goods Association (trade group)
NSGW: Native Sons of the Golden West (fraternal, mutual
benefit)
NSHDS: National Society for Hebrew Day Schools (religious,
education)
NSHR: North Shore (railroad)
NSI: Noblemen Society Inc. (high school fraternity)
NSI: National Sojourners, Inc. (also NS) (Masonic, military)
NSL: National Student League (political, 1930s)
NSL: St. Lawrence & Raquette River (railroad)
NSLMM: National Society of Lords of Maryland Manors
(lineage)
NSLS: National Service Life Society (mutual benefit)
NSM: National Socialist Movement (KKK)
NSMCD: National Society Magna Charta Dames (lineage)
NSNEW: National Society New England Women (see also
SNEW) (lineage)
NSO: National Safeman's Organization (trade group)
NSOPCD: National Society of Old Plymouth Colony
Descendants (lineage)
NSP: New School Presbyterian General Assembly (religious
denomination)
NSPE: National Society of Professional Engineers
(professional)
NSPPAA: Network of Schools of Public Policy, Affairs, and
Administration (education)
NSPR: National Society for Park Resources (professional)

NSRB: National Security Resources Board (governmental)
NSRMCA: National Star Route Mail Contractors Association
(lobbying organization)
NSS: Newburgh and South Shore Railway (railroad)
NSS: National Slovak Society (of the United States of America)
(mutual benefit)
NSSCNE: National Society Sons of Colonial New England
(lineage)
NSSDAP: National Society Sons and Daughters of Antebellum
Planters (lineage)
NSSDP: National Society of Sons and Daughters of the
Pilgrims (lineage)
NSSEA: National School Supply and Equipment Association
(trade group)
NSSF: National Shooting Sports Foundation (lobby)
NSSS: National Society of Saints and Sinners (lineage)
NSSUP: National Society Sons of Utah Pioneers (lineage)
NSTA: National Science Teachers Association (professional)
NSWDG: Naval Special Warfare Development Group (military)
NTA: National Textile Association (trade group)
NTAIBC: New Testament Association of Independent Baptist
Churches (religious denomination)
NTCC: New Testament Church of Christ (religious
denomination)
NTCM: National Travelers Club for Masons (fraternal)
NTEU: National Treasury Employees Union (labor union)
NTF: National Turkey Federation (trade group)
NTHS: National Technical Honor Society (academic honorary)
NTIS: National Technical Information Service (governmental)
NTM: New Thought Movement (cult)
NTR: National Transcontinental Railway (railroad)
NTR: Natchez Trace (railroad)
NTRS: National Therapeutic Recreation Society (professional)
NTS: Naval Training Station (military, World War I)
NTS: Nazarene Theological Seminary (higher education,
religious)
NTSB: National Transportation Safety Board (governmental)
NTZR: Natchez Railway (railroad)
NU: National Union (mutual benefit)
NU: Nashville University (Tennessee) (higher education)
NUAS: National Union Assurance Society (mutual benefit)
NUBC: National Union of Baptist Churches (religious
denomination)

NUI: National University of Illinois (higher education)
NUIM: National Union of Iron Moulders (labor union)
NUL: National Union League (political)
NUP: New Union Party (political party)
NUP: National Union Party (political party)
NVCA: National Venture Capital Association (trade group)
NVOA: National Veterans Organization of America (veterans)
NVR: Northern Vermont (railroad)
NVRR: Napa Valley (railroad)
NW: Norfolk & Western (also N&W) (railroad)
NW: Northwest Airlines (airline code)
NWA: National Weather Association (professional)
NWC: New World Communications (business)
NWCCU: Northwest Commission on Colleges and Universities (education, accrediting)
NWHM: National Women's History Museum (museum)
NWHL: National Women's Hockey League (sports)
NWLA: National Worship Leaders Association (religious, trade)
NWLB: National War Labor Board (governmental)
NWLH: Northwestern Legion of Honor (mutual benefit)
NWMP: North West Mounted Police (Canada) (governmental)
NWP: National Woman's Party (political party)
NWP: Northwestern Pacific (railroad)
NWR: Nashville & Western (railroad)
NWRA: National Waste & Recycling Association (trade group)
NWSA: National Woman Suffrage Association (civic)
NWSA: National Women's Studies Association (political)
NWSEO: National Weather Service Employees Organization (labor union)
NWU: National Writers Union (labor union)
NY&ERR: New York & Erie Rail Road (railroad)
NY&OM: New York & Oswego Midland (railroad)
NYA: New York & Atlantic (railroad)
NYA: National Youth Administration (New Deal) (governmental)
NYC: New York Central (railroad)
NYC: New York Company (lineage)
NYCB: New York City Ballet (dance)
NYCH: New York Cross Harbor (railroad)
NYCIP: New York Center for Independent Publishing (trade group)
NYCL: New York Consumers League (civic)
NYCN: New York Connecting (railroad)

NYCO: New York City Opera (musical)
NYCS: New York Central System (railroad)
NYCT: New York Container Terminal (railroad-related)
NYD: New York Dock (railroad)
NYEC: New York Etching Club (professional?)
NYEMS: New York Evangelical Missionary Society (religious)
NYER: New York & Eastern (railroad)
NYGBS: New York Genealogical and Biographical Society (academic)
NYGL: New York and Greenwood Lake Railway (railroad)
NYLB: New York & Long Branch (railroad)
NYLE: New York & Lake Erie (railroad)
NYMA: New York Military Academy (school)
NYMC: New York Medical College (higher education)
NYMS: New York Missionary Society (religious)
NYNJ: New York New Jersey (railroad)
NYO&W: New York, Ontario & Western (also O&W, OW) (railroad)
NYOG: New York & Ogdensburg (railroad)
NYP: New York Philharmonic (musical)
NYPL: New York Public Library
NYSCA: National Youth Sports Coaches Association (professional)
NYSP: New York State Police (governmental)
NYST: New York State Troopers (governmental)
NYSW: New York, Susquehanna & Western (railroad)
NYTBL: National Yeshiva Teachers Board of License (religious, education)
NYU: New York University (New York) (higher education)
NZ: Air New Zealand (airline code)
NZPCA: New Zealand Pony Clubs Association (equestrian)
NZWHA: New Zealand Warmblood Horse Association (equestrian)

O

O1889: Oklahoma 1889er Society (lineage)
O&W: New York, Ontario and Western (also NYO&W, OW) (railroad)
OA: Order of the Arrow (see also OofA) (secret society within Boy Scouts of America) (fraternal)
OA: Order of the Acorn (lineage)
OA: Order of the Amaranth (Masonic, charitable)
OA: Order of (the) Alhambra (fraternal, Catholic, charitable)
OA: Order of Ahepa (also OofA) (Greek-American civic)
OA: Order of Alfredians (fraternal, British descent, mutual benefit)
OA: Order of Americus (mutual benefit)
OA: Order of Amitie (mutual benefit)
OA: Order of Aegis (also OofA) (mutual benefit)
OA: Order of the Amazons (Masonic)
OA: Olympic Airways (Airlines) (airline code)
OAA: Order of African Architects (quasi-Masonic)
OAAA: Order of Americans of Armorial Ancestry (lineage)
OAC: Orthodox Anglican Church (religious denomination)
OAC: Order of American Cincinnatus (lineage)
OAC: Old Apostolic Church (religious denomination)
OACI: Organisation de L'aviation civile international (UN Agency)
OAD: Discalced Augustinians (religious order)
OAFC: Order of the American Fraternal Circle (mutual benefit)
OAH: Organization of American Historians (professional)
OAK: Order of American Knights (fraternal)
OAL: Olympic Airways (Airlines) (airline code)
OAM: Order of American Mechanics (fraternal)
OAO: Order of Ancient Oaks (fraternal)
OAPN: Order of Anti-Poke-Noses (anti-KKK)
OAR: Order of the Augustinian Recollects (religious order)
OAR: Old Augusta (railroad)
OARC: Ordo Aureae & Rosae Crucis (fraternal, Rosicrucian)
OAT: Order of Artistic Typists (honorary)
OAU: Order of the American Union (political)
OB: Order of the Bath (knighthood)
OB: Order of the Bath of the USA (lineage)

OB: Order of Bananas (social)
OB: Order of Bugs (fraternal)
OB: Order of the Builders (Masonic, youth)
OB: Order of Barristers (law) (academic honorary)
OB: Old Brethren (religious denomination)
OB: Order of Bethlehemites (mutual benefit)
OB: Order of Barristers (honorary)
OBA: Order, B'rith Abraham (mutual benefit)
OBA: Orange Benevolent Association (mutual benefit)
OBA: Oberhasli Breeders of America (goats)
OBGB: Old Brethren German Baptist (religious denomination)
OBK: Order of the Black Knight (German, mutual benefit)
OBS: Order of the Blessed Sacrament (religious order)
OBSC: Open Bible Standard Churches (religious denomination)
OBU: Old Baptist Union (religious denomination)
OBU: Order of the Benevolent Union (mutual benefit)
OC: Optimist Club (civic)
OC: Order of Camels (Masonic?)
OC: Oxford Class, Methodist Episcopal Church (religious, educational)
OC: Ohio Central System (railroad)
OC: Order of the Coif (law) (honorary)
OC: Ordo Crucis (religious order)
OC: Office of Censorship (governmental)
OCA: Orthodox Church in America (religious denomination)
OCA: Order of the Crown in America (lineage)
OCA: Organic Consumers Association (civic)
OCarm: Order of Our Lady of Mt. Carmel
(Carmelites)(Carmelite Sisters for the Aged and Infirm) (religious order)
OCarm (Carthusians Prvince of St. Elias) (religious order)
OCart: Carthusians (religious order)
OCC: Order of the Crown of Charlemagne in the United States of America (lineage)
OCC: Old Catholic Church (religious denomination)
OCC: Brothers of Our Lady of Mount Carmel, Calced Carmelites (religious order)
OCC: Office of the Comptroller of the Currency (governmental)
OCCA: Old Catholic Church of America (religious denomination)
OCCE: Old Catholic Church in Europe (religious denomination)

OCD: Brothers of Our Lady of Mount Carmel, Discalced
Carmelite Order (religious order)
OCD: Sisters of Our Lady of Mount Carmel, Carmelite Sisters,
Discalced Carmelite Nuns (religious order)
OCD: Order of Our Lady of Mt. Carmel (Carmelites) (religious
order)
OCD: Office of Civilian (or Civil) Defense (governmental)
OCDM: Office of Civil and Defense Mobilization
(governmental)
OCDS: Order of Our Lady of Mt. Carmel (Carmelites) (religious
order)
OCE: Oregon, California and Eastern Railway (railroad)
OCE: Omega Chi Epsilon (chemical engineering) (academic
honorary)
OCF: Order of Chosen Friends (also OofCF) (fraternal, mutual
benefit)
OCFU: Order of the Continental Fraternal Union (mutual
benefit)
OCHC: Order of Canadian Home Circles (mutual benefit)
OCI: Office of the Coordinator of Information (governmental)
OCIAA: Office of the Coordinator of Inter-American Affairs
(governmental)
OCist: Cistercians of the Ancient Observance (religious order)
OCJS: Order of the Constellation of Junior Stars (fraternal -
Eastern Stars, youth)
OCLMA: Order of Colonial Lords of Manors in America
(lineage)
OCPD: Office of Community Planning and Development
(governmental)
OCR: Order of Cistercians of the Strict Observance (Trappists)
(religious order)
OCR: Oklahoma Central (railroad)
OCR: Order of Confederate Rose (hereditary?)
OCR: Ottawa Central (railroad)
OCRD: Orthodox Christian Reformed Church (religious
denomination)
OCRR: Ottawa Central Railway (railroad)
OCSO: Order of Cistercians of the Strict Observance
(Trappists) (religious order)
OCTR: Octoraro Railway (railroad)
OCU: Order of Continental Union (mutual benefit)
OCUS: Ohio Credit Union System (trade group)

OD: Order of DeMolay (also ODM and OOD) (youth, Masonic)

OD: Order of Daedalians (military support)

OD: Order of Druids (fraternal, mystic)

OD: Order of Deacons (religious)

OD: Order of Desoms (Masonic, mutual benefit)

OD: Ordnance Corps (Army branch)

ODAHAC: Order of Descendents of the Ancient & Honorable Artillery Company (lineage)

ODAP: Order of Descendents of Ancient Planters (lineage)

ODE: Omicron Delta Epsilon (economic) (academic honorary)

ODK: Omicron Delta Kappa (leadership) (academic honorary)

ODM: Order of DeMolay (also OD and OOD) (youth, Masonic)

ODM: Office of Defense Mobilization (governmental)

OdeM: Order of Our Lady of Mercy (Mercedarians) (youth, religious order)

ODHS: Des Schwestern Verbandes (Sisters of the Federation) (religious order)

ODNI: Office of the Director of National Intelligence (governmental)

ODPP: Order of Descendents of Pirates and Privateers (lineage)

ODS: Order of the Daughters of Scotia (lineage)

ODS: Order of the Daughters of Scotland (lineage)

OE: Order of Emorians (related to Order of Evergreens) (life extension)

OE: Order of Evergreens (related to Order of Emorians) (life extension)

OE: Order of Equity (also OOE) (mutual benefit)

OE: Order of Egbo (secret, possibly Masonic)

OECD: Organisation for Economic Cooperation and Development (international)

OEO: Office of Economic Opportunity (political)

OES: Order of the Eastern Star (Masonic fraternal organization for women)

OES: Office of Economic Stabilization (governmental)

OESE: Office of Elementary and Secondary Education (governmental)

OESSH: Ordo Equestris Sancti Sepulcri Hierosolymitani (religious, knighthood)

OF: Air Finland Ltd. (airline code)

OFC: Odd Fellows Club (fraternal)

OFC: Order of the Fraternal Circle (mutual benefit)
OFFC: Order of the First Families of Connecticut (lineage)
OFFM: Order of the First Families of Maine (lineage)
OFFM: Order of the First Families of Maryland (lineage)
OFFM: Order of the First Families of Mississippi (lineage)
OFFNC: Order of the First Families of North Carolina (lineage)
OFFNH: Order of the First Families of New Hampshire (lineage)
OFFRIPP: Order of the First Families of Rhode Island and Providence Plantations (lineage)
OFFV: Order of First Families of Virginia (lineage)
OFHA: Odd Fellows Home Association (fraternal)
OFM: Order of Friars Minor (Franciscan Friars) (religious order)
OFMConv: Order of Conventual Franciscans (religious order)
OFMAS: Odd Fellows' Mutual Aid Society (fraternal, self-help)
OFMCap: Order of Friars Minor Capuchin (religious order)
OFMConv: Order of Friars Minor Conventual (Conventuals) (religious order)
OFMI: Franciscan Friars of Mary Immaculate (religious order)
OFPA: Order of the Founders and Patriots of America (lineage)
OFPM: Odd Fellows Patriarchs Militant (fraternal)
OFRA: Odd Fellows Relief Association (mutual benefit)
OFWB: Old Free Will Baptist Convention (religious denomination)
OFWW: Order of the First World War (lineage)
OGBB: Old German Baptist Brethren (religious denomination)
OGC: Order of the Golden Chain (mutual benefit)
OGC: Order of the Golden Cross (mutual benefit)
OGC: Order of the Golden Circle (fraternal)
OGC: Oberhasli Goat Club (livestock)
OGD: Hermetic Order of the Golden Dawn (also HOGD) (perhaps also EOGD – Esoteric Order of the Golden Dawn) (rosicrucian)
OGEE: Ogeechee Railway (railroad)
OGK: Order of the Golden Key (fraternal, secret)
OGL: Order of the Golden Links (mutual benefit)
OGR: Order of the Golden Rod (mutual benefit)
OGS: Order of the Golden Seal (mutual benefit)
OGS: Oratory of the Good Shepherd (religious community)
OGT: Order of Good Templars (Masonic)
OGT: Order of Good Times (culinary)

OH: Order of Hospitallers (Hospitaller Brothers of St. John of God) (religious order)
OH: Order of Heptasophs (also OofH) (mutual benefit)
OH: Order of Homebuilders (also OofH) (mutual benefit, secret)
OHA: Ontario Hockey Association (sports)
OHA: Oral History Association (learned)
OHAC: Order of the Honorable Artillery Company (lineage)
OHB: Order of Home Builders (mutual benefit)
OHC: Order of the Holy Cross (religious community)
OHC: Order of the Holy Cross (Benedictine) (religious community)
OHCR: Ohio Central (railroad)
OHGRC: The Order of the Hermetic Gold and The Rose + Cross (Rosicrucian, fraternal)
OHL: Ontario Hockey League (sports)
OHP: Order of the Holy Paraclete (religious community)
OHRY: Owego & Hartford (railroad)
OI: Order of Iroquois (also OofI) (mutual benefit)
OI: Optimist International (fraternal)
OIA: Order of Independent Americans (mutual benefit)
OIAL: Order Independent American Legion (fraternal, possibly mutual benefit)
OIC: Order of the Imitation of Christ (Bethany Ashram) (religious order)
OIH: Order of Iron Hall (fraternal, mutual benefit)
OII: Organization for International Investment (trade group)
OIW: Order of Indian Wars (of the United States) (lineage)
OJN: Order of Julian of Norwich (religious community)
OKF: Order Knights of Friendship (fraternal, mutual benefit)
OKM: Order of Knight Masons (fraternal)
OKP: Order of the Knights of Pythias (see KofP) (fraternal)
OHPA: Ohio and Pennsylvania (railroad)
OKR: Original Knight Riders (KKK)
OKAN: Okanagan Valley (railroad)
OKCE: Okarche Central Railway (railroad)
OKF: Order Knights of Friendship (mutual benefit)
OKKT: Oklahoma, Kansas and Texas (railroad)
OKStJ: Order of Knights of St. Joseph (mutual benefit)
OKU: Omicron Kappa Upsilon (dentistry) (honorary)
OL: Order of Liberty (mutual benefit)
OLAC: OnLine Audiovisual Catalogers, Inc. (business)
OLB: Omaha, Lincoln and Beatrice Railway (railroad)

OLF: Order of Lutheran Franciscans (religious order)
OLG: Order of Lady Glade (women, fraternal)
OLIG: Orchestra Library Information Group (musical)
OLM: Order of Lebanese Maronite (Baladites) (religious order)
OLRS: Order of the Little Red Schoolhouse (likely nativist)
OLS: Sisters of Our Lady of Sorrows (religious order)
OLVM: Our Lady of Victory Missionary Sisters (religious order)
OLYR: Olympic (railroad)
OM: Order of Mules (fraternal, civic)
OM: Order of Mogullions (mutual benefit)
OMA: Oakland Military Academy (school)
OMA: Oklahoma Military Academy (school or higher education)
OMA: Obesity Medicine Association (professional)
OMA: Open Mashup Alliance (trade group)
OMA: Order of Mutual Aid (mutual benefit)
OMB: Old Missionary Baptists (religious denomination)
OMB: Office of Management and Budget (governmental)
OMBA: Occidental Mutual Benefit Association (mutual benefit)
OMC: Omaha Medical College (Nebraska) (higher education)
OMD: Order of the Merovingian Dynasty (lineage)
OMI: Missionary Oblates of Mary Immaculate (religious order)
OMID: Ontario Midland (railroad)
OMP: Order of Mutual Protection (full name may be Artisans Order of Mutual Protection) (mutual benefit)
OMS: Officers' Materiel School (military, World War I)
OMS: Order of the Mystic Star (fraternal) (see also MS)
OMS: Oriental Missionary Society (religious)
OMSS: Organized Medical Staff Section (professional)
OMV: Oblates of the Virgin Mary (religious order)
ONCT: Ontario Central (railroad)
ONDCP: Office of National Drug Control Policy (governmental)
ONER: Ontario Eastern (railroad)
ONNI: Office of National Narcotics Intelligence (governmental)
ONT: Ontario Northland Railway (railroad)
ONW: Oregon and Northwestern (railroad)
OO: Order of Owls (also OOO, FOO) (fraternal, mutual benefit)
OO: Orange Order (militant Protestant)
OO: Order of the Orioles (also FOO) (fraternal)
OO: Order of the Orient (mutual benefit)

OOA: Order of Ahepa (American Hellenic Educational Progressive Association) (educational)

OOA: Old Order Amish (religious denomination)

OOB: Order of the Builders (also OB) (Masonic, youth)

OOB: Old Order Brethren (religious denomination)

OOC: Order of the Calanthe (mutual benefit)

OOD: Order of DeMolay (also OD and ODM) (youth, Masonic)

OOD: Order of Deacons (religious)

OOE: Order of Equity (also OE) (mutual benefit)

OOF: Order of Odd Fellows (see IOOF) (fraternal)

OofA: Order of Amaranth (Masonic)

OofA: Order of the Arrow (see also OA) (Boy Scout honorary)

OofA: Order of Aegis (also OA) (mutual benefit)

OofA: Order of Ahepa (also OA) (Greek-American civic)

OofCF: Order of Chosen Friends (also OCF) (fraternal)

OofF: Order of Foresters (mutual benefit)

OofH: Order of Heptasophs (also OH) (mutual benefit)

OofH: Order of Homebuilders (also OH) (mutual benefit, secret)

OofI: Order of Iroquois (also OI) (mutual benefit)

OofO: Order of Omega (academic honorary)

OofUF: Order of United Friends (mutual benefit)

OOGBB: Old Order German Baptist Brethren (religious denomination)

OOHP: Oriental Order of Humility and Perfection (fraternal)

OOL: Order of Odd Ladies (mutual benefit)

OOM: Old Order Mennonites (religious denomination)

OOO: Order of Owls (see OO) (fraternal, mutual benefit)

OORB: Old Order River Brethren (religious denomination)

OOSH: Des Schwestern Verbandes (Sisters of the Federation) (mutual benefit)

OOT: Order of Twelve (fraternal, ethnic)

OOU: Order of Unity (IOOF, mutual benefit)

OP: Order of Protection (mutual benefit)

OP: Order of Friars Preachers (Dominicans) (religious order)

OP: Dominican Sisters of the Immaculate Conception (Dominicans) (religious order)

OP: Sisters of Mary, Mother of the Eucharist (religious order)

OP: Adrian Dominican Sisters, Congregation of the Most Holy Rosary (religious order)

OP: Dominican Sisters, Congregation of Our Lady of the Rosary, Sisters of Sparkill, Sisters of the Third Order of St. Dominic (religious order)

OP: Dominican Sisters, Congregation of Our Lady of the Rosary, Sinsinawa, Wisconsin, Sisters of the Third Order of St. Dominic (religious order)

OP: Dominican Sisters, Congregation of Our Lady of the Rosary, Aberdeen, Sisters of the Third Order of St. Dominic (also a variety of other geographic designations) (religious order)

OP: Sisters of the Third Order of Penance of St. Dominic (religious order)

OP: Old Philologians (Alumni of Marylebone School)

OP: Opposition Party (political party)

OP: Objectivist Party (political party)

OP: Opposition (political party)

OP: Order of Pente (mutual benefit)

OP: Order of Pendo (mutual benefit)

OP-20-G: Office of the Chief of Naval Operations 20th Division of the Office of Naval Communications, G section/Communications Security (military)

OPA: Office of Price Administration (governmental)

OPC: Orthodox Presbyterian Church (religious denomination)

OPC: Office of Policy Coordination (governmental)

OPCC: Old Point Comfort College (Virginia) (higher education)

OPCMIA: Operative Plasterers' and Cement Masons' International Association (labor union)

OPCW: Organisation for the Prohibition of Chemical Weapons (international organization)

OPE: Oregon, Pacific and Eastern (railroad)

OPEC: Organization of Petroleum Exporting Countries (international, political)

OPG: Order of Pink Goats (The Ancient, Honorable and Fragrant Order of the Pink Goats) (also PG) (Rotarian)

OPH: National Grange of the Order of Patrons of Husbandry (fraternal)

OPI: Order of Perpetual Indulgence (also called SPI - Sisters of Perpetual Indulgence) (social protest)

OPIC: Overseas Private Investment Corporation (governmental)

OPIEU: Office and Professional Employees International Union (labor union)

OPK: Order of Protestant Knights (mutual benefit)

OPKTS: Order of the Poor Knights of the Temple of Solomon (see KT)

OPNAV: Office of the Chief of Naval Operations (military)

OPM: Office of Personnel Management (governmental)

OPP: Ontario Provincial Police (governmental)

OPraem: Canons Regular of Premontre, Norbertine Fathers (religious order)

OPR: Oregon Pacific (railroad)

OPT: Orange Port Terminal Railway (railroad)

OR: Operation Rescue (political/religious)

OR: Owasco River Railway (railroad)

OR: Order of Reubens (fraternal)

OR: Order of Rameses (fraternal)

OR: Omega Rho (operations research) (academic honorary)

ORA: Ormet (railroad)

ORA: Order of the Royal Argosy (mutual benefit)

ORA: Order of the Royal Ark (mutual benefit)

ORB: Old Regular Baptist (religious denomination)

ORC: Order of the Red Cross (fraternal, mutual benefit, Masonic)

ORC: Order of Railway Conductors (labor union)

ORC: Officers' Reserve Corps (military, World War I)

ORCCA: Old Roman Catholic Church in America (religious denomination)

ORG: Order of the Rainbow for Girls (Masonic, youth)

ORION: Our Race Is Our Nation (KKK)

ORM: Order of Red Men (fraternal)

ORMA: Oak Ridge Military Academy (school)

ORP: Order of Royal Purple (fraternal, mutual benefit)

ORR: Osage (railroad)

ORR: Office of Refugee Resettlement (governmental)

ORT: Order of Railway Telegraphers (labor union)

ORT: Society for Trades and Agricultural Labor (religious, educational)

OS: Order of Sparta (mutual benefit)

OS: Order of the Square (fraternal)

OS: Order of the Sanhedrin (mutual benefit)

OS: Order of Solon (mutual benefit)

OSA: Order of St. Augustine (Augustinians) (religious order)

OSA: Sisters of St. Rita (religious order)

OSA: Order of St. Anne (religious community)

OSA: Order of St. Anne at Bethany (religious community)

OSA: The Order of the Sons of America (Orden Hijos de America) (Hispanic/American civil rights)
OSA: Orthodox Society of America (mutual benefit)
OSA: Operation Save America (political/religious)
OSA: Old Settlers Association (lineage)
OSB: Old School Baptist Church a/k/a Anti-Mission Baptist (religious denomination)
OSB: Order of the Star of Bethlehem (mutual benefit)
OSB: Order of St. Benedict (Benedictines) (religious order/community)
OSB: Community of Our Lady & St. John (Benedictine) (religious community)
OSB: Community of St. Mary at the Cross (Order of St. Benedict) (religious community)
OSB: Order of the Shepherds of Bethlehem (mutual benefit)
OSB: Benedictine Sisters of Perpetual Adoration (religious order)
OSB: Benedictine Sisters of Pontifical Jurisdiction (religious order)
OSB: Missionary Benedictine Sisters (religious order)
OSB Cam.: Camaldolese Benedictines (religious order)
OSBA: Order of St. Benedict (Anglican) (religious order)
OSBS: Oblate Sisters of the Blessed Sacrament (religious order)
OSC: Order of Scottish Clans (St. Andrew's Societies) (see BOSC: Benevolent Order of Scottish Clans) (lineage)
OSC: Canons Regular of the Holy Cross (Crosiers) (religious order)
OSC: Nuns of the Order of St. Clare (Poor Clares) (religious order)
OSC: Community of St. Clare (religious community)
OSC: Crosier Fathers and Brothers (religious order)
OSC: Office of Special Counsel (governmental)
OSCam: Order of Saint Camillus (religious order)
OSCC: Order of Scions of Colonial Cavaliers (lineage)
OSD: Operation Stand Down (military support)
OSE: Order of St. Elisabeth (religious order)
OSE: Order of the Star in the East (cult)
OSERS: Office of Special Education and Rehabilitative Services (governmental)
OSF: Order of St. Francis (religious order)
OSF: Franciscan Sisters of the Eucharist (religious order)
OSF: Franciscan Brothers of Brooklyn (religious order)

OSF: Sisters of St. Francis of Perpetual Adoration (religious order)

OSF: Sisters of St. Francis of the Martyr St. George (religious order)

OSF: Bernardine Franciscan Sisters (religious order)

OSF: Sisters of St. Francis of the Immaculate Conception (religious order)

OSF: School Sisters of St. Francis (various locations) (religious order)

OSF: Order of Select Friends (mutual benefit)

OSF: Hospital Sisters of the Third Order of St. Francis (religious order)

OSF: Poor Sisters of St. Francis Seraph of the Perpetual Adoration (religious order)

OSF: Sisters of St. Francis of Penance and Christian Charity (religious order)

OSF: Sisters of St. Francis of Philadelphia (religious order)

OSF: Sisters of St. Francis of the Holy Cross (religious order)

OSF: Sisters of St. Francis of the Holy Family (religious order)

OSF: Congregation of the Sisters of St. Francis of Mary Immaculate of the Third Order (religious order)

OSF: Sisters of the Third Order Regular of St. Francis of Assisi (religious order)

OSGA: Old School General Assembly of the Presbyterian Church (religious denomination)

OSH: Order of St. Helena (religious community)

OSH: Order of the Shield of Honor (mutual benefit)

OSHA: Occupational Safety and Health Administration (governmental)

OSHCJ: Oblate Sisters of the Holy Child Jesus (religious order)

OSI: Order of the Sons of Italy (lineage)

OSI: Oblates of St. Joseph (Josephines of Asti) (religious order)

OSI: Office of Strategic Influence (governmental)

OSI: Open Society Institute (political)

OSIA: Order of the Sons of Italy in America (lineage)

OSL: Order of the Sons of Liberty (Civil War Southern sympathizers)

OSL: Oregon Short Line (railroad)

OSM: Order of Friars, Servants of Mary (Servites) (religious order)

OSM: Order of the Secret Monitor (see also BDJ – Brotherhood of David and Jonathan) (Masonic)

OSP: Oblate Sisters of Providence (religious order)

OSP: Office of Special Plans (governmental)
OSP: Order of the Sons of Progress (mutual benefit)
OSR: Order of the Solid Rock (mutual benefit)
OSRD: Office of Scientific Research and Development (governmental)
OSRR: Ohio Southern (railroad)
OSS: Office of Strategic Services (governmental)
OSSB: Order of the Star Spangled Banner (a/k/a Sons of '76; source of Know-Nothings) (nativist, anti-Catholic)
OSSG: Order of the Sons of St. George (mutual benefit)
OSSNHS: Order of the Sword & Shield National Honor Society (protective security) (honorary)
OSSR: Redemptoristines (religious order)
OSST: Order of the Most Holy Trinity (Trinitarians) (religious order)
OSTI: Office of Scientific and Technical Information (governmental)
OSTP: Office of Science and Technology Policy (governmental)
OTR: Oakland Terminal (railroad)
OSU: Ursuline Nuns of the Roman Union (Ursuline Sisters) (religious order)
OSU: Ohio State University (Ohio) (higher education)
OSU: Oregon State University (higher education)
OSU: Oklahoma State University (Oklahoma) (higher education)
OSWW: Order of the Second World War (lineage)
OSZ: Order of Sons of Zion (mutual benefit)
OT: Order of the Trapezoid (cult)
OT: Order of the Triangle (mutual benefit)
OT: Order of the Tontine (mutual benefit)
OTA: Office of Technology Assessment (governmental)
OTC: Order of Three Crusades 1096-1192 (lineage)
OTC: Officers' Training Camp (military, World War I)
OTF: Order of True Friends (mutual benefit)
OTK: Order of the True Kindred (Masonic, mutual benefit)
OTK: Order of The Key Honor Society (honorary, leadership)
OTMB: Old Time Missionary Baptist (religious denomination)
OTO: Ordo Templi Orientis (Order of the Templars of the East) (fraternal)
OTS: Officers' Training School (military, World War I)
OTS: Ordo Templi Satoris (cult)
OTT: Ottumwa Terminal (railroad)
OTVR: Otter Tail Valley (railroad)

OU: Order of Unity (mutual benefit)

OUA: Order of United Americans (nativist)

OUA: Order of United Artisans (mutual benefit)

OUAM: Order of United American Mechanics (nativist, anti-Catholic)

OUCH: Ouachita (railroad)

OUCTA: Order of United Commercial Travelers of America (mutual benefit)

OUF: Order of United Fellowship (mutual benefit)

OUF: Order of United Friends (mutual benefit)

OUHB: Order of United Hebrew Brothers (ethnic, mutual benefit)

OV: Orange Volunteers (militant Protestant)

OV: Order of the Visitation (religious order)

OV: Estonian Air (airline code)

OV: Order of Vesta (mutual benefit)

OVACBCG: Ohio Valley Association of Christian Baptist Churches of God (religious denomination)

OVO: Ottawa Valley Railway (railroad)

OVR: Ohio Valley (railroad)

OW: Order of Washington (lineage)

OW: New York, Ontario & Western (also NYO&W, O&W) (railroad)

OW: Order of the World (mutual benefit)

OWC: Ozark Wesleyan College (Missouri) (higher education)

OWHA: Ontario Women's Hockey Association (sports)

OWI: Office of War Information (governmental)

OWL: Secret literary society at University of Virginia

OWLC: Open World Leadership Center (governmental)

OWM: Office of War Mobilization (governmental)

OWSJ: Order of the White Shrine of Jerusalem (mutual benefit)

Oxy: Occidental College (higher education)

OYD: Order of Yellow Dogs (fraternal)

239

P

P4A: Patriots 4 America (nativist)

P-TA: Parent-Teachers' Association

P&E: Pacific and Eastern (railroad)

P&S: Pittsburg and Shawmut (railroad)

P&WV: Pittsburgh and West Virginia Railway (railroad)

PA: Press Assistants (labor union)

PAA: Playground Association of America (civic)

PAA: Polish Association of America (mutual benefit)

PAA: Pi Alpha Alpha (public administration) (academic honorary)

PAA: Pancretan Association of America (ethnic)

PAAIA: Public Affairs Alliance of Iranian Americans (lobby)

PAB: Planning Accreditation Board (education)

PAB: Pennsylvania Association of Broadcasters (trade group)

PAC: Pentecostal Assemblies of Canada (religious denomination)

PACE: Paper, Allied-Industrial, Chemical & Energy Workers International Union (labor union)

PACO: Pro Arte Chamber Orchestra of Boston (musical)

PACOM: Pacific Command (military)

PACY: Prairie Central Railway (railroad)

PAD: Phi Alpha Delta (fraternal, service)

PADD: Petroleum Administration for Defense Districts (governmental)

PAE: Peoria and Eastern Railway (railroad)

PAE: Phi Alpha Epsilon (architectural engineering) (academic honorary)

PAF: Pan-American Foundation (political front)

PAHA: Polish American History Association (learned)

PAIS: Pennsylvania Association of Independent Schools (education)

PAL: Paducah & Louisville (railroad)

PAL: Philippine Airlines Inc. (airline code)

PAM: Presbyterian Association of Musicians (religious, musical)

PAM: Pittsburgh, Allegheny and McKees Rocks (railroad)

PAM: Polish Alma Mater (mutual benefit)

PAMA: Performing Arts Medicine Association (civic)

PAMS: Production, Advertising, Merchandising Service (business)
PanAm: Pan-American World Airways (company)
PAPi: Phi Alpha Pi (religious)
PARY: Prairie Trunk Railway (railroad)
PAS: Pan Am Southern (railroad)
PAS: Percussive Arts Society (musical)
PASTCF: Presbyterian Association on Science, Technology and the Christian Faith (religious)
PAT: Phi Alpha Theta (history) (honorary fraternity)
PATCO: Professional Air Traffic Controllers Organization (labor union)
PATH: Port Authority Trans Hudson (railroad)
PATH: Professional Association of Therapeutic Horsemanship (equestrian)
PAUCA: Providence Association of Ukrainian Catholics in America (mutual benefit)
PAUT: Pennsylvania and Atlantic (railroad)
PAW: Pride At Work (labor union)
PAW: People for the American Way (political)
PAW: Publishers Association of the West (professional)
PAWS: Performing Animal Welfare Society (civic, political)
PAWS: Progressive Animal Welfare Society (civic, political)
PAX: Pi Alpha Xi (horticulture) (academic honorary)
PB: Primitive Baptists (religious denomination)
PB: Progressive Baptist (religious denomination)
PB: Plymouth Brethren (religious denomination)
PB: Psi Beta (psychology and two-year colleges) (academic honorary)
PBA: Patrolmen's (or Police) Benevolent Association (labor, mutual benefit)
PBA: Police Beneficiary Association (mutual aid)
PBA: Polish Beneficial Association (mutual benefit)
PBA: Polish Baptist Association (religious denomination)
PBC: Primitive Baptist Conference (of New Brunswick, Maine, and Nova Scotia) (religious denomination)
PBC: Pillsbury Baptist Bible College (Minnesota) (higher education)
PBCNE: Portuguese Baptist Convention of New England (religious denomination)
PBD: Phi Beta Delta (international education) (academic honorary)
PBGC: Pension Benefit Guaranty Corp. (governmental)

PBK: Phi Beta Kappa (college honorary)

PBL: Philadelphia Belt Line (railroad)

PBNE: Philadelphia, Bethlehem & New England (railroad)

PBR: Patapsco and Back Rivers (railroad)

PBRR: Prairie Belt (railroad)

PBS: Public Broadcasting Service (media, quasi-governmental)

PBS-USA: The Prayer Book Society of the USA (religious)

PBU: Presbyterian Beneficial Union (mutual aid)

PBU: Primitive Baptist Universalists (Universalism) (religious denomination)

PBVM: Sisters of the Presentation of the Blessed Virgin Mary (Presentation Sisters) (religious order)

PBVR: Port Bienville (railroad)

PC: The Pony Club (equestrian, UK)

PC: Pay Corps, US Navy (military, World War I)

PC: Penn Central Transportation Company (railroad)

PC: Palmer College (Florida) (higher education)

PC: Poor Catholics (religious order)

PCA: Presbyterian Church in America (religious denomination)

PCA: Patriarchal Circle of America (fraternal, mutual benefit)

PCA: Pony Club Australia (equestrian)

PCANSW: Pony Club Association of New South Wales (equestrian)

PCAV: Pony Club Association of Victoria (equestrian)

PCBAA: Presbyterian Church Business Administrators Association (religious, professional)

PCC: Pentecostal Churches of Christ (religious denomination)

PCCA: Presbyterian College Chaplains Association (religious)

PCCMP: Presbyterian Council for Chaplains and Military Personnel (religious)

PCDS: Pennsylvania College of Dental Surgery (higher education)

PCG: Philadelphia Church of God (religious denomination)

PCG: Pentecostal Church of God (religious denomination)

PCHA: Pacific Coast Hockey Association (sports)

PCHL: Pacific Coast Hockey League (sports)

PCI: Protestant Community of Inspiration (religious denomination)

PCLOB: Privacy and Civil Liberties Oversight Board (governmental)

PCN: Pentecostal Church of the Nazarene (religious denomination)

PCP: Personal Choice Party (political party)

PCPE: Panzer College of Physical Education (New Jersey) (higher education)

PCR: Pacific Coast Railway (railroad)

PCRBA: Pineywoods Cattle Registry & Breeders Association (cattle)

PCRC: Panama Canal Railway (railroad)

PCU: Portuguese Continental Union (of the United States of America) (mutual benefit)

PCUS: Presbyterian Church of the United States (religious denomination)

PCUSA: Presbyterian Church USA (religious denomination)

PCY: Pittsburgh, Chartiers and Youghiogheny Railway (railroad)

PDA: Parenteral Drug Association (professional)

PDC: Philadelphia Dental College (Pennsylvania) (higher education)

PDCA: Purebred Dexter Cattle Association of North American (cattle)

PDCA: Painting and Decorating Contractors of America (trade group)

PDP: Phi Delta Phi (law) (honorary)

PDP: Pi Delta Phi (French) (academic honorary)

PDRR: Pee Dee (railroad) Corporation (railroad)

PE: Pacific Electric Railway (railroad)

PE: Pi Epsilon (environmental science) (academic honorary)

PEARL: Professional Electrical Apparatus Recyclers League (trade group)

PEC: Protestant Episcopal Church (religious denomination)

PECF: Protestant Episcopal Cathedral Foundation (religious)

PECUSA: Protestant Episcopal Church in the United States of America (religious denomination)

PEDS: Pilgrim Edward Doty Society (lineage)

PEER: Presbyterian Endowment Education & Resource Network (religious)

PEER: Public Employees for Environmental Responsibility (professional)

PEG: Progressive Endowment Guild (mutual benefit)

PEGA: Progressive Endowment Guild of America (mutual benefit)

PEGCC: Private Equity Growth Capital Council (lobby)

PEHS: Protestant Episcopal Historical Society (religious)

PEIR: Prince Edward Island Railway (railroad)

Penn: University of Pennsylvania (higher education)

PEO: Protect Each Other Sisterhood (or Philanthropic
Educational Organization)
(fraternal, mutual benefit, women)
PERF: Police Executive Research Forum (professional)
PES: Phi Eta Sigma (honorary fraternity)
PES: Party of European Socialists (political)
PESPEK: Protestant Episcopal Society for the Promotion of
Evangelical Knowledge (religious)
PER: Port Everglades Railway (railroad)
PET: Pi Epsilon Tau (petroleum engineering) (honorary
fraternity)
P-EU: Photo-Engravers' Union (labor union)
PF: Pioneer and Fayette (railroad)
PF: United Order of Pilgrim Fathers (lineage)
PF: Pilgrim Fraternity (youth)
PFA: Presidential Families of America (lineage)
PFA: Polish Falcons of America (fraternal, mutual benefit)
PFA: Pioneer Fraternal Association (mutual benefit)
PFA: Professional Fraternity Association (umbrella
organization)
PFC: Protected Fireside Circle (mutual benefit)
PFCS: Pilgrim Francis Cooke Society (lineage)
PFE: Pacific Fruit Express (railroad)
PFI: Pellet Fuels Institute (trade group)
PFIA: Police and Firemen's Insurance Association (mutual
benefit)
PFO: Pioneer Fraternal Order (mutual benefit)
PFO: People's Favorite Order (mutual benefit)
PFofA: Patriotic Friends of America (fraternal, possibly farm
laborers, mutual benefit)
PFP: Peace and Freedom Party (political party)
PFWBC: Pentecostal Free Will Baptist Church (religious
denomination)
PFYBO: People's Five Year Benefit Order (mutual benefit)
PG: Programmers Guild (labor union)
PG: Order of Pink Goats (The Ancient, Honorable and
Fragrant Order of the Pink Goats) (also OPG) (Rotarian)
PG: Bangkok Airways Co. Ltd. (airlines code)
PG: Programmers Guild (trade group)
PGA: Professional Golfers Association (trade group)
PGA: Producers Guild of American (trade group)
PGAA: Playground Association of America (professional)
PGD: Phi Gamma Delta (fraternity)

PGE: Pacific Great Eastern (railroad)
PGM: Pi Gamma Mu (social sciences) (honorary fraternity)
PGN: Phi Gamma Nu (fraternal, service)
PGRV: Pigeon River (railroad)
PH: The Order of Patrons of Husbandry (Grange) (fraternal)
PHAA: Pinto Horse Association of American (equestrian)
PHC: Protected Home Circle (mutual benefit)
PHC: Pilgrim Holiness Church (religious denomination)
PHCF: Potter's House Christian Fellowship (religious denomination)
PHCR: Port Colbourne Harbour Railway
PHD: Port Huron and Detroit (railroad)
PHES: Prince Hall Eastern Star (Masonic, ethnic)
PHF: Prince Hall Freemasonry (Masonic, ethnic)
PHF: Public Health Foundation (research, civic)
PHL: Pacific Harbor Line (railroad)
PHMS: Philadelphia Home Missionary Society (religious)
PHNS: Public Health Nursing Service (of the American Red Cross)
PHP: Presbyterian Hunger Program (religious)
PhRMA: Pharmaceutical Research and Manufacturers of America (Trade group)
PHS: United States Public Health Service (governmental)
PHS: Plymouth Hereditary Society (lineage)
PHS: Presbyterian Historical Society (religious)
PHSA: Pearl Harbor Survivors Association (fraternal, veterans)
PI: Paducah and Illinois (railroad)
PIA: Perfect Initiates of Asia (mutual benefit)
PIA: Pakistan International Airlines (airline code)
PIA: Printing Industries of America (trade group)
PIC: Professional Interfraternity Conference (umbrella organization)
PIC: Pacific Islander Council (ethnic)
PICAO: Provisional International Civil Aviation Organization (international)
PICK: Pickens (railroad)
PIDS: Philippine Institute for Development Studies (political)
PILP: Presbyterian Investment and Loan Program (religious)
PIPA: Polo Instructors and Players Association (equestrian)
PIPSA: Pacific Islands Political Studies Association (political)
PIR: Pittsburgh Industrial (railroad)
PIRA: Physics Instructional Resource Association (education)
Pitt: University of Pittsburgh (higher education)

PIX: Psi Iota Xi (fraternal, service)
PJR: Port Jersey (railroad)
PJRL: Penn Jersey Rail Lines (railroad)
PK: Promise Keepers (religious)
PK: Phi Kappa (high school fraternity)
PK: Pakistan International Airlines (airline code)
PKA: Protestant Knights of America (mutual benefit)
PKA: Protected Knights of America (mutual benefit)
PKA: Pi Kappa Alpha (college fraternity)
PKA: Phi Kappa Alpha (leadership) (academic honorary)
PKL: Pi Kappa Lambda (music) (academic honorary)
PKM: Phi Kappa Mu (fraternal, service)
PKP: Pi Kappa Psi (college fraternity)
PKP: Phi Kappa Phi (academic honorary)
PKS: Phi Kappa Sigma (college fraternity)
PKT: Phi Kappa Theta (religious)
PLA: Provident League of America (mutual benefit)
PLA: Public Library Association (trade group)
PLC: Public Land Commission (governmental)
PLCA: Pipe Line Contractors Association (trade group)
PLE: Pittsburgh & Lake Erie (railroad)
PLEF: Pythian Sisters (fraternal)
PLMA: Private Label Manufacturers Association (trade group)
PLO: Palestine Liberation Organization (guerilla organization)
PLP: Progressive Labor Party (political)
PLP: Pentecostal League of Prayer (religious denomination)
PLPA: Professional Lacrosse Players Association (labor union)
PLR: Patriotic League of the Revolution (fraternal)
PLT: Pi Lambda Theta (education) (academic honorary)
PLTA: Philosophy Learning and Teaching Organization
(education)
PLU: Phi Lambda Upsilon (chemistry) (academic honorary)
PLW: Pittsburgh, Lisbon & Western (railroad)
PM: Patriarchs Militant (Independent Order of Odd Fellows)
(fraternal)
PM: Sisters of the Presentation of Mary (religious order)
PM: Pere Marquette (railroad)
PMA: Phi Mu Alpha (musical/fraternal)
PMA: Progressive Miners Association (labor?)
PMA: Pacific Maritime Association (trade group)
PMA: Produce Marketing Association (trade group)
PMA: Promotion Marketing Association (trade group)
PMC: Primitive Methodist Church (religious denomination)

PMC: Pentecostal Missionary Church of Christ (4th watch) (religious denomination)

PMC: People's Methodist Church (religious denomination)

PMC: Pan Methodist Commission (religious)

PME: Pi Mu Epsilon (mathematics) (academic honorary)

PMI: Plumbing Manufacturers International (trade group)

PMLIO: People's Mutual Life Insurance Order (mutual benefit)

PMMBA: Pryor Mountain Mustang Breeders Association (equine)

PMPA: Precision Machined Products Association (trade group)

PMS: Presbyterian Monthly Satire (religious)

PN: Piedmont & Northern (railroad)

PN: Pennsylvania Northeastern (railroad)

PNA: Polish National Alliance (mutual benefit)

PNA: Pennsylvania Newspaper Association (trade group)

PNAB: Polish National Alliance of Brooklyn (mutual benefit)

PNBC: Progressive National Baptist Convention (religious denomination)

PNC: Platteville Normal College (Wisconsin) (higher education)

PNCC: Polish National Catholic Church (religious denomination)

PNCEA: Paulist National Catholic Evangelization Association (religious)

PNE: Pi Nu Epsilon (music) (academic honorary)

PNR: Panhandle Northern (railroad)

PNU: Polish National Union of America (mutual benefit)

PNW: Prescott & Northwestern (railroad)

PNWR: Portland and Western (railroad)

PO: Populist Party (political party)

PofH: Patrons of Husbandry (Grange) (fraternal)

POA: Patriotic Order of Americans (patriotic, mutual benefit)

POA: Patriots of America (political, free silver)

POAK: Port of Oakland Railway (railroad)

POF: Pennsylvania Order of Foresters (mutual benefit)

POG: Provincial Old Guard (fraternal, Masonic)

POH: Patrons of Husbandry (Grange) (fraternal)

POHC: Pittsburgh & Ohio Central (railroad)

POPi: Pi Omega Pi (business education) (academic honorary)

POS: Priory of Sion (bogus)

POSA: Patriotic Order of the Sons of America (nativist, mutual benefit)

POSofA: (see POSA – Patriotic Order of the Sons of America) (nativist, mutual benefit)

POTB: Port of Tillamook (railroad)
POUR: President's Organization for Unemployment Relief (political)
POV: Pittsburgh & Ohio Valley (railroad)
POW: Progressive Order of the West (mutual benefit)
POWER: Progressive Organization for Workplace and Employee Rights (labor union)
PP: Piscataqua Pioneers (lineage)
PP: Printing Pressmen (labor union)
PP: Progressive Party (political party)
PP: Patriot Party (political party)
PP: People's Party (political party)
PP: Populist Party (political party)
PP: Prohibition Party (political party)
PP: Progressive Party (a/k/a Bull Moose Party) (political party)
PPA: Proletarian Party of America (political party)
PPA: Protestant Protective Association (militant Protestant)
PPA: Professional Panhellenic Association (umbrella organization)
PPA: Professional Photographers of America (trade group)
PPB: Pacific Pioneer Broadcasters (professional)
PPBA: Portuguese Protective and Benevolent Association (mutual benefit)
PPC: Presbyterian Partnership of Conscience (religious)
PPFA: Planned Parenthood Federation of American (civic)
PPFA: Professional Picture Framers Association (professional)
PPG: Pittsburgh Plate Glass (business)
PPOSW: Patriotic & Protective Order of the Stags of the World (fraternal, mutual benefit)
PPP: Prudent Patricians of Pompeii (of the United States of America) (mutual benefit)
PPS: Partnership for Public Service (advocacy)
PPU: Peoria and Pekin Union Railway (railroad)
PR: Pavers and Rammermen (labor union)
PR: Progressive Party (political party)
PR: Pershing Rifles (military honorary)
PR: Pax Romana (religious)
PR: Philippine Airlines, Inc. (airline code)
PRAA: Playground and Recreation Association of America (civic)
PRC: Park Region College (Minnesota) (higher education)
PRC: Presbyterian Reformed Church (religious denomination)
PRC: Paul Revere Club (cult)

PRC: Postal Regulatory Commission (governmental)
PRCA: Protestant Reformed Churches in America (religious denomination)
PRCU: Polish Roman Catholic Union of America (also PRCUA) (mutual benefit)
PRCUA: Polish Roman Catholic Union of America (also PRCU) (mutual benefit)
PREC: Puerto Rico Education Council (education)
PRFC: Plymouth Rock Fanciers Club (poultry)
PRISM: Pacific Roundtable on Industry, Society and Management (business)
PRL: Penn Eastern Rail Lines (railroad)
PRMA: Pharmaceutical Research and Manufacturers of American (trade group)
PrMC: Primitive Methodist Church (religious denomination)
PRMI: Presbyterian-Reformed Ministries International (religious denomination)
PRNP: Puerto Rican Nationalist Party (political party)
PRODEMCA: Friends of the Democratic Center in Central America (political)
PRPi: Phi Rho Pi (forensics, junior college) (academic honorary)
PRR: Pennsylvania Railroad (railroad)
PRSA: Public Relations Society of America (professional)
PRSL: Pennsylvania-Reading Seashore (railroad)
PRSP: Puerto Rican Socialist Party (political party)
PRV: Pearl River Valley Railway (railroad)
PRYL: Port Royal Railroad
PS: Pythian Sisters (or Sisterhood) (fraternal)
PS: Plantagenet Society (lineage)
PS: Panacea Society (religious)
PS: Pittsburgh & Shawmut Railroad
PS: Phi Sigma (biology) (honorary fraternity)
PS: The Pilgrim Society (lineage)
PS: Philathletes Society (research, Masonic)
PS: Princes of Syracuse (youth, fraternal)
PS: Ukraine International Airlines (airline code)
PSA: Pi Sigma Alpha (political science) (academic honorary)
PSA: Pacific Sociological Association (professional)
PSA: Psychological Society of America (professional)
PSAP: Puget Sound and Pacific Railroad
PSC: Paul Smith's College (higher education)
PSC: Professional Services Council (trade group)
PSCU: Pennsylvania Slovak Catholic Union (mutual benefit)

249

PSDA: Print Services & Distribution Association (trade group)
PSI: Phi Sigma Iota (foreign languages) (academic honorary)
PSIA: Professional Ski Instructors of America (professional, sport)
PsiU: Psi Upsilon (college fraternity)
PSK: Phi Sigma Kappa (college fraternity)
PSL: Party for Socialism and Liberation (political party)
PSL: Peabody Short Line (railroad)
PSLL: Plymouth Short Line (railroad)
PSMI: Portland School of Medical Instruction (Maine) (higher education)
PSN: Project Safe Neighborhoods (advocacy)
PSS: Society of St. Sulpice (religious order)
PSSH: Plumbers', Steamfitters', and Steamfitters' Helpers' (labor union)
PST: Phi Sigma Tau (philosophy) (honorary fraternity)
PST: Phi Sigma Theta (honorary fraternity)
PT: Portland Terminal (railroad)
PTA: Parents and Teachers Association (see P-TA) (civic)
PTA: Pianoforte Tuners' Association (trade group)
PTE: Pi Theta Epsilon (occupational therapy) (academic honorary)
PTG: Piano Technicians Guild (trade, musical)
PTK: Phi Theta Kappa (junior college) (academic honorary)
PTK: Phi Theta Kappa (fraternal, service)
PTR: Port Terminal Railroad of SC (railroad)
PTS: Pi Tau Sigma (mechanical engineering) (honorary fraternity)
PTS: Phi Tau Sigma (food science) (academic honorary)
PTS: Princeton Theological Seminary (higher education)
PUA: Polish Union of America (mutual benefit)
PUL: Philadelphia Union League (men's club)
PUO: Phi Upsilon Omicron (consumer science) (academic honorary)
PVA: Pioneer Valley Academy (school)
PVA: Paralyzed Veterans of America (veterans)
PVMI: Parish Visitors of Mary Immaculate (religious order)
PVRR: Pioneer Valley Railroad
PVS: Pecos Valley Southern (railroad)
PW: Providence & Worcester (railroad)
PWA: Public Works Administration (New Deal) (governmental)
PWAA: Polish Women's Alliance of America (mutual benefit)
PWIA: Personal Watercraft Industry Association (trade group)

PWU: Potash Workers Union (labor union)
PWV: Pittsburgh & West Virginia (railroad)
PX: Psi Chi (psychology) (honorary fraternity)
PYC: Presbyterian Youth Connection (youth, religious)
PZ: Phi Zeta (veterinary medicine) (honorary fraternity)

Q

Q&S: Quill & Scroll (also QS and QSS) (high school honorary)
QA: Quarrymen's Association (labor union)
QA: Queens of Avilion (religious, girls)
QAAA: Quebec Amateur Athletic Association (sports)
QAHA: Quebec Amateur Hockey Association (sports)
QAIMNS: Queen Alexandra's Imperial Military Nursing Service (UK) (governmental)
QAR: Queen Anne's Revenge (Blackbeard's flagship)
QBT: Quincy Bay Terminal Company (railroad)
QC: Quebec Central Railway (railroad)
QCI: Quota Club International (women)
QEBH: Secret senior honor society at the University of Missouri (honorary)
QF: Qantas Airways Ltd. (airline code)
QFA: Qantas Airways Ltd. (airline code)
QHL: Quebec Hockey League (sports)
QM: Quartermaster (military, World War I)
QMC: Quartermaster Corps (Army branch)
QR: Qatar Airways (airline code)
QRC: Quail Run Christian School (school)
QRR: Quincy Railroad
QS: Quill & Scroll Society (also Q&S and QSS) (high school honorary)
QSHL: Quebec Senior Hockey League (sports)
QSS: Quill & Scroll Society (high school honorary)
QRS: Bangor & Aroostook Railway (railroad car marking)
QTR: Qatar Airways (airline code)

R

R: Republican (political party)
R&C: Raleigh & Charleston Railroad
R&D: Richmond & Danville (railroad)
RA: Rebekah Assemblies (fraternal)
RA: Railroad Administration (governmental, WWI)
RA: Royal Academy (possibly Royal Academy of the Arts or Royal Academy of Music)
RA: Royal Arcanum (fraternal, mutual benefit)
RA: Religious of the Assumption (religious order)
RA: Resettlement Administration (governmental, New Deal)
RA: Royal Ambassadors (religious, youth)
RA: Readjuster (political party)
RA: Resettlement Administration (governmental)
RA: Royal Adelphia (mutual benefit)
RAAC: Royal Australian Air Corps (military)
RAAF: Royal Australian Air Force (military)
RAC: Royal Arch Chapter (fraternal)
RAC: Recording Artists Coalition (labor union)
RACN: Raccoon River Railroad
RACRJ: Religious Action Center of Reform Judaism (lobby)
RAF: Royal Air Force (military, British)
RAJ: Russian Association of Japanologists (learned)
RAM: Royal Arch Masons (Masonic)
RAM: Royal Air Maroc (airline code)
RAMC: Royal Army Medical Corps (military, British, World War I)
RAMC: Restored Apostolic Mission Church (religious denomination)
RAN: Royal Australian Navy (military)
RAND: RAND Corporation (acronym of Research and Development) (research)
RANU: Regular Army and Navy Union (veterans)
RAOA: Railway Accounting Officers Association (trade organization)
RAOB: Royal Antediluvian Order of Buffaloes (fraternal, British, service)
RAPC: Royal Arch Purple Chapter (Protestant Irish, fraternal)
RAPS: Regulatory Affairs Professional Society (professional)

RandR: Refoundation and Revolution (political)
RAS: Royal Aid Society (mutual benefit)
RB: Reformed Baptist (religious denomination)
RB: Regular Baptist (religious denomination)
RB: Rochester Brotherhood (fraternal)
RB: Rebel Brigades (KKK)
RBA: Romanian Baptist Association (religious denomination)
RBAI: Royal Black Association of Ireland (Protestant Irish)
RBB: Royal American Shows (rail car symbol)
RBC: Regular Baptist Church (religious denomination)
RBDA: Regional Bond Dealers Association (trade group)
RBMHF: Rhythm and Blues Music Hall of Fame (musical)
RBMN: Reading, Blue Mountain & Northern Railroad
RBO: Russian Brotherhood Association (of the USA) (Mutual benefit)
RBOX: RailBox/RailGon (also ABOX and GONX) (Rail car leasing company)
RBP: Royal Black Preceptory (a/k/a Royal Black Knights) (Masonic)
RBS: Royal Benefit Society (mutual benefit)
RC: Republican Club (political)
RC: Roman Catholic (religious denomination)
RC: Red Cross (civic)
RC: Republican Club (political)
RC: Religious of the Cenacle (Cenacle Sisters) (religious order)
RC: Rivendell Community (religious community)
RC: Rosslyn Connecting Railroad
RC: Rangers of the Cross (KKK)
RC: Regnum Christi (lay order)
RC: Rivendell Community (religious)
RCA: Reformed Church in America (religious denomination)
RCA: Red Cross Auxiliary
RCA: Radio Corporation of America (corporation)
RCA: Royal College of Art (UK university)
RCAC: Royal Canadian Army Cadets (military)
RCAF: Royal Canadian Air Force (military)
RCAMS: Roman Catholic Archdiocese for the Military Services, USA (religious, military support)
RCC: Red Cross of Constantine (also RCofC) (Masonic)
RCC: Religion Communicators Council (religious, professional)
RCCG: Redeemed Christian Church of God (religious denomination)
RCF: Aeroflot – Cargo (airline code)

RCI: Revival Centres International (religious denomination)
RCI: Ricker Classical Institute (Maine) (higher education)
RCIU: Retail Clerks International Union (labor union)
RCJ: Rogationists of the Heart of Jesus (religious order)
RCK: Red Cross Knights (Knight of the Red Cross of Constantine (Masonic)
RCKL: Royal Conclave of Knights and Ladies (mutual benefit)
RCL: Royal Canadian Legion (veterans)
RCMP: Royal Canadian Mounted Police (governmental)
RCO: Rose Cross Order of the Orient (Rosicrucians, fraternal)
RCofC: Red Cross of Constantine (also RCC) (Masonic)
RCPUSA: Revolutionary Communist Party of the USA (political)
RCR: Randall Cattle Registry Inc. (cattle)
RCRY: Raritan Central Railway (railroad)
RCU: Retail Clerks' Union (labor union)
RCUS: Reformed Church in the United States (religious denomination)
RD: Rebecca Degree (fraternal)
RDA: Riding for the Disabled Association (equestrian)
RDG: Reading Railroad
RE: Red Eagles (mutual benefit)
REA: Rural Electrification Administration (New Deal) (governmental)
REA: The Retired Enlisted Association (veterans)
REAP: Research, Educate, Advocacy, People (union reform group)
REC: Reformed Episcopal Church (religious denomination)
RENAMO: Mozambican National Resistance (guerilla organization)
REOA: Royal Exalted Order of the Ameranth (Masonic)
REOF: Royal and Exalted Order of Fleas (fraternal)
RF: Rosicrucian Fraternity (fraternal, religious)
RF: Royal Fraternity, The (mutual benefit)
RF&P: Richmond, Fredericksburg and Potomac Railroad (also RFP)
RFA: Royal Field Artillery (military, British, World War I)
RFA: Radio Free Asia (governmental)
RFB: Royal Fellows of Bagdad (sales, political)
RFC: Reconstruction Finance Corporation (quasi-governmental)
RFCI: Resilient Floor Covering Institute (trade group)
RFE: Radio Free Europe (governmental)

RFG: Royal Fraternal Guardians (mutual benefit)
RFJI: Research Foundation for Jewish Immigration, Inc. (religious)
RFP: Richmond, Fredericksburg & Potomac Railroad (also RF&P)
RFS: Resident and Fellow Section (professional)
RG: Rainbow Girls (youth, Masonic)
RG: Varig Airlines (airline code)
RG: Royal Guardians (fraternal, service, mutual benefit)
RGS: Good Shepherd Sisters (religious order)
RGS: Rio Grande Southern Railroad
RGW: Rio Grande Western Railroad
RH: Royal Highlanders (mutual benefit)
RHA: Rebekah Home Association (fraternal)
RHC: Rock Hill College (Maryland) (higher education)
RI: Rotary International (fraternal, civic)
RI: Chicago, Rock Island and Pacific (also ROCK) (railroad)
RIAA: Recording Industry Association of America (trade group)
RIAJ: Recording Industry Association of Japan (trade group)
RIANZ: Recording Industry Association of New Zealand (trade group)
RIC: Rhode Island College (higher education)
RIHMS: Rhode Island Home Missionary Society (religious)
RILA: Retail Industry Leaders Association (trade group)
RIMAS: Russian Independent Mutual Aid Society (mutual benefit)
RIMS: Risk and Insurance Management Society (trade group)
RIRC: Rhode Island Red Club (poultry)
RIRJ: Research Institute of Religious Jewry (religious)
RISC: Regulatory Information Service Center (governmental)
RISD: Rhode Island School of Design (Rhode Island) (higher education)
RIT: Rochester Institute of Technology (New York) (higher education)
RITA: Research and Innovative Technology Administration (governmental)
RJ: Royal Jordanian Airlines (airline code)
RJA: Royal Jordanian Airlines (airline code)
RJC: Republican Jewish Coalition (lobby)
RJCV: R. J. Corman Railroad/West Virginia Line (railroad)
RK: Roman Knights (Rosicrucian)
RKA: Royal Knights of America (unknown but did exist)

RKKD: Royal Knights of King David (mutual benefit)
RL: Rebecca (Rebekah) Lodge (fraternal)
RL: Rutland Line (railroad)
RL: Royal League (Canadian hockey minor league)
RL: Royal League (mutual benefit)
RL: Radio Liberty (governmental)
RLA: Rebekah Ladies Auxiliary (fraternal)
RLA: Robert Land Academy (school)
RLBA: Randall Lineback Breed Association (livestock)
RLDS: Reorganized Church of Jesus Christ of Latter-day Saints (religious denomination)
RM: Red Men (fraternal)
RM: Reformed Methodist Church (religious denomination)
RM: Reformed Mennonites (religious denomination)
RMA: Reserve Military Aviator (military, World War I)
RMA: Randolph-Macon Academy (school)
RMA: Riverside Military Academy (school)
RMBI: Royal Masonic Benevolent Institution (Masonic, mutual benefit)
RMBS: Rocky Mountain Business Seminar (business)
RMC: Royal Military College of Canada (higher education, military)
RMEC: Recovery Ministries of the Episcopal Church (religious)
RMHA: Rocky Mountain Horse Association (equine)
RMK: Rocky Mountain Knights (KKK)
RMOKH: Religious and Military Order of the Knights of the Holy Sepulchre (also seen as RMOKHSJ) (religious)
RMOKHSJ: Religious and Military Order of the Knights of the Holy Sepulchre (also seen as RMOKH) (religious)
RN: Royal Neighbors of America (also RNA) (mutual benefit)
RNA: Royal Neighbors of America (also RN) (mutual benefit)
RNC: Republican National Committee (political organization)
RNU: Ruthenian National Union (mutual benefit)
RNWMP: Royal North West Mounted Police (Canada) (governmental)
RNZAF: Royal New Zealand Air Force (military)
RNZRSA: Royal New Zealand Returned and Services Organization (veterans)
RO: Rosicrucian Order, a/k/a AMORC (also RO-AUM) (Masonic, fraternal)
ROA: Retired Officers Association (veterans)
ROA: Reserve Officers Association (military support)
RO-AUM: Rosicrucian Order (also RO) (Masonic, fraternal)

ROAUS: Reserve Officers Association of the United States (military)

ROCA: Russian Orthodox Church in American (religious denomination)

ROCK: Chicago, Rock Island & Pacific (also RI) (railroad)

ROCMAS: Russian Orthodox Catholic Mutual Aid Society (mutual benefit)

ROCWMAS: Russian Orthodox Catholic Women's Mutual Aid Society (mutual benefit)

ROFDA: Retailer Owned Food Distributors & Associates (trade group)

ROGD: Rosicrucian Order of the Golden Dawn (fraternal, Rosicrucian)

ROJ: Royal Order of Jesters (Masonic)

ROL: Revolutionary Organization of Labor (political)

ROL: Royal Order of Lions (also ROOL) (fraternal, antecedent of Lions Clubs International)

ROOL: Royal Order of Lions (also ROL) (fraternal, antecedent of Lions Clubs International)

ROP: Royal Order of Purple (probably Order of Royal Purple - female branch of Elks in Canada) (fraternal)

ROPA: Regional Orchestra Players Association (professional)

ROS: Royal Order of Scotland (Masonic)

ROTC: Reserve Officers' Training Corps (military)

RP: Reformed Presbyterian Church, a/k/a Covenanters (religious denomination)

RP: Readjuster Party (political party)

RPA: Renal Physicians Association (professional)

RPAC: Revolution Political Action Committee (lobby, libertarian)

RPC: Railway Postal Clerks (labor union)

RPCGA: Reformed Presbyterian Church General Assembly (religious denomination)

RPCNA: Reformed Presbyterian Church of North America (religious denomination)

RPCUS: Reformed Presbyterian Church in the United States (religious denomination)

RPG: Sister Adorers of the Precious Blood (religious order)

RPI: Rensselaer Polytechnic Institute (New York) (higher education)

RPI: Recognition Professionals International (professional)

RPNGA: Rebekah Past Noble Grands Association (fraternal)

RPRC: Richmond Pacific Railroad

RPS: Rhodes Preparatory School (school)
RPUSA: Reform Party of the United States of America (political party)
RR: Raritan River (railroad)
RR&C: Railroad and Construction Service (military, World War I)
RRA: Reconstructionist Rabbinical Association (religious)
RRB: Railroad Retirement Board (governmental)
RRC: Restored Reformed Church (religious denomination)
RRC: Reconstructionist Rabbinical College (religious, higher education)
RRC: Residency Review Committee (accrediting)
RRCI: Redmont Railway (railroad)
RRCO: Rochelle Railroad
RRR: Riders of the Red Robe (KKK)
RRRR: Royal Riders of the Red Robe (KKK)
RRVU: Red River Valley University (North Dakota) (higher education)
RRVW: Red River Valley and Western Railroad
RS: Relief Society (women)
RS: Roberval and Saguenay Railway (railroad)
RSA: Royal Standard of America (mutual benefit)
RSAA: Receptive Services Association of America (trade group)
RSAC: Recreational Software Advisory Council (trade group)
RSB: Rochester Subway (railroad)
RSCJ: Society of the Sacred Heart (religious order)
RSGF: Royal Society of Good Fellows (possibly same as AOGF – Ancient Order of Good Fellows) (mutual benefit)
RSLA: Returned & Services League of Australia (veterans)
RSM: Royal and Select Masons (sometimes "Selected" instead of "Select") (Masonic)[4]
RSM: Religious Sisters of Mercy (religious order)
RSM: Sisters of Mercy (religious order)
RSM: Sisters of Mercy of the Americas (religious order)
RSMA: Railway Supply Manufacturers Association (trade group)
RSNA: Radiological Society of North America (professional)
RSNR: Red Springs and Northern Railroad
RSofGF: (possibly) Royal Society of Good Fellows (fraternal)
RSOR: Riceboro Southern Railway (railroad)

---

[4] Gerald Edgar points out that this is the abbreviation for Royal Select Master, an office within the York Rite of Masonry. It has also been seen as Royal Select Masons.

RSP: Roscoe, Snyder and Pacific Railway (railroad)
RSR: Rochester & Southern (railroad)
RSSG: Royal Society of Saint George (lineage)
RSTV: Rite of St. Vaclara (a misspelling of Vaclava) (also RStV) (unknown)
RStV: Rite of St. Vaclava (also seen as RSTV) (unknown)
RStV: Rite of St. Vitus (also seen misspelled at St. Vita) (mystical)
RSV: Rite of St. Vitus (mystical)
RSW: Rathbone Sisters of the World (fraternal)
RT: Royal Templars of Temperance (also RTofT and RTT) (political/social)
RT: River Terminal (railroad)
RTA: Railway Tie Association (trade group)
RTC: Round Table Club (fraternal, service)
RTJ: Royal Tribe of Joseph (fraternal, mutual benefit)
RTN: Russian Television Network (religious, political)
RTofT: Royal Templars of Temperance (also RT and RTT) (political/social)
RTT: Royal Templars of Temperance (see RTofT and RT) (political/social)
RTT: Romania Think Tank (political)
RUP: Raza Unida Party (political party)
RUT: Rutland Railroad
RV: Rahway Valley Railroad (also RVRR)
RVPR: Riverport Railroad
RVRR: Rahway Valley Railroad (also RV)
RW: Reconciling Works (religious)
RW&B: Red, White and Blue (also RWB) (nativist, anti-Catholic)
RWB: Red, White and Blue (also RW&B) (nativist, anti-Catholic)
RWDSU: Retail, Wholesale and Department Store Union (labor union)
RWF: Roger Williams Fellowship (religious denomination)
RWS: Red Wing Seminary (Minnesota) (higher education)
RWU: Roger Williams University (Tennessee) (higher education)
RX: Rho Chi (pharmacy) (academic honorary)
RYR: Ryanair, Ltd. (airline code)

S

S: Silver Party (political party)

S&B: Scabbard and Blade (military collegiate honorary)

SA: Society of the Atonement (Graymoor Friars and Sisters) (religious order)

SA: Socialist Action (political party)

SA: Socialist Alternative (political party)

SA: Savannah and Atlanta Railroad

SA: Sons of Adam (also SofA) (fraternal)

SA: Salvation Army (religious denomination)

SA: South African Airways (airline code)

SA: Franciscan Sisters of the Atonement (religious order)

SA: Society of Actuaries (professional)

SAA: Society of American Archivists (professional organization)

SAA: South African Airways (airline code)

SABR: Society for American Baseball Research, Inc. (sports0

SAC: Society of the Catholic Apostolate (Pallottines) (religious order)

SAC: Second Advent Church (religious denomination)

SAC: Society of the Army of the Cumberland (veterans)

SAC: Strategic Air Command (military)

SACS: Southern Association of Colleges and Schools (education, accrediting)

SAD: Society of the Ark and Dove (lineage)

SADD: Students Against Drunk Driving (civic)

SAE: Sigma Alpha Epsilon (fraternity)

SAEE: Society for Arts Entrepreneurship Education (musical)

SAF: Scandinavian American Fraternity (mutual benefit, fraternal)

SAFE-BioPharma: Biological Pharmaceutical Association (see also Pharmaceutical Research and Manufacturers of America (PhRMA) (Trade group)

SAFS: Small Arms Firing School (military, World War I)

SAG: Screen Actors Guild (labor union)

SAG: Society of the Army of Georgia (veterans)

SAG-AFTRA: Screen Actors Guild – American Federation of Television and Radio Artists (merged organization) (labor union)

SAGES: Society of American Gastrointestinal Endoscopic Surgeons (professional)

SAH: Society of Architectural Historians (learned)
SAH: Slovak American Home (ethnic, musical)
SAHS: Swiss-American Historical Society (learned)
SAI: Sigma Alpha Iota (fraternal/musical)
SAI: Society of American Indians (fraternal)
SAIS: Southern Association of Independent Schools (education)
SAL: Sons of the American Legion (lineage)
SAL: Seaboard Air Line Railroad
SAL: Sigma Alpha Lambda (leadership) (academic honorary)
SAMHSA: Substance Abuse and Mental Health Services
Administration (governmental)
SAN: Sandersville (railroad)
SAPB: Sisters Adorers of the Precious Blood (religious order)
SAPi: Sigma Alpha Pi (leadership) (academic honorary)
SAPT: Savannah Port Terminal Railroad
SAR: Sisters of the American Revolution (lineage)
SAR: Sons of the American Revolution (also NSAR) (lineage)
SAR: Sigma Alpha Rho (high school fraternity)
SARA: Society of American Registered Architects (professional)
SAS: Saint Andrew's Society (lineage)
SAS: St. Ambrogio Society (social)
SAS: Scandinavian Airlines System (airline code, business)
SAS: Society of American Silversmiths (craft)
SASA: South African Sheepdog Association (canine)
SAT: Society of the Army of the Tennessee (veterans)
SATC: Student Army Training Corps (military, WWI)
SAVMA: Student American Veterinary Medical Association
(student)
SAWV: Spanish American War Veterans (veterans)
SAWV: Society of the Army of West Virginia (veterans)
SB: Strict Baptists (religious denomination)
SB: Separate Baptist (religious denomination)
SB: South Buffalo (railroad)
SB: Separate Baptists (religious denomination)
SB: Spiritual Baptists (religious denomination)
SB: Sons of Benjamin (IOSB: Independent Order of the Sons
of Benjamin (Jewish, fraternal)
SB: Spartan Band (Burnett's 13th Texas Cavalry) (military, Civil
War)
SB: Social Brethren (religious denomination)
SBA: Security Benefit Association (mutual benefit)
SBA: Small Business Administration (governmental)
SBBA: Spanish Barb Breeders Association (equine)

SBC: Southern Baptist Convention (religious denomination)
SBC: Separate Baptists in Christ (religious denomination)
SBC: Sue Bennett College (Kentucky) (higher education)
SBCA: Satellite Broadcasting and Communications Association (trade group)
SBCL: Saint Boniface (also seen as Bonifazius) Catholic Union (religious, mutual benefit)
SBD: Seaboard System Railroad
SBD: Sigma Beta Delta (business administration) (academic honorary)
SBD: Hereditary Order of the Signers of the Bush Declaration of March 22, 1775 (lineage)
SBF: Southwide Baptist Fellowship (religious denomination)
SBF: Society of Blue Friars (fraternal)
SBHA: Spanish Barb Horse Association (equine)
SBIC: Separate Baptists in Christ (religious denomination)
SBK: South Brooklyn (railroad)
SBL: Society of Biblical Literature (religious)
SBL: Society B. Lafayette (lineage)
SBLN: Sterling Belt Line Railway (railroad)
SBM: St. Louis, Brownsville and Mexico (railroad)
SBofA: Scandinavian Brotherhood of America (lineage)
SBOA: Slovakian Brotherhood of America (lineage)
SBPS: Southern Baptist Publication Society (religious)
SBRR: Stourbridge Railroad Company (railroad)
SBS: Stoneleigh-Burnham School (Massachusetts) (school)
SBS: Sisters of the Blessed Sacrament (religious order)
SBTC: Southern Baptists of Texas Convention (religious denomination)
SBVR: South Branch Valley Railroad
SC: Society of the Cincinnati (lineage)
SC: Sisters of Charity (religious order)
SC: Sisters of Charity (UK) (religious community)
SC: Signal Corps (Army branch)
SC: Sisters of Charity of Saint Elizabeth (religious order)
SC: Brothers of the Sacred Heart (religious order)
SC: Spokane College (Washington) (higher education)
SC: Storer College (West Virginia) (higher education)
SC: Sumter and Choctaw Railway (railroad)
SC: Stamford College (Texas) (higher education)
SCA: Society for Creative Anachronism (historical role play) (educational)
SCA: Society for Cultural Anthropology (professional)

SCAA: Specialty Coffee Association of America (trade group)
SCAI: Society for Cardiovascular Angiography and Interventions (professional)
SCAW: Supreme Camp of American Woodmen (fraternal, mutual benefit, ethnic)
SCB: Southeast Conservative Baptists (religious denomination)
SCB: Society for Conservation Biology (professional)
SCBG: Santa Cruz, Big Trees and Pacific Railway (railroad)
SCC: Sisters of Christian Charity (religious order)
SCC: Skirball Cultural Center (religious)
SCC: Southern Claims Commission (governmental)
SCC: Supply Chain Council (professional)
SCCA: Sports Car Club of American (motorsports)
SCCE: Society of Corporate Compliance and Ethics (professional)
SCCM: Society of Critical Care Medicine (professional)
SCCU: Slovak Catholic Cadets Union (mutual benefit)
SCD: Society of Christian Doctrine (religious)
SCDA: Society of the Colonial Dames of America (lineage)
SCDM: Society for Clinical Data Management (professional)
SCHC: Society of the Companions of the Holy Cross (religious order)
SCI: Southern Christian Institute (Mississippi) (higher education)
SCIGA: San Clemente Island Goat Association (goats)
SCHC: Companions of the Society of the Holy Cross (religious order)
SCIOTS: Ancient Egyptian Order of Sciots (Masonic)
SCJ: Congregation of Priests of the Sacred Heart (Sacred Heart Fathers) (religious order)
SCL: Sisters of Charity of Leavenworth (religious order)
SCMA: Society of Chemical Manufacturers and Affiliates (trade group)
SCOA: Supreme Council Order of the Amaranth (Masonic)
SCORC: Signal Corps Officers' Reserve Corps (military, World War I)
SCORE International: Sanctioning Committee Off Road Events International (motorsports)
SCOTS: Signal Corps Officers' Training School (military, World War I)
SCOTUS: Supreme Court of the United States (governmental)
SCP: Society of California Pioneers (lineage)
SCP: Scriptural Counterfeits Project (religious)

SCPP: Steel and Copper Plate Printers (labor union)
SCR: Sydney Coal Railroad
SCR: South Central Railroad
SCRF: South Carolina Central Railroad
SCRW: Seaway Commercial Railway (railroad)
SCS: Slovak Catholic Sokol (mutual benefit, physical fitness)
SCS: Slavonic Catholic Society (also appears as SKS) (ethnic, mutual benefit)
SCS: Swedish Colonial Society (lineage)
SCSARD: Sovereign Colonial Society Americans of Royal Descent (lineage)
SCSU: Southern Connecticut State University (higher education)
SCT: Sioux City Terminal Railway (railroad)
SCTA: Southern California Timing Association (motorsports)
SCTK: Supreme Conclave of True Kindred (fraternal)
SCTR: South Central Tennessee Railroad
SCUB: Supreme Commandery of the United Brotherhood (mutual benefit)
SCUP: Society for College and University Planning (professional)
SCV: Sons of (the) Confederate Veterans (lobby)
SCVCW: Sons of Confederate Veterans of the Civil War (lineage)
SCW: Society of Colonial Wars (lineage)
SCWU: Shirt and Collar Workers' Union (labor union)
SD/USA: Social Democrats USA (political)
SDA: Sigma Delta Alpha (fraternity, ethnic)
SDA: Seventh Day Adventist (religious denomination)
SDA: Society of Descendents of the Alamo (lineage)
SDA: Society of Design Administrators (professional)
SDA: San Diego and Arizona Railroad
SDA: Shop, Distributive and Allied Employees Assn. (trade union, Australia)
SDA: Shrine Directors of North America (fraternal, Shriners)
SDA: Soap and Detergent Association (trade group)
SDA: Surface Design Association (professional)
SDA: St. Dominic Academy (New Jersey) (school)
SDA: Schools Development Authority (New Jersey, governmental)
SDA: Sons and Daughters of America (mutual benefit)
SDA: SD Card Association (trade group)
SDAC: Seventh Day Adventist Church (religious denomination)

SDARM: Seventh Day Adventist Reform Movement (religious denomination)
SDB: Salesians of St. John Bosco (religious order)
SDB: Seventh Day Baptists (religious denomination)
SDBB: Somerset Terminal Railroad
SDBGC: Seventh Day Baptist General Conference of the United States and Canada (religious denomination)
SDC: Seventh Day Christians (religious denomination)
SDC: Sisters of Divine Charity (religious order)
SDCC: Society of the Descendants of the Colonial Clergy (lineage)
SDCS: Stage Directors and Choreographers Society (labor union)
SDFH: Society of the Descendants of the Founders of Hartford (lineage)
SDIV: San Diego and Imperial Valley Railroad
SDJ: Sons and Daughters of Justice (mutual benefit)
SDK: Society of Descendants of Knights of the Most Noble Order of the Garter (lineage)
SDKG: Society of Descendants of Knights of the Garter (lineage)
SDL: Sons and Daughters of Liberty (fraternal, mutual benefit)
SDLP: Social Democratic and Labour Party (UK, political)
SDNA: Shrine Directors of North America (religious)
SDNR: San Diego Northern Railway (railroad)
SDOP: Self-Development of People (religious)
SDOP: Sons and Daughters of Oregon Pioneers (lineage)
SDP: Social Democratic Party (political party)
SDP: Sons and Daughters of Protection (nativist, mutual benefit)
SDPi: Sigma Delta Pi (Spanish and Portuguese) (academic honorary)
SDR: Sons and Daughters of the Revolution (lineage)
SDS: Saint David's Society (lineage)
SDS: Students for a Democratic Society (political action)
SDS: Society of the Divine Savior (Salvatorians) (religious order)
SDS: Sisters of the Divine Savior (religious order)
SDSC: Society of Descendents of Signers of the Constitution (lineage)
SDSE: Society of the Descendants of the Schwenkfeldian Exiles (lineage)

SDSH: Sisters of the Society Devoted to the Sacred Heart (Sacred Heart Sisters) (religious order)
SDSU: Soo Line Railroad
SDUSA: Social Democrats, USA (political)
SDV: Clerics of the Divine Vocation (Vocationist Fathers and Brothers) (religious order)
SE: Stationary Engineers (labor union)
SEA: Society for the Elimination of Acronyms (social movement)
SEAMUS: Society for Electro-Acoustic Music in the United States (musical)
SEBC: Societe des Eleveurs de Bovins Canadiens (cattle)
SEBS: Sons of England Benevolent Society (fraternal, mutual benefit, hereditary)
SEC: Scottish Episcopal Church (religious denomination)
SEC: Southern Episcopal Church (religious denomination)
SEC: Supreme Emblem Club (of the United States of America) (hobby)
SEC: Sephardic Educational Center (religious)
SEC: Securities and Exchange Commission (governmental)
SECC: Societe des Eleveurs de Cheveaux Canadiens (equine)
SEIA: Solar Energy Industry Association (trade group)
SEIU: Service Employees International Union (labor union)
SEKR: Southeast Kansas Railroad
SEM: School of Ecclesiastic Music (religious, musical)
SEM: Society for Economic Measurement (professional)
SEMA: Southeastern Military Academy (school)
SEP: Socialist Equality Party (political)
SEPA: Southeastern Pennsylvania Transportation Authority (SEPTA) (railroad)
SER: Society for Ecological Restoration (civic)
SERA: Sierra Railroad
SERC: Signal Enlisted Reserve Corps (military, World War I)
SERV: Society of Ethical and Religious Vegetarians (religious, lifestyle)
SES: Society Espirito Santo (religious)
SES: Socialist Educational Society (political)
SESAC: (see SESCAC)
SESCAC: (musical copyright trade organization – meaning of acronym unknown)
SETAC: Society of Environmental Toxicology and Chemistry (professional)
SEU: Stereotypers' and Electrotypers' Union (labor union)

SF: Select Friends (unknown)
SF: Sons of the Holy Family (religious order)
SFA: Special Forces Association (military)
SFA: Scandinavian Fraternity of America (mutual benefit)
SFAL: SF and L Railway (railroad)
SFAW: Solid Fuels Administration for War (governmental)
SFB: Sphinx Fraternal Brotherhood (high school fraternity)
SFIA: Society for Industrial Archaeology (also SIA) (professional)
SFLIS: Stoga (Sloga?) Fraternal Life Insurance Society (mutual benefit, ethnic)
SFLR: Shore Fast Line Railroad
SFP: Franciscan Sisters of the Poor (religious order)
SFR: Southern Freight Railroad
SFS: Santa Fe Southern Railway (railroad)
SFWC: Supreme Forest Woodmen Circle (mutual benefit)
SEU: Slovak Evangelical Union (mutual benefit)
SFSU: San Francisco State University (higher education)
SFW: Society of the Foreign Wars of the United States (veterans)
SFWC: Supreme Forest Woodmen Circle (fraternal)
SG: Sunshine Girls (youth, fraternal)
SG: Brothers of Christian Instruction of St. Gabriel (religious order)
SGA: St. Gregory's Abby (religious community)
SGA: Spanish Goat Association (goats)
SGB: Sovereign Grace Baptists (religious denomination)
SGE: Sigma Gamma Epsilon (geology) (academic honorary)
SGFC: Sovereign Grace Fellowship of Canada (religious, Canadian)
SGIM: Society of General Internal Medicine (professional)
SGLR: Seminole Gulf Railway (railroad)
SGM: Soeurs Grises de Montreal (Grey Nuns of Montreal) (Sisters of Charity of Montreal) (religious order)
SGM: Sovereign Grace Ministries (religious denomination)
SGMA: Sporting Goods Manufacturers Association (trade group)
SGN: Soeurs Grises de Quebec (Sisters of Charity of Quebec; Grey Nuns) (religious order)
SGQ: Soeurs Grises de Quebec (Sisters of Charity of Quebec; Grey Nuns) (religious order)
SGS: St. George's Society (lineage)

SGT: Sigma Gamma Tau (aerospace engineering) (honorary fraternity)

SGUS: Slovak Gymnastic Union Sokol of the USA (mutual benefit)

SGVY: Saginaw Valley Railway (railroad)

SH: Steelton and Highspire Railroad

SH: Order of the Sons of Hermann (fraternal, mutual benefit)

SH: Shield of Honor (mutual benefit)

SH: Sons of Hermann (fraternal)

SHA: Southern Historical Association (learned)

SHAFR: Society for Historians of American Foreign Relations (professional)

SHC: Society of the Holy Cross (religious community)

SHCJ: Society of the Holy Child Jesus (religious order)

SHF: Sisters of the Holy Family (religious order)

SHI: Stolen Horse International (equestrian)

SHJ: Society for Humanistic Judaism (religious)

SHM: Society for Hospice Medicine (professional)

SHM: Society of Hospital Medicine (professional)

SHM: Social History of Medicine (learned)

SHN: Sisterhood of the Holy Nativity (religious community)

SHR: Sulphur Horse Registry (equine)

SHRM: Society for Human Resource Management (professional)

SHS: Society of the Holy Spirit of the State of California (mutual benefit)

SHS: Subsistence Homesteads Division (governmental)

SI: Sisters of the Incarnation (religious community

SI: Sons of Italy (see also SofI) (ethnic, mutual benefit)

SI: Spokane International Railway (railroad)

SI: Soroptimist International (fraternal)

SI: Sertoma International (service – hearing impairment)

SIA: Society for Industrial Archaeology (also SFIA) (professional)

SIA: Singapore Airlines Limited (airline code)

SID: Society for Investigative Dermatology (professional)

SIFMA: Securities Industry and Financial Markets Association (trade group)

SIGNIS: World Catholic Association for Communication (religious, professional)

SIHR: Society for International Hockey Research (sports)

SILS: St. Ignatius Loyola (school or college, usually) (school/higher education)

SIM: Sudan Interior Ministry (religious)
SIM: The Society for the Increase of the Ministry (religious)
SIMS: Societa Italiana di Mutto Soccorso (mutual benefit)
SIND: Southern Indiana Railway (railroad)
SIP: Society of Indiana Pioneers (lineage)
SiPSi: Sigma Pi Sigma (high school sorority)
SIR: Sigma Iota Rho (international relations) (academic honorary)
SIR: Sons In Retirement (fraternal)
SIR: Society of Interventional Radiology (professional)
SIRC: Staten Island Railroad
SIRR: Southern Industrial Railroad
SIRX: Southern Illinois Railcar (rail car leasing company)
SIS: Scotch-Irish Society (of the United States of America (lineage)
SIS: Steamboat Inspection Service (governmental)
SIS: Signals Intelligence Service (governmental)
SIS: The Spine Intervention Society (professional)
SIU: Seafarers International Union of North America (labor union)
SJ: Society of Jesus (Jesuits) (religious order)
SJ: Sons of Jonadab (temperance)
SJBA: Sephardic Jewish Brotherhood of America (Jewish, mutual benefit)
SJE: Society of Jewish Ethics (religious)
SJH: Sisters of Jesus our Hope (religious order)
SJMS: St. John's Military School (school)
SJP: Students for Justice in Palestine (political)
SJT: St. Joseph Terminal Railroad
SJVR: San Joaquin Valley Railroad
SK: Scandinavian Airlines System (airline code)
SKD: Sigma Kappa Delta (English at two year colleges) (academic honorary)
SKIP: Special Kindness in Packages (military support)
SKOL: South Kansas and Oklahoma Railroad
SKPR: Southern Kent and Pacific Railroad
SKS: South Kent School (school)
SKS: Slavonic Catholic Society (also SCS) (mutual benefit)
SKUM: Sigma Kappa Upsilon Mu (college fraternity)
SL: Sons of Liberty (nativist)
SL: Sisters of Life (religious order)
SL: Sisters of Loretto (or Loreto) at the Foot of the Cross (religious order)

SL: Sexennial League (mutual benefit)
SL: Salt Lake City Southern Railroad
SL: Spartacist League (political)
SLA: Sigma Lambda Alpha (landscape architecture) (academic honorary)
SLA: Special Libraries Association (umbrella organization)
SLAL: South Plains Lamesa Railroad
SLAW: St. Lawrence Railroad
SLC: San Luis Central Railroad
SLEHC: St. Luke's Episcopal Health Charities (religious)
SLF: Saint Laurence Foundation (religious)
SLG: Community of the Sisters of the Love of God (religious community)
SLGG: Sidney and Lowe Railroad
SLGW: Salt Lake, Garfield and Western Railroad
SLH: Sugarloaf and Hazelton Railroad
SLID: Student League for Industrial Democracy (political)
SLP: Socialist Labor Party (political party)
SLPA: Socialist Labor Party of America (political party)
SLPS: Swedish Lutheran Publication Society (religious)
SLQ: St. Lawrence and Atlantic Railroad
SLR: St. Lawrence and Atlantic Railroad
SLRG: San Luis and Rio Grande Railroad
SLS: Society of Laparoendoscopic Surgeons (professional)
SLSDC: St. Lawrence Seaway Development Corporation (governmental)
SLSF: St. Louis & San Francisco (also FRISCO) (railroad)
SLSM: Society of Our Lady St. Mary (religious community)
SLTV: St. Louis Turn Verein (ethnic, athletic)
SLW: Sisters of the Living Word (religious order)
SLWC: Stillwater Central Railroad
SLX: Sigma Lambda Chi (construction management) (academic honorary)
SLZC: Swedish Lutheran Zion Church
SM: Sons of Malta (also SofM) (fraternal/religious)
SM: Society of Mary (Marianists) (religious order)
SM: Society of Mary (Marists)(Marist Fathers and Brothers) (religious order)
SM: Marists in New Zealand (religious order)
SM: Sisters of Mercy (religious order)
SM: St. Mary's Railroad
SMA: School of Military Aeronautics (military, World War I)
SMA: San Manuel Arizona Railroad

SMA: Society of African Missions (religious order)
SMAA: Scandinavian Mutual Aid Association (mutual benefit)
SMACC: Sheet Metal and Air Conditioning Contractors
National Association (trade group)
SMB: Societa di Mutuo Beneficio (mutual benefit)
SMBA: Slovenian Mutual Benefit Association (mutual benefit)
SMC: Scarritt-Morrisville College (Missouri) (higher education)
SMC: Southern Methodist Church (religious denomination)
SMD: Society of Mayflower Descendents (lineage)
SMD: Sigma Mu Delta (fraternal)
SMEA: Scripture Meditation Evangelistic Association (religious)
SMK: Southern Mountain Knights (KKK)
SML: Student Missionary League (religious)
SMM: Montfortian Religious (includes The Company of Mary
(Montfort Missionaries), The Daughters of Wisdom, The
Brothers of Saint Gabriel) (religious orders)
SMMI: Sisters Minor of Mary Immaculate (religious order)
SMNR: Southern Manitoba Railway (railroad)
SMOC: Supreme Mechanical Order of the Sun (labor, mutual
benefit)
SMOM: Sovereign Military Order of Malta (a/k/a Order of
Malta) (religious, charitable)
SMOTJ: Sovereign Military Order of the Temple of Jerusalem
(religious, fraternal)
SMPTE: Society of Motion Picture & Television Engineers
(labor union)
SMR: Spanish Mustang Registry (equine)
SMRR: Sisseton Milbank Railroad
SMS: Societa di Mutuo Soccoroso (mutual benefit)
SMSM: Missionary Sisters of the Society of Mary – Marist
Missionary Sisters (religious order)
SMT: Sisters of the Mysterious Ten (fraternal, ethnic)
SMT: Society for Music Theory (musical)
SMU: Southern Methodist University (Texas) (higher education)
SMV: Santa Maria Valley Railroad
SMWIA: Sheet Metal Workers International Association (labor
union)
SMWU: Sheet Metal Workers Union (labor union)
SN: Saint Nicholas Society (lineage)
SN: Sons of Norway (hereditary, mutual benefit)
SN: Sacramento Northern Railway (railroad)
SN: Sabena World Airways (airline code)
SNA-AUM: Shrine of North America (fraternal, Masonic)

SNBS: Slovene National Benefit Society (mutual benefit)
SNC: Springfield Normal College (Missouri) (higher education)
SNC: Saratoga & North Creek (railroad)
SNCC: Student Non-violent Coordinating Committee (political)
SNCT: Seattle and North Coast Railroad
SND: Sisters of Notre Dame (religious order)
SNDdeN: Sisters of Notre Dame de Namur (religious order)
SNER: Southern New England Railway (railroad)
SNEW: National Society of New England Women (usually
NSNEW – National Society of New England Women) (lineage)
SNF: Serb National Federation (ethnic, mutual benefit)
SNHS: Science National Honor Society (academic honorary)
SNIA: Storage Networking Industry Association (trade group)
SNIS: State Normal and Industrial School (North Dakota)
(higher education)
SNJM: Sisters of the Holy Names of Jesus and Mary (religious
order)
SNL: St. Nicholas League (youth, religious)
SNMA: Student National Medical Association (education)
SNMMI: Society of Nuclear Medicine and Molecular Imaging
(professional)
SNTC: Students' Naval Training Corps (military, World War I)
SNY: SMS Rail Lines of NY (railroad)
SO: Sisters Online (religious order)
SO: South Orient (railroad)
SO: Sons of Odin (KKK)
SOA: Society of Actuaries (professional)
SOA: U. S. Army School of the Americas (military)
SOB: Society of Bearded Numismatists (probably not a serious
organization)
SoB: Society of the Bell (business organization)
SofA: Sons of Adam (also seen as SA) (fraternal)
SOCis: Cistercians of the Ancient Observance (religious order)
SOCCENT: Special Operations Command, Central Command
(military)
SOCOM: United States Special Operations Command (military)
SOCONY: Standard Oil Company of New York (business)
SoCRA: Society of Clinical Research Associates (professional)
SOCTI: Soldiers Of the Cross Training Institute (KKK)
SoCV: Sons of Confederate Veterans (lineage)
SODA: Short-course Off-road Drivers Association
(motorsports)
SofE: Sons of England (lineage)

SofI: Sons of Italy (see also SI) (ethnic, mutual benefit)
SoL: Sons of Liberty (fraternal)
SofM: Sons of Malta (also SM) (fraternal, religious)
SofP: Sons of Pericles (Order of the Sons of Pericles) (also SP)
(youth, ethnic)
SofP: Sons of Poland (also SP) (mutual benefit)
SofStG: Sons of St. George (fraternal, mutual benefit,
hereditary)
SofV: Sons of Veterans (lineage)
SOKP: Society of Kentucky Pioneers (lineage)
SOLI: Society of Our Lady of the Isles (religious community)
SOLT: Society of Our Lady of the Most Holy Trinity (religious
order)
SOM: Somerset Railroad Corp. (railroad)
SOMA: Sharing of Ministries Abroad (religious)
SOO: Soo Line Railroad
SOOB: Social Order of the Beauceant (women, fraternal,
religious)
SOP: Sons of Pericles - junior order of AHEPA (American.
Hellenic Educational Progressive Association) (ethnic)
SOPR: South Pierce Railroad
SOR: Southern Ontario Railway (railroad)
SOS: Society of Ordained Scientists (religious order)
SOS: Sisters of the Snow (Daughters of Our Lady of the Snow)
(religious order)
SOSJ: Sovereign Order of St. John of Jerusalem (religious)
SOTB: Sacred Order of Twilight Brothers (performance art
composition; not an organization per se)
SOU: Southern Railway (railroad)
SOUTHCOM: U. S. Southern Command (military)
SOV: Sons of Veterans (lineage)
SOWR: Supreme Order of White Rabbits (fraternal)
SP: Socialist Party (political party)
SP: Sons of Poland (also SofP) (mutual benefit)
SP: Sisters of Providence (also FCSP) (religious order)
SP: Sisters of Providence of Saint Mary-of-the-Woods (religious
order)
SP: Southern Pacific Transportation Company (railroad)
SP: Southern Party (political party)
SP: Sons of Pericles (Order of the Sons of Pericles) (also SofP,
SOP) (youth, ethnic)
SP: Silver Party (political party)
SP&S: Spokane, Portland & Seattle (railroad)

SPA: Socialist Party of America (political party)
SPA: Sigma Phi Alpha (dental hygiene) (academic honorary)
SPAA: St. Patrick's Alliance of America (fraternal, mutual benefit)
SPAB: Supply Priorities and Allocation Board (governmental)
SPARS: Society of Professional Recording Services (trade group)
SPB: Society of the Precious Blood (religious community)
SPB: Surplus Property Board (governmental)
SPCA: Society for the Prevention of Cruelty to Animals (political, civic)
SPCK: Society for the Promotion of Christian Knowledge (religious)
SPCSCPG: Society for the Prevention of Calling Sleeping Car Porters "George" (once humorous)
SPE: Sigma Phi Epsilon (college fraternity)
SPEBSQSA: Society for the Preservation and Encouragement of Barbershop Quartet Singing in America (now BHS: Barbershop Harmony Society) (arts)
SPEG: Spencerville and Elgin Railroad
SPEP: Society for Phenomenology and Existential Philosophy (professional, learned)
SPF: Society for the Propagation of the Faith (religious)
SPG: Society for Propagation of the Gospel (religious)
SPG: Society for Propagating the Gospel among the Indians and others in North America (religious)
SPG: Society for Propagating the Gospel in Foreign Parts (religious)
SPI: Sisters of Perpetual Indulgence (also called Order of Perpetual Indulgence (OPI)) (social protest)
SPK: Sigma Pi Kappa (historic preservation) (academic honorary)
SPOOM: Society for the Preservation Of Old Mills (cultural)
SPPA: Society for the Preservation of Poultry Antiquities (poultry)
SPQR: Senatus Populesque Romanus (The Senate and the Roman People) (governmental)
SPR: Southern Pacific Railroad (business)
SPRE: Society of Park and Recreation Educators (professional)
SPS: Spokane, Portland and Seattle Railway (railroad)
SPS: Sigma Pi Sigma (physics) (honorary fraternity)
SPS: Safety Pharmacology Society (professional)
SPS: Senior Physician Section (professional)

SPSR: Spokane, Portland and Seattle Railway (railroad)
SPUS: Socialist Party of the United States (political party)
SPUSA: Socialist Party USA (political party)
SPW: Space Wing (military)
SQ: Singapore Airlines Limited (airline code)
SQVR: Sequatchie Valley Railroad
SR: Sons of the Revolution (lineage)
SR: Scottish Rite (Masonic)
SR: Societas Rosicrusiana (religious)
SR: Silver Republican (political party)
SR: Swissair (airline code)
SR: Sentinels of the Republic (lobby)
SR&D: Selma, Rome and Dalton (railroad)
SRA: Shrine Recorders Association of North America (Masonic)
SRA: States Rights Association (political)
SRA: Seabury Resources for Aging (religious)
SRAC: Sabbath Rest Advent Church (religious denomination)
SRB: Scouts Royale Brotherhood (high school fraternity)
SRBC: Susquehanna River Basin Commission (governmental)
SRC: Strasburg Railroad
SRDP: States' Rights Democratic Party (a/k/a Dixiecrats) (political party)
SRIA: Societas Rosicruciana in Anglia (fraternal, Rosicrucians, cult)
SRIA: Societas Rosicruciana in America (fraternal, Rosicrucians, cult)
SRICF: Societas Rosicruciana in Civitatibus Foederatis (fraternal, Rosicrucians, cult)
SRM: Society of Red Men (fraternal)
SRN: Sabine River and Northern Railroad
SRNJ: Southern Railroad of New Jersey (railroad)
SRP: Society of Recorder Players (musical)
SRP: Silver Republican Party (political party)
SRS: Scouts Royale Sisterhood (high school sorority)
SRS: Statistical Reporting Service (governmental)
SRT: Sons of the Republic of Texas (lineage)
SRW: Society of Recreation Workers (professional)
SRY: Southern Railway of British Columbia (railroad)
SRYC: Sierra Railway of California (railroad)
SS: Sewing Society of the Methodist Episcopal Church (religious)
SS: Society of St. Sulpice (religious order)

SS: Sand Springs Railway (railroad)
SS: Senate of Sparta (mutual benefit)
SS: Schuylkill Seminary (Pennsylvania) (higher education)
SSA: Society of the Sacred Advent (religious community)
SSA: Social Security Administration (New Deal) (governmental)
SSA: Society of Saint Augustine (religious order)
SSA: Sisters of St. Anne (religious order)
SSA: Syrian Studies Association (learned)
SSAL: Sunday School Athletic League (religious)
SSAO: Southern Sons Army of One (KKK)
SSAP: Society of St. Anna the Prophen (religious community)
SSATB: Secondary School Admission Test Board (education)
SSAtP: Society of St. Anna the Prophet (religious community)
SSAW: Student Strike Against War (political, 1930s)
SSAWV: Sons of Spanish American War Veterans (lineage)
SSB: Society of the Sisters of Bethany (religious community)
SSB: Sabbath School Board (of the Seventh Day Baptist
General Conference) (religious)
SSB: Strategic Support Branch (governmental)
SSBA: Sons of Scotland Benevolent Association (fraternal,
ethnic, mutual benefit)
SSBU: South Slavic Benevolent Union (mutual benefit)
SSC: Missionary Society of St. Columba (Columbans) (religious
order)
SSC: Society of the Sacred Cross (religious community)
SSC: Southern State College (South Dakota) (higher education)
SSC: Seven Stars of Consolidation (mutual benefit)
SSCC: Congregation of the Sacred Hearts of Jesus and Mary
(religious order)
SSCJ: Sisters, Servants of the Most Sacred Heart of Jesus
(religious order)
SSCM: Sisters of Saints Cyril and Methodius (religious order)
SSCM: Society for Seventeenth Century Music (musical)
SSDK: Savannah State Docks Railroad
SSE: Society of St. Edmund Fathers, Edmundites (religious
order)
SSF: Society of St. Francis (religious community)
SSG: Sons of St. George (lineage)
SSG: Sisters of St. Gregory (religious order)
SSG: Society of Select Guardians (mutual benefit)
SSH: South Shore Railroad
SSH: Society of the Sacred Heart (religious order)
SSHA: Social Studies History Association (learned)

SSHR: Sulphur Springs Horse Registry (equine)
SSJ: St. Joseph's Society of the Sacred Heart (Josephite Fathers and Brothers) (religious order)
SSJ: Sisters of St. Joseph (religious order)
SSJ: Sisters of St. Joseph of the Sacred Heart (religious order)
SSJ: Josephite Fathers and Brothers (religious order)
SSJ: Sisters of Saint Joseph of Springfield (religious order)
SSJD: Sisterhood of St. John the Divine (religious community)
SSJD: Society of St. John the Divine (religious community)
SSJE: Society of St. John the Evangelist (religious community)
SSJR: Sheffield Station Junction Railway (railroad)
SSJ-TOSF: Sisters of St. Joseph of the Third Order of St. Francis (religious order)
SSLV: Southern San Luis Valley Railroad
SSM: Sisterhood of St. Mary (religious community)
SSM: Society of St. Margaret (religious community)
SSM: Society of the Sacred Mission (religious community)
SSM: Sisters of the Sorrowful Mother (religious order)
SSMA: Soldiers & Sailors Memorial Association (civic)
SSMA: Southwest Spanish Mustang Association (equine)
SSMN: Sisters of St. Mary of Namur (religious order)
SSMO: Sisters of St. Mary of Oregon (religious order)
SSN: Scholars Strategy Network (professional)
SSND: School Sisters of Notre Dame (religious order)
SSO: Scotch Society Order (fraternal)
SSP: Society of St. Paul (religious order)
SSP: Society of St. Paul (religious community)
SSP: Sigma Sigma Phi (osteopathic medicine) (honorary)
SSP: Scottish Socialist Party (political)
SSPC: The Society for Protective Coatings (professional)
SSPC: Missionary Sisters of St. Peter Claver (religious order)
SSPi: Sigma Sigma Pi (energy engineering) (honorary fraternity)
SSpSAP: Holy Spirit Adoration Sisters (religious order)
SSS: Congregation of the Blessed Sacrament (Sacramontines) (religious order)
SSS: Servants of the Blessed Sacrament (religious order)
SSS: St. Stanislaus Society (religious)
SSS: Selective Service System (governmental)
SSS: Southern Sociological Society (learned)
SSSA: Soil Science Society of America (professional)
SSSF: School Sisters of Saint Francis (religious order)
SSSJ: Student Struggle for Soviet Jewry (youth, religious)
SSTh: Sisters of St. Therese of the Child Jesus (religious order)

SStG: Society of St. George (fraternal)
SSU: Sunday School Union of the Methodist Episcopal Church (religious)
SSW: St. Louis Southwestern Railway (railroad)
SSWGB: Society of the Second War with Great Britain (lineage)
ST: Sons of Temperance (political)
ST: Missionary Servants of the Most Holy Trinity (religious order)
ST: Missionary Cenacle Family (also MSBT) (religious order)
ST: Pan Am Railways (railroad)
ST: Springfield Terminal Railway (railroad)
ST: Society of Taborites (mutual benefit)
ST: Society of Toxicology (professional)
STBH: Supreme Tribe of Ben Hur (mutual benefit)
STD: Sigma Tau Delta (English) (honorary fraternity)
ST.GSofNY: St. George's Society of New York (lineage)
ST&LA: Socialist Trade & Labor Alliance (labor union)
STL: The Society for Truth & Light (political/religious)
STLE: St. Louis & Evansville Railroad Company (railroad)
STLH: St. Lawrence and Hudson Railway (railroad)
STMA: St. Maries River Railroad
STRT: Stewartstown Railroad
STS: Saint Tamina Society (fraternal)
STS" Society of Thoracic Surgeons (medical)
STT: Sigma Theta Tau (nursing) (academic honorary)
STX: Sigma Tau Chi (communications) (academic honorary)
SU: Usruline Sisters (religious order)
SU: Southern University (Alabama) (higher education)
SU: Spokane University (Washington) (higher education)
SU: Straight University (Louisiana) (higher education)
SU: Aeroflot Russian Airlines (airline code)
SU: Aeroflot – Cargo (airline code)
SUAB: Southern Alabama Railroad
SUI: Society of United Irishmen(also UI - United Irishmen) (revolutionary)
SUN: Sunset Railroad
Sunoco: Sun Oil Company (business)
SUNY: State University of New York (higher education)
SUPR: Southern United Professional Racing (motorsports)
SUR: State University Railroad
SUS: Step Up for Soldiers (military support)
SUSA: Sokol U. S. A. (mutual benefit)

SUSTA: Southern United States Trade Association (trade group)
SUV: Sons of Union Veterans of the Civil War (also SUVCW) (lineage)
SUVCW: Sons of Union Veterans of the Civil War (also SUV) (lineage)
SV: Sons of the Veterans of the United States of America (lineage)
SV: Sisters of Life (religious order)
SV: Shenandoah Valley Railroad
SV: Saudi Arabian Airlines (airline code)
SVA: Saudi Arabian Airlines (airline code)
SVA: Sons of Veterans Auxiliary (lineage)
SVD: Divine Word Missionaries (religious order)
SVI: Southern Railway of Vancouver (railroad)
SVIL: Saltville Railroad
SVRA: Sportscar Vintage Racing Association (motorsports)
SVRR: Shamokin Valley Railroad
SVS: Society for Vascular Surgery (professional)
SVUSA: Sons of Veterans of the United State of America (see SV and SUV) (lineage)
SW: Southwestern Railroad
SW: Strategic Wing (military)
SWA: Southwest Airlines Co. (airline code)
SWACHA: Southwestern Automated Clearing House Association (trade group)
SWANA: Solid Waste Association of North America (trade group)
SWAPO: South-West Africa People's Organization (guerilla organization)
SWC: Simon Wisenthal Center (religious, political)
SWCS: Soil and Water Conservation Society (advocacy)
SWE: Society of Women Engineers (professional)
SWG: Society of Women Geographers (learned)
SWGR: Seagraves, Whiteface and Lubbock Railroad
SWHG: Social Welfare History Group (learned)
SWHR: Society for Women's Health Research (learned)
SWKR: San Pedro and Southwestern Railroad
SWM: Order of Heptasophs (mutual benefit)
SWO: Socialist Workers Organization (political)
SWP: Socialist Workers Party (political)
SWP: Southwest Pennsylvania Railroad

SWPP: Society of Workforce Planning Professionals (professional)
SWRA: Specialty Wine Retailers Association (trade group)
SWS: Society of Wetland Scientists (professional)
SWSA: Salisbury Winter Sports Association (sports)
SX: Missionary Society of St. Francis Xavier (Xaverians) (religious order)
SX: Sigma Xi (scientific research) (honorary)
SYMWA: Spend Your Money With Americans (KKK)
SYMWAO: Spend Your Money With Americans Only (KKK)
SYRR: Sandusky River Railroad
SZ: Sigma Zeta (computer sciences and mathematics) (academic honorary)

T

T&B: Troy and Boston Railroad
TA: Tailhook Association (military support)
TA&B: Total Abstinence & Benevolent Society (religious, mutual benefit)
TAA: The Ameraucana Alliance (poultry)
TAA: The Aluminum Institute (trade group)
TACCS: Transnational Association of Christian Colleges and Schools (religious, education)
TAEA: Tangipahoa and Eastern Railroad
TAFU: The Acme Fraternal Union (see also AFU) (mutual benefit)
TAG: Tennessee, Alabama, and Georgia (railroad)
TAI: The Accreditation Institution (education)
TAI: Texas Acupuncture Institute (higher education)
TAI: Tuskegee Airmen, Inc (military support)
TAK: Theta Alpha Kappa (philosophy and religion) (academic honorary)
TAK: Traditionalist American Knights (KKK)
TAMFS: That All May Freely Serve (religious, activist)
TAP: Theta Alpha Phi (theatre) (academic honorary)
TAP: Air Portugal (airline code)
TAPi: Tau Alpha Pi (engineering) (academic honorary)
TAPPI: Technical Association of the Pulp and Paper Industry (trade group)
TBER: Terra Haute, Brazil and Eastern Railroad
TBH: Tribe of Ben Hur (mutual benefit)
TBN: Trinity Broadcasting Network (company)
TPPi: Tau Beta Pi (engineering) (academic honorary)
TBS: Tau Beta Sigma (music/band) (academic honorary)
TBV: Trinity & Brazos Valley Railway (railroad)
TC: Triangle Club (political)
TC: Tank Corps (military, World War I)
TC: Tennessee Central Railway (railroad)
TC: Transportation Corps (Army branch)
TCA: The Cantors Assembly (religious, musical)
TCA: Tennessee Concrete Association (trade group)
TCBR: Tecumseh Branch Connecting Railroad
TCC: True Catholic Church (religious denomination)

TCC: The Christian Community (religious)
TCG: Order of the Teachers of the Children of God (religious community)
TCG: Tucson, Cornelia and Gila Bend Railroad
TCG: Trusted Computing Group (trade group)
TChi: Theta Chi (fraternity)
TCIU: Transportation Communication International Union (labor union)
TCKR: Turtle Creek Industrial Railroad
TCL: Tall Cedars of Lebanon (Masonic)
TCM International Institute (Indiana) (higher education)
TCM: Training Christians for Ministry (religious)
TCM: Tech Council of Maryland (trade group)
TCNJ: The College of New Jersey (higher education)
TCRY: Tri-City Railroad
TCT: Texas City Terminal Railroad
TCU: Transportation Communications International Union (labor union)
TCU: Texas Christian University (Texas) (higher education)
TDC: True Dutch Church (religious denomination)
TDIU: Team Drivers International Union (labor union)
TDK: Theta Delta Kappa (fraternal)
TDS: Theta Delta Sigma (fraternal)
TDU: Teamsters for a Democratic Union (labor reform group)
TCWR: Twin Cities and Western Railroad
TDX: Theta Delta Chi (college fraternity)
TE: Tacoma Eastern Railway (railroad)
TE: FlyLAL – Lithuanian Airlines (airline code)
TEA: The Eclectic Assembly (see also EA) (mutual benefit)
TEC: The Episcopal Church (religious denomination)
TEC: Teens Encounter Christ (religious, youth)
TEKE: Tau Kappa Epsilon (see TKE) (college fraternity)
TEM: Temiskaming and Northern Ontario (railroad)
TENN: Tennessee Railroad
TES: The Endocrine Society (professional)
TEUU: Gulfcoast Transit (railroad)
TEX: Tau Epsilon Chi (high school sorority)
Texaco: Texas Oil Company (business)
TEXC: Texas Central Railroad
TF: Thrivent Financial (religious, mutual benefit)
TFM: Transportacion Ferroviaria Mexicana (railroad)
TG: Thai Airways International Public (airline code)

TGD: Thelemic Order of the Golden Dawn (also TOGD) (fraternal)
TGF: The Grand Fraternity (mutual benefit)
TH: Territory of Hawaii (military)
TH: Temple of Honor and Temperance (also TPLF) (IOOF) (fraternal)
TH: Temple of Honor (IOOF)
THA: Thai Airways International Public (airline code)
THB: Toronto, Hamilton and Buffalo Railway (railroad)
THT: Templars of Honor and Temperance (temperance, fraternal, secret)
THY: Turkish Airways, Inc. (airline code)
TIEK: True Invisible Empire Knights (KKK)
TILX: Trinity Rail Management (rail car lessor)
TI: Turners Island (railroad)
TI: Tobacco Institute (trade group)
TIBR: Timber Rock Railroad
TIETAK: True Invisible Empire Traditionalist Knights of the Ku Klux Klan (KKK)
TIPP: Tippecanoe Railway (railroad)
TIRL: Tonawanda Island Railroad
TISH: Tishomingo Railroad
TK: Order of True Kindred (Masonic)
TK: Tuetonic (sic) Knights (KKK)
TK: Texas Knights (of the Ku Klux Klan) (KKK)
TK: Turkish Airways, Inc. (airline code)
TKE: Tau Kappa Epsilon (college fraternity)
TKEN: Tennken Railroad
TKKKK: Templar Knights of the Ku Klux Klan
TKO: Theta Kappa Omega (high school fraternity)
TL: Trotskyist League (political)
TL: Templars of Liberty (anti-Catholic, mutual benefit)
TL: Teachers Life (mutual benefit)
TLCR: Texas Longhorn Cattlemen's Registry (cattle)
TLHU: Tile Layers and Helpers Union (labor union)
TLMIA: Triple Link Mutual Indemnity Association (mutual benefit)
TLO: Tribal Liaison Office (political)
TLPE: Temple of Honor and Temperance (of IOOF) (fraternal)
TLW: Tavern League of Wisconsin (trade group)
TM: Texas Mexican Railway (railroad)
TM: Transcendental Meditation (cult)

TMA: Turnaround Management Association (professional)
TMA: The Mason's Annuity (mutual benefit)
TMC: Tile and Mantel Contractors Association (trade group)
TMCA: Transportation Marketing & Communications Association (trade group)
TMER&L: The Milwaukee Electric Railroad and Light Company (railroad)
TMI: Texas Military Institute, the Episcopal School of Texas (school)
TMRW: Tacoma Rail (railroad)
TN: Texas and Northern Railway (railroad)
TNM: Missouri Pacific Railway (railroad)
TNMR: Texas-New Mexico Railroad
TNO: Texas and New Orleans (railroad)
TNR: Kansas City Southern Railway (railroad)
TNSR: Nashtown and Southern Railroad
TO: Teepee Order (also AIO – American Indian Order) (fraternal)
TO&E: Texas, Oklahoma and Eastern (railroad)
TOA: Teepee Order of America (fraternal, ethnic)
TOASFAA: Templar's Order of the American Star, Free & Accepted Americans (see also FAA – Free & Accepted Americans, etc.) (nativist)
TOC: Toledo & Ohio Central Railway (railroad)
TOE: Texas, Oklahoma and Eastern Railroad
TOGD: Thelemic Order of the Golden Dawn (also TGD) (fraternal)
TOR: Franciscan Friars of the Third Order Regular (religious order)
TOR: Franciscan Sisters of Penance of the Sorrowful Mother (religious order)
TORC: The Off-Road Championship (motorsports)
TOS: Temple of Set (perhaps Seti?) (also TS) (fraternal)
TOS: The Optical Society (professional)
TOSF: Third Order of St. Francis (religious)
TOTE: Improved Order of Redmen (fraternal)
TOV: Tooele Valley Railway (railroad)
TP: Transhumanist Party (political)
TP: Texas and Pacific Railway (railroad)
TP: Air Portugal (airline code)
TPA: Travelers Protective Association of America (also TPAA) (mutual benefit)
TP&W: Toledo, Peoria & Western (railroad)

TPAA: Travelers Protective Association of America (also TPA) (mutual benefit)
TPKU: Toledo, Peoria & Western (railroad)
TPLF: Temple of Honor and Temperance (also TH) (Odd Fellows) (fraternal)
TPNY: Taxpayers Party of New York (political party)
TPT: Conrail (railroad)
TPW: Toledo, Peoria & Western (railroad)
TR: Tomahawk Railway (railroad)
TR: True Reformers (United Order of True Reformers – UOTR) (ethnic, fraternal)
TRAIN: TrainingFinder Real-time Affiliate Integrated Network (service)
TRB: Descendants of the Illegitimate Sons and Daughters of the Kings of Britain (The Royal Bastards) (lineage)
TRC: Trona Railway (railroad)
TRC: Theta Rho Clubs (Rebekahs) (youth, fraternal)
TRICARE: Civilian Health and Medical Program of the Uniformed Services (see also CHAMPUS) (governmental)
TRF: Thoroughbred Retirement Foundation (equestrian)
TRIN: Trinidad Railway (railroad)
TRK: Traditional Rebel Knights (KKK)
TRLS: Tapping Reeve Law School (educational)
TROA: The Retired Officers Association (military)
TRRY: Trillium Railway (railroad)
TS: Theosophical Society (religious denomination)
TS: Tammany Society (fraternal)
TS: Thespian Society (youth, educational)
TS: Tidewater Southern (railroad)
TS: Tau Sigma (honorary fraternity)
TS: Temple of Set (Seti?) (also TOS) (fraternal)
TS: True Sisters (fraternal)
TS: Triological Society (professional)
TSA: Transportation Security Administration (governmental)
TSBA: Texas Small Business Association (trade group)
TSBY: Tuscola and Saginaw Bay Railway (railroad)
TSCC: Tharp Springs Christian College (Texas) (higher education)
TSCRA: Texas and Southwestern Cattle Raisers Association (trade group)
TSD: Tau Sigma Delta (architecture) (academic honorary)
TSE: Texas Southeastern Railway (railroad)
TSEU: Theatrical Stage Employees' Union (labor union)

TSRR: Tennessee Southern Railroad
TSU: Tulsa-Sapulpa Union Railroad
TT: Toledo Terminal Railroad
TTER: Tomiko, Tilden & Eastern (railroad)
TTIS: Transkentucky Transportation Railroad
TTMA: Texas Talent Musicians Association (professional)
TTR: Tijuana and Tecate Railway (railroad)
TTSI: Thanks to Scandinavia, Inc. (religious)
TTX: Trailer Train Corporation (rail car lessor)
TUP: The United Presbyterians (religious denomination)
TVA: Tennessee Valley Authority (New Deal) (governmental)
TVRR: Tulare Valley Railroad
TW: Trans World Airlines (airline code)
TWA: Trans World Airways (company)
TWC: The Wesleyan Church (religious denomination)
TWI: The Way International (cult)
TWIU: Tobacco Workers' International Union (labor union)
TWK: Trinity White Knights (KKK)
TWK: Tennessee White Knights (KKK)
TWU: Transport Workers Union of America (labor union)
TWUA: Textile Workers Union of America (labor union)
TX: Theta Chi (fraternity)
TX: Theta Xi (fraternity)
TXB: Theta Chi Beta (study of religion) (honorary fraternity)
TXNW: Texas North Western Railway (railroad)
TXOR: Texas and Oklahoma Railroad
TZPR: Tazewell and Peoria Railroad

U

U: Unionist Party (political party_

UA: United Association of Journeymen and Apprentices of the Plumbing and Pipefitting Industry of the United States and Canada (Plumbers and Pipefitters Union) (labor union)

UA: Unitarian Association (religious denomination)

UA: United Aid (mutual benefit)

UA: United Americans (political)

UA: United Airlines, Inc. (airline code)

UAB: United African Brotherhood (fraternal, ethnic, mutual benefit)

UAC: United Apostolic Church (religious denomination)

UAFA: United Armed Forces Association (military)

UAFWB: United American Free Will Baptists (religious denomination)

UAFWBC: United American Free Will Baptist Church (religious denomination)

UAFWBC: United American Free Will Baptist Conference (religious denomination)

UAHC: Union of American Hebrew Congregations (religious denomination)

UAL: United Airlines, Inc. (business)

UAL: United Airlines, Inc. (airline code)

UALE: United Association for Labor Education (professional)

UAM: United American Mechanics (mutual benefit)

UAMC: Universal African Motor Corps (ethnic)

UAN: United American Nurses (labor union)

UAOD: United Ancient Order of Druids (fraternal, mutual benefit)

UAV: United American Veterans (veterans)

UAM: United American Mechanics (nativist, anti-Catholic)

UAW: United Automobile, Aerospace & Agricultural Implement Workers of America International Union (labor union)

UB: United Baptists (religious denomination)

UB: United Brethren in Christ (religious denomination)

UB&SofL: United Brothers and Sisters of Light (fraternal, mutual benefit)

UBA: United Benevolent Association (mutual benefit)

UBA: Union Beneficial Association (mutual benefit)

UBC: United Brotherhood of Carpenters and Joiners of America (also UBCJA) (labor union)

UBCJA: United Brotherhood of Carpenters and Joiners of America (also UBC) (labor union)

UBCN: Universal Black Cross Nurses (ethnic)

UBE: Union of Black Episcopalians (religious)

UBF: Unregistered Baptist Fellowship (religious denomination)

UBF-SMT: United Brethren of Friendship and Sisters of the Mysterious Ten (ethnic, mutual benefit)

UBF: United Brothers of Friendship (fraternal, ethnic)

UBRE: United Brotherhood of Railway Employees (labor union)

UBS: Union Bank of Switzerland and Swiss Bank Corporation (merged company)

UC: Union Club (men's club)

UC: Upsala College (New Jersey) (higher education)

UCB: United Carolina Bank (business)

UCBerkeley: University of California – Berkeley (higher education)

UCBWN: United Church Board for World Missions (religious)

UCC: United Church of Christ (religious denomination)

UCC: United Church of Canada (religious denomination)

UCC: Union Christian College (higher education)

UCC: United Christian Church (religious denomination)

UCC: Ukrainian Catholic Church (religious denomination)

UCCC: United Covenant Churches of Christ (religious denomination)

UCCE: Universal Craftsmen Council of Engineers (Masonic, trade)

UCDavis: University of California – Davis (higher education)

UCG: United Church of God (religious denomination)

UCHCM: United Cloth Hat and Cap Makers of North America (labor union)

UCIrvine: University of California – Irvine (higher education)

UCLA: University of California – Los Angeles (California) (higher education)

UCLM: Unity of Czech Ladies and Men (mutual benefit)

UCM: Universal Church of the Master (cult)

UCMS: United Christian Missionary Society (religious)

UConn: University of Connecticut (Connecticut) (higher education)

UCP: United Citizens Party (political party)

UCPA: United Cerebral Palsy Associations, Inc. (charity)
UCPC: Upper Cumberland Presbyterian Church (religious denomination)
UCR: Utah Coal Route (railroad)
UCRY: Utah Central Railway (railroad)
UCS: Union of Concerned Scientists (political)
UCSB: University of California, Santa Barbara (higher education)
UCSF: University of California, San Francisco (higher education)
UCT: United Commercial Travelers of America (also UCTA) (mutual benefit)
UCTA: United Commercial Travelers of America (also UCT) (mutual benefit)
UCV: United Confederate Veterans (veterans)
UD: University of Dallas (Texas) (higher education)
UDA: Ulster Defence Association (guerilla movement – Northern Ireland)
UDC: United Daughters of the Confederacy (lineage)
UDMS: United Domestic Missionary Society (religious)
UDWK: United Dixie White Knights of the Ku Klux Klan (KKK)
UE: United Electrical, Radio and Machine Workers of America (labor union)
UE: Union Endowment (mutual benefit)
UEBC: Ukrainian Evangelical Baptist Convention (religious denomination)
UEBCC: Ukrainian Evangelical Baptist Convention of Canada (religious, Canadian)
UECNA: United Episcopal Church of North America (religious denomination)
UEL: United Empire Loyalists (lineage)
UEL: United Endowment League (mutual benefit)
UERMWA: United Electrical, Radio and Machine Workers of America (labor union)
UELAC: United Empire Loyalists' Association of Canada (lineage)
UF: United Friends (mutual benefit)
UF: United Friars (fraternal)
UFA: Ukrainian Fraternal Association (mutual benefit)
UFBCC: Union of French Baptist Churches of Canada (religious – Canadian)
UFCW: United Food and Commercial Workers (labor union)

UFL: Union Fraternal League (mutual benefit)
UFL: United Fraternal League (mutual benefit)
UFM: United Friends of Michigan (mutual benefit)
UFSD: Union Free School District (educational)
UFT: United Federation of Teachers (labor union)
UFW: United Farm Workers of America (labor union)
UFWB: United Free Will Baptists (religious denomination)
UFWBLA: Unaffiliated Free Will Baptist Local Association (religious denomination)
UGA: University of Georgia (higher education)
UGT: United Gospel Tabernacle (religious denomination)
UGW: United Garment Workers (labor union)
UHA: Ukrainian Historical Association (learned)
UHCA: United Holy Church of American (religious denomination)
UHF: Universal Harmony Association (cult)
UHRA: United Hebrew Relief Association (ethnic, mutual benefit, charitable)
UHMS: Undersea and Hyperbaric Medical Society (professional)
UI: United Irishmen (also SUI – Society of United Irishmen) (revolutionary)
UIC: University of Illinois at Chicago (higher education)
UITT: United Independent Technology Technicians of America (labor union)
UJA: United Jewish Appeal (religious)
UJC: United Jewish Communities (religious)
UJOTASP: United Junior Order of the Ancient Sacred Phoenix (probably fraternal)
UK: University of Kentucky (higher education)
UKA: United Klans of America (KKK)
UKC: United Kennel Club (sports)
UKDA: United Knights and Daughters of America (fraternal, mutual benefit)
UL: Urban League (civic)
UL: Universal Life (religious)
UL: Union League (men's club)
UL: Sri Lankan Airlines Limited (airline code)
ULA: United League of America (mutual benefit, fraternal)
ULB: Union of Latvian Baptists (religious denomination)
ULC: Union League Club (social)
ULP: Upsilon Lambda Phi (high school fraternity)
ULS: United Lutheran Society (mutual benefit)

UMass: University of Massachusetts (Massachusetts) (collegiate)
UMC: United Methodist Church (religious denomination)
UMC: United Methodist Clergy (religious)
UMC: United Methodist Communications (religious)
UMC: University Medical College (Missouri) (higher education)
UMI: Ukrainian Music Institute (ethnic, musical)
UMiC: United Missionary Church (religious denomination)
UMJC: Union of Messianic Jewish Congregations (religious denomination)
UMP: Upper Merion and Plymouth Railroad
UMS: United Missionary Society (religious)
UMW: United Methodist Women (religious)
UMW: United Mine Workers (of America) (labor union)
UMWA: United Mine Workers of America (labor union)
UNA: Ukrainian National Association (mutual benefit)
UNAA: Ukrainian National Aid Association (mutual benefit)
UNAPOC: United National Association of Post Office Clerks (labor union)
UNC: University of North Carolina (North Carolina) (higher education)
UNESCO: United National Educational, Scientific, and Cultural Organization (UN Agency)
UNH: University of New Hampshire (higher education)
UNI: Unity Railways (railroad)
UNIA: Universal Negro Improvement Association (fraternal, ethnic)
Unico: (Italian word for unique) (civic)
UNICRI: United Nations Interregional Crime and Justice Research Institute (UN activity)
UNIDIR: United Nations Institute for Disarmament Research (UN activity)
UNIDO: United Nations Industrial Development Organization (UN agency)
UNIS: United Nations International School (New York) (school)
UNITAR: United Nations Institute for Training and Research (UN activity)
UNITE: Union of Needle trades, Industrial and Textile Employees (labor union)
UNLIS: United National Life Insurance Society (mutual benefit)
UNMiss: United Nations Mission (governmental)
UNOCHA: Office for the Coordination of Humanitarian Affairs (UN agency)

UNODC: United Nations Office on Drugs and Crime (UN agency)
UNOOSA: United Nations Office for Outer Space Affairs (UN agency)
UNRISD: United Nations Research Institute for Social Development (UN activity)
UNSK: United Northern and Southern Knights (KKK)
UNSSC: United Nations System Staff College (UN activity)
UNU: United Nations University (UN activity)
UNWTO: World Tourism Organization (UN agency)
UNYC: Union of Nazarene Yisraelite Congregations (religious denomination)
UO: Union Orange (Northern Irish, political)
UOA: United Order of Americans (mutual benefit)
UOC: United Oprington Club (poultry)
UOE: United Order Effort (religious cult)
UOE: United Order of Equity (mutual benefit)
UOF: United Order of Foresters (mutual benefit)
UofA: United Americans (also UA) (political)
UofC: University of Chicago (higher education)
UOofGC: United Order of Grand Commandery (see UOGC) (Masonic)
UOGC: United Order of Grand Commandery (see UO of GC) (Masonic)
UOH: United Order of Hope (mutual benefit)
UOJCA: Union of Orthodox Jewish Congregations of America (religious denomination)
UOofGC: United Order of the Golden Cross (became part of WOW) (fraternal, temperance, mutual benefit)
UOofIOL: United Order of Independent Odd Ladies (fraternal)
UOPF: United Order of the Pilgrim Fathers (mutual benefit)
UOTR: United Order of True Reformers (ethnic, fraternal)
UOTS: United Order of True Sisters (religious, Jewish, women, civic)
UP: United Presbyterians (religious denomination)
UP: Union Pacific Railroad (railroad)
UP: Union Party (political party)
UP: United Press (journalism)
UP: Union of Prayer (religious)
UPA: Unity Party of America (political party)
UPA: United Patriots of America (nativist, anti-Moslem)
UPCC: United Pentecostal Churches of Christ (religious denomination)

UPCI: United Pentecostal Church International (religious denomination)
UPCNA: United Presbyterian Church in North America (religious denomination)
UPD: Upsilon Phi Delta (health administration) (academic honorary)
UPDA: Uganda People's Democratic Army (guerilla group)
UPE: Upsilon Pi Epsilon (computer sciences) (honorary fraternity)
UPEACE: University for Peace (UN activity)
UPenn: University of Pennsylvania (Pennsylvania) (higher education)
UPS: United Parcel Service (business)
UPS: United Parcel Service (airline code)
UPU: Universal Postal Union (UN agency)
UPWA: Union of Polish Women of America (mutual benefit)
UPWA: United Packinghouse Workers of America (labor union)
URC: United Reformed Church (religious denomination)
URCL&PW: United Rubber, Coal, Linoleum, and Plastic Workers of America (labor union)
URCNA: United Reformed Churches in North America (religious denomination)
URNG: Guatemalan National Revolutionary Unity (guerilla organization)
US: Ursuline Sisters (religious order)
US: US Airways (airline code)
US: Piedmont Airlines, Inc. (airline code)
USA: United States Army (military)
USA: United Steelworkers of America (labor union)
USA: United States of America (governmental)
USA: US Airways, Inc. (airline code)
USAAF: United States Army Air Force (military – pre WWII)
USAAS: United State Army Ambulance Service (military, World War I)
USAC: Utah State Agricultural College (higher education)
USAC: United States Auto Club (motorsports)
USACOM: U. S. Atlantic Command (military)
USAE: USA Equestrian (equestrian)
USAF: United States Air Force (military)
USAFA: U. S. Air Force Academy (higher education, military)
USAFE: United States Air Forces in Europe (military)
USAFR: U. S. Air Force Reserves (military)

USAFRC: United States Air Force Reserve Command (military)
USAFSS: United States Air Force Security Services (governmental)
USAID: Agency for International Development (governmental)
USAPA: US Airlines Pilots Association (labor union)
USAR: United States Army Reserve (military)
USARA: United States Adventure Racing Association (sports)
USARC: United States Arctic Research Commission (governmental)
USAREC: US Army Recruiting Command (military)
USAREUR: U. S. Army European Command (military)
USARHAW: United States Army Hawaii (military)
USARPAC: United States Army Pacific (military)
USASA: United States Army Security Agency (also ASA) (governmental)
USAWOA: US Army Warrant Officers Association (military)
USAX: Fort Eustis Military Railroad
USB: United Society of Believers (in Christ's Second Appearing) (Shakers) (religious denomination)
USBA: United States Brewers' Association (trade group)
USBI: United States Bureau of Investigation (antecedent of FBI) (governmental)
USBIC: United States Business and Industry Council (lobby)
USBF: United States Benefit Fraternity (mutual benefit)
USBF: United States Benevolent Fraternity (mutual benefit)
USBGS: U. S. Belted Galloway Society (cattle)
USC: University of Southern California (higher education)
USC: Union of Slavic Churches (of Evangelical Christians and Slavic Baptists of Canada (religious, Canadian)
USCA: United States Cavalry Association (equestrian)
USCAP: United States and Canadian Academy of Pathology (professional)
USCC: United States Christian Commission (Civil War agency)
USCC: United States Chamber of Commerce (trade group)
USCCB: United States Conference of Catholic Bishops (religious)
USCG: United States Coast Guard (governmental)
USCE: United Society of Christian Endeavor (religious)
USCENTCOM: U. S. Central Command (military)
USCERT: United States Computer Emergency Readiness Team (governmental)
USCG: United States Coast Guard (governmental)

USCGA: United States Coast Guard Academy (Connecticut) (college, governmental)
USCGR: United States Coast Guard Reserves (military)
USCHS: United States Catholic Historical Society (religious)
USCS: United States Custom Service (governmental)
USCSC: United States Civil Service Commission (governmental)
USCT: United States Colored Troops (military, civil war)
USCTA: United States Combined Training Association (equestrian)
USD: United States' Daughters (of 1812) (lineage)
USDA: Department of Agriculture (governmental)
USDB: United Seventh-Day Brethren (religious denomination)
USDB: United States Disciplinary Barracks (military)
USDF: United States Dressage Federation (equestrian)
USEA: United States Eventing Association (equestrian)
USEF: United States Equestrian Federation (equestrian)
USET: United States Equestrian Team (equestrian)
USFA: United States Food Administration (governmental)
USFI: Fourth International (political)
USFIP: United States Forces in the Philippines (military)
USFMB: United States Federal Maritime Board (governmental)
USFWS: United States Fish and Wildlife Service (governmental)
USGBC: United States Green Building Council (professional)
USGS: United States Geological Survey (governmental)
USGS: United States Grazing Service (governmental)
USHJA: United States Hunter/Jumper Association (equestrian)
USHL: United States Hockey League (sports)
USHRA: United States Hot Rod Association (motorsports)
USIA: United States Information Agency (governmental)
USJB: Union Saint-Jean Baptiste (religious, ethnic)
USJC: United States Junior Chamber (Jaycees) (service)
USK: United States Klans (KKK)
USLCMBA: U. S. Letter Carriers Mutual Benefit Association (mutual benefit)
USLF: St. Louis-San Francisco Railway (railroad)
USLF: United States Lipizzan Federation (equine)
USLMRA: United States Lawn Mower Racing Association (motorsports)
USLP: United States Labor Party (political party)
USLSS: United States Life-Saving Service (governmental)
USLX: United Railway Equipment (rail car lessor)
USMA: United States Military Academy at West Point (New York) (higher education, governmental)

USMAPrep: United Sates Military Academy Preparatory School (school)
USMB: United States Metric Board (governmental)
USMC: United States Marine Corps (military)
USMC: United States Maritime Commission (governmental)
USMCR: United States Marine Corps Reserve (military)
USMGA: United States Mounted Games Association (equestrian)
USMLO: U.S. Marxist-Leninist Organization (political)
USMP: United States Marijuana Party (political party)
USMS: United States Marshals Service (governmental)
USMTC: United States Military Telegraph Corps (military)
USMTN: U. S. Military Television Network (military support)
USN: United States Navy (military)
USNA: United States Naval Academy (Maryland) (college, governmental)
USNAS: United States Naval Air Station (military)
USNL: US Navy League (military) (see also NL)
USNMC: United States Navy Medical Corps (military, World War I)
USNR: United States Navy Reserve (military)
USNRF: United States Naval Reserve Force (military, World War I)
USNTS: United States Naval Training Station (military, World War I)
USNX: Norfolk Naval Shipyard (railroad)
USO: United Service Organizations (military support)
USOC: United States Olympic Committee (sports)
USOE: United States Office of Education (governmental)
USofA: United Steelworkers of America (labor union)
USOGA: United States Oil & Gas Association (lobby)
USOTUS: United Societies of the United States (mutual benefit?)
USOWI: United States Office of War Information (governmental)
USPA: United States Polo Association (equestrian)
USPC: United States Pony Clubs, Inc. (youth, equestrian)
USPEA: U. S. Poultry & Egg Association (trade group)
USPG: United Society for the Propagation of the Gospel (religious)
USPHS: United States Public Health Service (governmental)
USPP: United States Pacifist Party (political)
USPP: United States Pirate Party (political)

USPRA: United States Psychiatric Rehabilitation Association (professional)

USPS: United States Postal Service (governmental)

USPSL&C: Union of Stone Pavers, Sidewalk Layers, and Curb Setters (labor union)

USRA: United States Railway Administration (World War I) (governmental)

USRCS: United States Revenue Cutter Service (governmental)

USRRB: United States Railroad Retirement Board (governmental)

USS: United States Steel Co. (business)

USS: Union of Scandinavian Singers (musical)

USSB: United States Shipping Board (governmental)

USSC: United States Sanitary Commission (Civil War agency)

USSC: United States Sub Chaser (military, World War I)

USSS: United States Secret Service (governmental)

USSSA: United States Specialty Sports Association (sports)

USSTAF: United States Strategic Air Forces (military)

USTA: United States Telecom Association (trade group)

USTP: United States Treasury Police (governmental)

USTTA: United States Travel and Tourism Administration (governmental)

USUSA: United Societies of the United States of America (religious)

USVLS: United States Volunteer Life Saving Corps (youth, civic)

USWA: United Steelworkers of America (labor union)

USWPF: United States Women's Polo Federation (equestrian)

USWV: United Spanish War Veterans (veterans)

USY: United Synagogue Youth (religious, youth)

UT: University of Tennessee (Tennessee) (higher education)

UT: University of Texas (Texas) (higher education)

UTAH: Utah Railway (railroad)

UTC: University of Tennessee at Chattanooga (Tennessee) (higher education)

UTJ: Union for Traditional Judaism (religious)

UTLX: Union Tank Car (rail car lessor)

UTS: Union Theological Institute (higher education)

UTU: United Transportation Union (labor union)

UTUIA: United Transportation Union Insurance Association (mutual benefit)

UU: Unitarian Universalist (Church) (religious denomination)

UU: Unconditional Unionist (political party)

UUHS: Unitarian Universalist Historical Society (religious, learned)
UUP: Unconditional Union Party (political party)
UV: Unione Veneziana (ethnic, mutual benefit)
UVA: University of Virginia (Virginia) (higher education)
UVL: Union Veterans League (veterans)
UVL: Union Veterans Legion (veterans)
UVM: University of Vermont (higher education)
UVU: Union Veterans Union (veterans)
UWA: Ukrainian Workingmen's Association (mutual benefit)
UWSA: United We Stand America (political party)
UWUA: Utility Workers Union of America (labor union)
UWWC: United War Work Campaign (World War I)(patriotic)
UZC: United Zion Church (religious denomination)

V

V&M: Vermont and Massachusetts Railroad
VA: US Department of Veterans Affairs (Veterans Administration) (governmental)
VA: Vision America (political)
VAA: Verhovay Aid Association (mutual benefit)
VAAFA: Vietnamese American Armed Forces Association (military support)
VAF: Vernacular Architecture Forum (professional)
VALE: Valley Railroad
VAMD: Virginia and Maryland Railroad
VAS: Vera Amicitia Sempiterna est (mutual benefit)
VBR: Virginia Blue Ridge Railway (railroad)
VC: Vashon College (Washington) (higher education)
VC: Virginia Central Railway (railroad)
VC: Vermont Central Railroad
VC: Veterinary Corps (Army branch)
VC: Vesta Circle (mutual benefit)
VCA: Veteran Corps of Artillery (lineage)
VCA: Vision Council of America (trade group)
VCRR: Ventura County Railroad
VCS: Veterans for Common Sense (veterans)
VCU: Virginia Commonwealth University (higher education)
VDMS: Vermont Domestic Missionary Society (religious)
VE: Visalia Electric Railroad
VEF: Vietnam Education Foundation (governmental)
VETS: Veterans' Employment and Training Service (governmental)
VF: Voice of the Faithful (religious)
VFI: Volunteers for Israel (religious)
VFIA: Verhovay Fraternal Insurance Association (ethnic, mutual benefit)
VFMA: Valley Forge Military Academy (school)
VFW: Veterans of Foreign Wars (veterans)
VFW: Veterans of Future Wars (political)
VGEC: Vergers' Guild of the Episcopal Church (religious)
VGN: Virginian Railway (railroad)
VGSA: Viola da Gamba Society of America (musical)
VHA: Veteran Health Administration (governmental)

VHM: Visitation Nuns (Nuns of the Visitation of Mary) (religious order)
VHPA: Vietnam Helicopter Pilots Association (veterans)
VIR: Virgin Atlantic Airways Limited (airline code)
VIS: Village Improvement Society (generic)
VMC: Royal Arcanum (fraternal)
VMI: Virginia Military Institute (Virginia) (higher education)
VMS: Volunteer Medical Service (health care, WWI)
VNAF: Vietnamese Air Force (Republic of Vietnam/South Vietnam) (military)
VNG: Vermont National Guard (military, World War I)
VO: Vasa Order (of America) (also VOA) (mutual benefit)
VOA: Vasa Order (of America) (also VO) (mutual benefit)
VOA: Volunteers of America (civic)
VOA: Voice of America (governmental)
VOSJ: Venerable Order of Saint John (chivalric)
VP: Vegetarian Party (political party)
VP: Veterans Party (political party)
VPA: Veterans Party of America (political party)
VPI: Virginia Polytechnic Institute (higher education)
VPL: Voluntary Parenthood League (civic)
VPP: Vermont Progressive Party (political party)
VR: Valdosta Railway (railroad)
VRD: Virgin America Inc. (airline code)
VRR: Vaughan Railroad
VS: Valley & Siletz (railroad)
VS: Virgin Atlantic Airways Limited (airline code)
VSA: Violin Society of America (musical)
VSA: Victorian Society in America (learned)
VSO: Valdosta Southern Railroad
VSOR: Vicksburg Southern Railroad
VT: Virginia and Truckee (railroad)
VT: Virginia Tech (higher education)
VTF: Veteran Tickets Foundation (military)
VTR: Vermont Railway (railroad)
VVA: Vietnam Veterans of America (veterans)
VVAW: Vietnam Veterans Against the War (political)
VVW: Veterans of the Vietnam War (veterans)
VX: Virgin America Inc. (airline code)

W

W: Whig Party (political party)

W8: Cargojet Airways Ltd. (airline code)

W&A: Western & Atlantic (railroad)

W&J: Washington & Jefferson College (higher education)

W&L: Washington & Lee University (Virginia) (higher education)

W&LE: Wheeling and Lake Erie Railway (also WLE) (railroad)

W&M: The College of William and Mary (higher education)

W&P: Willamette & Pacific Railroad

W&P: Winchester & Potomac Railroad

WA: Wide Awakes (also FAA – Free and Accepted Americans, AB – American Brethren, etc.) (nativist)

WA: Working America (labor union)

WA: Western Railway of Alabama (railroad)

WA: Woodchopper's Association (mutual benefit)

WAA: Western Association of Architects (professional)

WAAC: Women's Army Auxiliary Corps (military)

WAAF: Women of the Army Air Force (military)

WAB: Wabash Railroad

WAC: Women's Army Corps (military)

WAC: We Are Church (religious)

WADA: World Anti-Doping Agency (sports)

WAER: Wabash and Erie (railroad)

WAG: Wellsville, Addison and Galeton (railroad)

WAHO: World Arabian Horse Organization (equestrian)

WAL: Western Allegheny Railroad

WAND: Wisconsin and Michigan Railway (railroad)

WaPo: Washington Post (newspaper)

WAPOR: World Association for Public Opinion Research (professional)

WAR: Warrenton Railway (railroad)

WAR: Worldwide Army Rangers (military support)

WAS: Waynesburg Southern (railroad)

WAS: Women's Aid Society (religious)

WASC: Western Association of Schools and Colleges (education)

WASC-ACCJC: WASC Accrediting Commission for Community and Junior Colleges (education, accrediting)

WASC-ACSCU: WASC Accrediting Commission for Senior Colleges and Universities (education, accrediting)

WashU: Washington University in St. Louis (higher education)

WASPs: Women Air Force Service Pilots (military, WWII)

WATC: Washington Terminal (railroad)

WATL: Women's Anti-Tuberculosis League (charity)

WATR: Waterville Railroad

WAW: Waynesburg & Washington Railroad

WAWH: Western Association of Women Historians (learned)

WB: Women's Bureau (governmental)

WB: Western Bees (fraternal)

WBA: Workingmen's Benevolent Association (mutual benefit)

WBA: Workmen's Benefit Association (mutual benefit)

WBA: Women's Benefit Association (mutual benefit)

WBA: Wyandotte Breeders of America (poultry)

WBC: Women's Bowling Congress (sports)

WBC: Wilkes-Barre Connecting Railroad

WBC: War Bureau of Consultants (governmental)

WBCR: Wabash Central Railroad Corporation (railroad)

WBF: Workmen's Benefit Fund (mutual benefit)

WBF: World Baptist Fellowship (religious denomination)

WBF: Workmen's Benefit Fund (mutual benefit)

WBFA: Western Bohemian Fraternal Association (mutual benefit)

WBG: World Bank Group (UN agency)

WBHS: Worker Brothers of the Holy Spirit (religious community)

WBM: Women's Board of Missions of the Congregational Church (religious)

WBS: Wesley Bible Seminary (higher learning, religious)

WBTS: Waco, Beaumont, Trinity and Sabine Railway (railroad)

WBW: Washington Benevolent Society (fraternal, mutual benefit)

WC: Workmen's Circle (mutual benefit)

WC: War Council of the American National Red Cross (quasi-governmental, WWI)

WC: Women's Club

WC: Woodmen's Circle (auxiliary of Woodmen of the World) (mutual benefit)

WC: Wisconsin Central Ltd. (railroad)

WC: Wesleyan Church (religious denomination)

WC: Wesley College (Texas) (higher education)

WCC: World Council of Churches (religious)

WCCMS: World Council of Conservative/Masorti Synagogues (religious denomination)
WCCS: War Camp Community Service (patriotic)
WCEA: Western Catholic Education Association (religious, education)
WCES: Western Church Extension Society of the Protestant Episcopal Church (religious)
WCHL: Western Canada Hockey League (sports)
WCJCS: World Council of Jewish Communal Services (religious)
WCL: Women's Committee for the Loan (patriotic)
WCOF: Women's Catholic Order of Foresters (mutual benefit)
WCOR: Wellsboro & Corning Railroad Company (railroad)
WCRL: West Chester Railroad
WCSU: Western Connecticut State University (Connecticut) (higher education)
WCTU: Women's Christian Temperance Union (social cause, women)
WCU: Western Catholic Union (mutual benefit)
WCUZ: World Confederation of United Zionists (religious)
WD: War Department (governmental)
WDMS: Western Domestic Missionary Society (religious)
WE: Wheeling & Lake Erie (railroad)
WEAI: Western Economic Association International (professional)
WEAL: Western Allegheny (railroad)
WEC: White Eagle Club (political)
WEC: Waldensian Evangelical Church (religious denomination)
WEF: Water Environment Federation (umbrella organization)
WEIA: Women's Educational and Industrial Association (political)
WEL: Women's Electoral Lobby (Australia) (women)
WELS: Wisconsin Evangelical Lutheran Synod (religious denomination)
WEP: Wisconsin Electric Power (company)
WET: White Entertainment Today (KKK)
WFA: World Federalist Association (political)
WFA: War Food Administration (governmental)
WFBC: Wisconsin Fellowship of Baptist Churches (religious denomination)
WFC: War Finance Corporation (governmental)
WFDY: World Federation of Democratic Youth (political front)

WFIS: Washington Federation of Independent Schools (education)

WFJ: Western Fruit Jobbers (trade organization)

WFLA: Western Fraternal Life Association (mutual benefit)

WFM: Western Federation of Miners (labor union)

WFMS: Women's Foreign Missionary Society of the Methodist Episcopal Church (religious)

WFP: Working Families Party (political party)

WFS: West Florida Seminary (higher education)

WG: Women's Guild of the Congregational Church (religious)

WGA: Writers Guild of America, West (labor union)

WGAE: Writers Guild of America, East (labor union)

WGCF: World Guernsey Cattle Federation (cattle)

WGCR: Wiregrass Central Railroad

WGM: World Gospel Mission (religious denomination)

WGR: Willamina & Grand Ronde Railway (railroad)

WHA: World Hockey Association (sports)

WHAC: Wesleyan Holiness Association of Churches (religious denomination)

WHC: World Harp Congress (musical)

WHL: Western Hockey League (sports)

WHL: World Hockey League (sports)

WHMS: Women's Home Missionary Society of the Congregational Church (religious)

WHN: Wharton & Northern Railroad

WHO: World Health Organization (UN agency)

WHOE: Walking Horse & Eastern Railroad

WHPF: White House Police Force (governmental)

WHRC: Windsor and Hantsport Railway (railroad)

WHSG: Wadleigh High School for Girls (school)

WHWC: Wesleyan Holiness Women Clergy (religious)

WI: Women's Institute (UK) (women)

WI: Washboards International (musical)

WI: Woodcraft Indians (youth)

WIAC: Warriors-Internationalists Affairs Committee (fraternal)

WIB: War Industries Board (governmental, WWI)

WIBC: Women's International Bowling Congress (sports)

WICPP: Women's International Committee for Permanent Peace (civic, political)

WICT: Wisconsin & Calumet (railroad)

WILPF: Women's International League for Peace and Freedom (women, civic)

WINS: Colorado Workers for Innovations and New Solutions (labor union)
WIPO: World Intellectual Property Organization (UN agency)
WIS: Women in Industry Service (governmental)
WIWR: Wisconsin Western Railroad
WJ: West Michigan Railroad
WK: White Knights (KKK)
WKKK: Women of the KKK
WKPA: Western Knights Protective Association (mutual benefit)
WKRL: Western Kentucky Railway (railroad)
WKSC: White Knights of the Southern Cross (KKK)
WL: Workers' League (political)
WL: Woodmen Life (mutual benefit)
WLA: Women's Land Army "Farmerettes" (patriotic)
WLC: Women's Literary Club (social)
WLCJ: Women's League for Conservative Judaism (religious)
WLE: Wheeling and Lake Erie Railway (also W&LE) (railroad)
WLFB: Wolfeboro Railroad
WLI: Women's League for Israel (religious)
WLIS: Women's Life Insurance Society (mutual benefit)
WLO: Waterloo Railroad (railroad)
WLU: Western Labor Union (labor union)
WM: Western Maryland Railway (railroad)
WMA: Wentworth Military Academy (school)
WMBA: World Mutual Benefit Association (mutual benefit)
WMC: Wesleyan Methodist Church (religious denomination)
WMC: Will Mayfield College (Missouri) (higher education)
WMC: Working Men's Club (religious)
WMC: World Methodist Council (religious)
WMC: War Manpower Commission (governmental)
WMCSMC: Women's Missionary Council of the Southern Methodist Church (civic, religious)
WME: Worldwide Marriage Encounter (religious)
WMO: World Meteorological Organization (UN agency)
WMS: Women's Missionary Society (religious)
WMSC: White Mountain Scenic Railroad
WMSCG: World Mission Society Church of God (religious denomination)
WMSR: Western Maryland Scenic Railroad
WMU: Women's Missionary Union (religious, Southern Baptist)
WMWN: Weatherford, Mineral Wells and Northwestern Railway (railroad)

WN: Wisconsin Northern Railroad
WN: Southwest Airlines (airline code)
WNF: Winfield Railroad
WNFR: Winnifrede Railroad
WNWRA: Women's National War Relief Association (military support)
WNYP: Western New York & Pennsylvania Railroad
WOD: Washington & Old Dominion (railroad)
WOGC: W(orld?) Order of the Golden Cross (see WO of GC) (fraternal)
WO of GC: W(orld?) Order of the Golden Cross (probably became UOGC) (fraternal)
WOHO: Wabash and Ohio Railroad
WOM: Women of the Moose (see also WOTM) (fraternal)
WOTM: Women of the Moose (see also WOM) (fraternal)
WOW: Woodmen of the World (fraternal, mutual benefit)
WOW: Women of Woodcraft (auxiliary to Woodmen of the World) (fraternal, mutual benefit)
WOWLIS: Woodmen of the World Life Insurance Society (mutual benefit)
WP: Western Pacific (railroad)
WP: Whig Party (political party)
WP: Workers Party (political party)
WP: White Pride (KKK)
WPA: Works Progress Administration (New Deal) (governmental)
WPA: William Penn Association (fraternal, ethnic, mutual benefit)
WPAOG: West Point Association of Graduates (military)
WPB: War Production Board (governmental)
WPC: Westminster Presbyterian Church (religious denomination)
WPD: War Plans Division, United States Army (military)
WPEC: World Plan Executive Council (religious)
WPI: Worcester Polytech Institute (Massachusetts) (higher education)
WPFA: William Penn Fraternal Association (mutual benefit)
WPI: Worcester Polytechnic Institute (higher education)
WPP: Women's Peace Party (political, civic)
WPP: White Patriots Party (KKK)
WPRR: Willamette and Pacific Railroad
WPS: Women Physicians Section (professional)
WPSA: Western Political Science Association (professional)

WPT: Wabash Pittsburgh Terminal Railway (railroad)
WPUS: Workers Party of the United States (political party)
WRC: Women's Relief Corps (GAR auxiliary) (veterans)
WRLA: Western Retail Lumber Association (trade group)
WRR: Woodmen Rangers & Rangerettes (youth, mutual benefit)
WRS: War Research Service (governmental)
WRU: Western Reserve University (Ohio) (higher education)
WRWK: Warwick Railway (railroad)
WS: Winthrop Society (lineage)
WS: Ware Shoals Railroad
WS: Western Samaritans (mutual benefit)
WSA: Women's Suffrage Association (political)
WSA: Western Slavonic Association (mutual benefit)
WSA: War Shipping Administration (governmental)
WSB: Wage Stabilization Board (governmental)
WSCF: World Student Christian Federation (religious)
WSCS: Women's Society for Christian Service (religious)
WSGA: Wyoming Stock Growers Association (trade group)
WSHS: Worker Sisters of the Holy Spirit (religious community)
WSJR: Goderick-Exeter Railway (railroad)
WSLA: Western Samaritan Life Association (mutual benefit)
WSM: Wisconsin School of Mines (higher education)
WSM: World Socialist Movement (political)
WSN: Washington Southern Railway (railroad)
WSOR: Wisconsin and Southern Railroad
WSORR: World Series of Off-Road Racing (motorsports)
WSP: Welsh Society of Philadelphia (lineage)
WSP: Workers Socialist Party (political party)
WSP: Welcome Society of Pennsylvania (lineage)
WSPA: Western States Petroleum Association (trade group)
WSPUS: World Socialist Party of the US (political party)
WSR: Warren and Saline River Railroad
WSWA: Wine and Spirits Wholesalers of American (trade group)
WTA: Wesleyan Tabernacle Association (religious denomination)
WTC: Wilson Teachers College (District of Columbia) (higher education)
WTJR: Wichita Tillman & Jackson Railway (railroad)
WTL: West Texas and Lubbock Railroad
WTO: World Trade Organization (UN agency)
WTOH: Western Ohio Railroad

WTR: Work To Ride (equestrian)
WTRM: Warren and Trumbull Railroad
WTRY: Wilmington Terminal Railroad
WTS: Wesleyan Theological Seminary (higher education, religious)
WTSE: West Shore Railroad
WTUL: Women's Trade Union League (labor, civic)
WU: Weather Underground (political group)
WU: Workers United (labor union)
WU: Western Union (company)
WUA: World Umpires Association (labor union)
WUFE: World Union of Free Enterprise National Socialists (political)
WUHA: Western Union Holiness Association (religious denomination)
WUNS: World Union of National Socialists (political party)
WUPJ: World Union for Progressive Judaism (religious)
WUSM: Washington University School of Medicine (Maryland) (higher education)
WUT: Wichita Union Terminal Railway (railroad)
WVC: William and Vashti College (Illinois) (higher education)
WVC: West Virginia Central (railroad)
WVC: War Veterans Committee (fraternal)
WVI: World Vision International (religious)
WVN: West Virginia Northern (railroad)
WVR: Willamette Valley Railroad
WVSR: West Virginia Southern Railway (railroad)
WVU: West Virginia University (West Virginia) (higher education)
WW: Woodmen of the World (fraternal)
WW: Winchester & Western (railroad)
WWB: Writers' War Board (governmental)
WWE: World Wrestling Entertainment (business)
WWF: World Wrestling Federation (entertainment)
WWIT: WorldWIT (online organization of professional women) (women)
WWML: Wood, Wire and Metal Lathers (labor union)
WWP: Wounded Warrior Project (military support)
WWP: Workers World Party (political)
WWPAC: Women Warriors Political Action Committee (lobby)
WWR: Washington Western (railroad)
WWRC: Wilmington & Western Railroad
WWV: World War Veterans (veterans, fraternal)

WWW: "Wimachtendienk Wingolouchsik, Witahemowee"
Order of the Arrow (youth, secret, Boy Scouts)
WYCO: Wyoming & Colorado Railroad
WYS: Wyandotte Southern Railroad

X

X: Ancient Mystic Order of Samaritans (Odd Fellows) (fraternal)
XBP: Chi Beta Phi (science/math) (honorary fraternity)
XE: Chi Epsilon (civil engineering) (honorary fraternity)
XEB: Chi Epsilon Beta/Club Eligible Bachelors (high school fraternity)
XEPi: Chi Epsilon Pi (meteorology) (academic honorary)
XO: Chi Omega (sorority)
XPS: Xeroderma Pigmentosum Society (self-help)
XSB: Xavier Society for the Blind (religious)
XSI: Chi Sigma Iota (counseling) (academic honorary)
XSPi: Xi Sigma Pi (forestry) (academic honorary)
XU: Xavier University (higher education)
XULA: Xavier University of Louisiana (higher education)

Y

YAF: Young Americans for Freedom (political action)
YAN: Yancey Railroad
YAOC: Ye Ancient Order of Corks (fraternal, Masonic)
YARR: Youngstown and Austintown Railroad
YB: Youngstown Belt Railway (railroad)
YBF: Yul Brynner Head & Neck Cancer Foundation, Inc. (civic)
YC: Yankton College (South Dakota) (higher education)
YCC: Youth Conservation Corps (civic youth)
YDHR: York Durham Heritage Railway (railroad)
YEONC: Ye Ancient Order of Noble Corks (fraternal, service)
YFC: Youth For Christ USA (religious, youth)
YHA: Youth Hostels Association (youth, recreation)
YIP: Youth International Party (a/k/a Yippies) (political party)
YL: Youth Liberation (political action)
YLMB: Young Ladies Mission Band of the Congregational Church (religious)
YLMIA: Young Ladies Mutual Improvement Association (self-help)
YLS: Young Ladies Sodality (religious)
YMAMI: Young Men's Association for Mutual Improvement (self-help)
YMBA: Young Mortgage Bankers Association (business)
YMCA: Young Men's Christian Association (religious)
YMCU: Young Men's Christian Union (religious)
YMG: Young Men's Guild (religious)
YMHA: Young Men's Hebrew Association (religious)
YMI: Young Men's Institute (religious, fraternal)
YMIA: Young Men's Italian Association (fraternal)
YMIA: Young Men's Immaculate Association (fraternal, ethnic)
YMMIA: Young Men's Mutual Improvement Association (self-help)
YMMS: Young Men's Missionary Society of New York (religious)
YP: Young Pioneers (political action)
YPG: Young People's Guild (religious)
YPMS: Young People's Missionary Society of Western New York (religious)

YPS: Young Physicians Section (professional)
YPSCE: Young people's Society of Christian Endeavor of the Congregational Church (religious)
YPSL: Young People's Socialist League (political)
YR: York Rite (Shriners, Masonic)
YRC: York Railway (railroad)
YRPL: Yelm Roy Prairie Line (railroad)
YRSC: York Rite Sovereign College (Masonic)
YS: Youngstown and Southern (railroad)
YSLR: Yolo Shortline Railroad
YSU: Youngstown State University (higher education)
YV: Yosemite Valley (railroad)
YVRR: Yadkin Valley Railroad
YW: Yreka Western Railroad
YWBA: Young Women's Buddhist Association (religious)
YWCA: Young Women's Christian Association (religious)
YWCTU: Young Women's Christian Temperance Union (political)
YWG: Young Women's Guild (religious)
YWHA: Young Women's Hebrew Association (religious)
YX: Midwest Express/Midwest Airlines (airline code)

Z

ZBT: Zeta Beta Tau (college fraternity)
ZBS: Zivena Beneficial Society (mutual benefit)
ZCBJ: Western Bohemian Fraternal Association (mutual benefit)
ZCC: Zion Christian Church (religious denomination)
ZCMI: Zion Co-operative Mercantile Institute (Mormon)
ZFB: Zeta Phi Beta (sorority)
ZI: Zonta International (women, fraternal)
ZOA: Zionist Organization of America (religious)
ZOG: Zelta Omega Gamma (fraternity?)
ZPsi: Zeta Psi (fraternity)
ZIT: Zeta Iota Tau (fraternity)
ZTA: Zeta Tau Alpha (sorority)
ZW: Air Wisconsin Airlines Corporation (airline code)

www.ingramcontent.com/pod-product-compliance
Lightning Source LLC
Chambersburg PA
CBHW050507270326
41927CB00009B/1933